The Victoriou
Living in Grace an

1 John 4:16

Eddie Snipes

A book by:
Exchanged Life Discipleship

Published by GES Book Publishing
Carrollton, GA

Copyright © 2013 by Eddie Snipes, Exchanged Life Discipleship,
and GES Book Publishing

http://www.exchangedlife.com

ISBN: 978-0-9832247-6-1
Rev A.

Contact the author by visiting http://www.eddiesnipes.com or http://www.exchangedlife.com

Unless otherwise stated, the scripture in this book have been taken from the New King James Version. Copyright © 1982 by Thomas Nelson, Inc. Used by permission. All rights reserved.

Table of Contents

Preface

This book seeks to lay the foundation for a solid spiritual life that every Christian should have. We are more than conquerors through Christ, yet most do not experience the joy of our walk or the victory that has already been given to us. If someone had taught me these things early in my Christian walk, so many years of wandering through the spiritual desert could have been avoided. My hope is that you will gain the correct perspective so you can be teachable and avoid needless toils that produce no lasting results.

Certain topics will be visited more than once in this book, and this is by design. Some truths need to be viewed from more than one perspective to see how important they are in the Christian life.

One example is brokenness. This topic is introduced early in the book so the Christian can see it as a foundation of spiritual growth, but then it's revisited when it ties closely into other biblical truths. The goal is to show the value of brokenness as it fits into our overall spiritual life, and not merely as a topic we read and forget.

Re-emphasizing a truth from varying perspectives as it ties into other truths helps the reader to not forget, but also to see how God's word consistently ties together. Biblical principles need to be introduced, allowed to gel in our minds, and then solidified by tying them together with other relating scriptures.

As Christians, we are pilgrims and sojourners, but our journey through life is one of excitement and joy. You can – and should – live as an overcomer. Jesus said that each disciple is a friend, and it is the goal of this book to teach you how to walk in God's fellowship and never again view Him as a God far away.

The Foundation of Grace

1 Corinthians 3:11
> For no other foundation can anyone lay than that which is laid, which is Jesus Christ.

Before anyone can reach for spiritual maturity, they must first ensure they are building upon the right foundation. To build upon human effort or mere religion is a house destined for trouble. Only the life built upon Christ can withstand the trials of life and thrive in any circumstance. The Bible says that He is the chief cornerstone and our Rock. Religion is man trying to attain to God based upon the foundation of his own efforts. Faith is founded upon the solid foundation of Christ. He is our sufficiency.

Consider the history of religion. In every culture religion – even that which claims the name of Christ – has oppressed the masses. It has also fought against those who stood upon Christ alone. Nothing has changed. Sin oppresses. Religion oppresses. Man oppresses. But Christ sets people free. Consider **John 8:36**

> Therefore if the Son makes you free, you shall be free indeed.

Christianity shouldn't be a prison. Sadly, most people find their beliefs to be a burden instead of a benefit. Christian rules and procedures can become shackles instead of releasing them. Consider the passage below where Jesus spelled out His ministry to the people in **Luke 4:14-21**

> [17] And He was handed the book of the prophet Isaiah. And when He had opened the book, He found the place where it was written:
> [18] "The Spirit of the LORD *is* upon Me, Because He has anointed Me To preach the gospel to *the* poor; He has sent Me to heal the brokenhearted, To proclaim liberty to *the* captives And recovery of sight to *the* blind, To set at liberty those who are oppressed;
> [19] To proclaim the acceptable year of the LORD."
> [20] Then He closed the book, and gave *it* back to the attendant and sat down. And the eyes of all who were in the synagogue

were fixed on Him.

[21] And He began to say to them, "Today this Scripture is fulfilled in your hearing."

I want to draw your attention to a few key points that often get lost in the bustle of the average Christian's life. Jesus came to set you free, heal your heart, open your eyes, and proclaim the good news that you are now accepted before the Lord.

Human nature is fallen and corrupt and this has corrupted our flesh. Before Christ, our fallen nature oppressed us by sin and put us under the bondage of the law. The law proclaims guilt to any who have failed in any point. As the Bible says, though we keep the whole law, but offend in one area, we are guilty of the law – all the law. Just as a thief or murderer cannot proclaim all the good things they have done in order to be justified of one offense, neither can we. The law has no mercy.

Yet in Christ, we are set free from the law. This was the message of Christ. To proclaim our freedom from the bondage of sin, liberty from the weight of the law, and our acceptance with God. If you are in Christ, you are completely accepted by God. But true Christianity doesn't stop there. That acceptance opens the door to grace – God's unmerited, unearned favor. To understand the magnitude of what we have been given, let's start by looking at **John 17:23**

I in them, and You in Me; that they may be made perfect in one, and that the world may know that You have sent Me, and have loved them as You have loved Me.

Stop and meditate on this passage for a moment. How much does God love us? "You have loved them as You have loved Me." Let that sink into your heart. How much does God love the Son? The Father and the Son are one. Jesus has been given a name above every name.[1] In this short prayer Jesus reveals a profound truth that few understand. God loves you just as much as He loves Jesus.

This understanding of grace is the heart of walking in the Spirit. If you don't understand grace, you will always fall short of walking in the Spirit. You will fall short of overcoming sin and the

---

[1] Philippians 2:9

weaknesses that weigh you down. Not understanding grace is what makes Christianity into a prison. To be freed from the chains of sin only to erect a new prison of religion is not liberty.

Most people approach their faith from the outside in. They begin with doing external things in an attempt to make an internal change. What is your biggest weakness? It could be anger, greed, self-centeredness, lust, or some type of immoral behavior. We live in a world filled with sensuality, so let's use lust for an example. Suppose a man is struggling with lust. Here is how the average person attempts to overcome.

The man begins by feeling guilty for looking at things he knows have led him to impure thoughts or even immoral behavior. He resolves to do better. "I'm not going to look at women anymore," he tells himself. He then turns on the TV and what does he see on the next commercial? Sex sells, so he will be bombarded with it. Driving to work, what type of person will be on the billboard promoting a product? Then he sees more on the sports page of the newspaper. When he checks the weather on the internet, he sees more sensuality on the ads on the page. It is impossible to escape temptation while living in a world that thrives in it.

For a while he does better, but each exposure stirs burning feelings that agitate the very desires he is trying to control. In time, something in his soul begins craving what his mind has sworn off. The desire grows, wars against his mind, and in a moment of weakness he gives in. He promised the Lord he would live a holy life, so now he has guilt upon guilt. He sinned by lusting. He sinned by breaking his promise to God. Depending on the situation, he may have sinned with another person.

What will be his response to God? Fear. Shame. He will avoid God until he feels worthy enough to start praying again. Each failure creates more frustration and discouragement. Eventually he will declare that Christianity doesn't work and quit trying. Yet he won't find peace in surrendering to the flesh, so once he becomes miserable enough, he'll repent and start trying again.

Is this the Christian life God intended? Is this the type of life you have lived? Or are living? This is the life most Christians struggle through. People put on a spiritual demeanor and wear the mask of happiness, but when you really get to know people you find that they are no different than you. Some hide it better than others.

Nearly every Christian goes through this struggle, but few emerge to find the promise. They are like children in the desert. They find no satisfaction, but spend years and years wandering in circles wondering why God's promises are never fulfilled. They may claim the promises and pray for God's word to be made real, but each promise remains just out of reach.

When sharing my testimony a man once asked me, "Why doesn't God do that for me? I've prayed my entire life for deliverance, but God never answers."

It was a question I had no answer for, but it caused me to do a lot of searching. Why does God answer some prayers and not others? Sometimes God answers the need of someone's heart when they never even sought Him. Why? I believe this book will help answer that question.

The truth is, God will answer. God has promised that He will not turn away from the broken heart. And that is the key – brokenness. If you talk to those who have discovered the deeper walk of faith one thing is almost always in common – they have come to the end of themselves. God brought them to the place in their lives where they finally realized that 'I' can't do it. In fact, they must come to the place where they realize they can't do anything of eternal value, but are completely dependent upon Christ. That is when Jesus becomes real and true faith begins. This is where we experience friendship with God instead of just an escape from wrath.

People also approach acceptance with God from the outside in. In order to feel accepted, the average person has a mental checklist. Do good to someone – check. Read my daily devotion – check. Spend fifteen minutes in prayer – check. Go to church – check. When we do enough checks and avoid getting on the naughty list, we feel like God approves of us. A merit system Christianity never gets out of the penalty box.

This type of religion is based on legalism – or an attempt to keep the law. We all have various ways we view God's law, but in reality, people feel like God loves them when they feel they have kept the law, and feel like God is scorning them when they fall short. The truth is that the law cannot produce anything good in us, for the Bible says that the weakness of the law is the flesh – man's human nature.[2]

----

[2] Romans 8:3

In fact, the Bible says that the law serves two main functions, to be a teacher who brings us to Christ,[3] and it does so by condemning us to make us guilty before God.[4]

The law cannot be used as a tool to merit righteousness, for it requires absolute perfection. It is the revelation of God's perfect character, and because we were created in His image, the law demands we conform perfectly to God's character. But human nature has corrupted our ability; therefore, all have sinned and fallen short of the glory of God.[5]

The law does not merit righteousness – it puts forth the demand for righteousness. Do we get a reward because we don't speed on the highway? No, but if we do speed, the law penalizes us. Does our civil law reward us for not murdering or stealing? No. The law penalizes those who steal or kill. This is the nature of law, yet for some reason, when It comes to God, we expect a merit for the areas we keep the law and don't realize that the law's purpose is not a merit system, but the demand for perfection.

If we try to live under the law, and we act perfectly in hundreds of areas, but fail in a single moment of weakness, we are guilty. Consider the example we looked at for the man trying to overcome lust. He might spend months resisting every temptation. He might do better than he ever thought possible. But in a moment of weakness, what happens? He fails. Weeks or months of good behavior is wiped out by a single point of failure. And that is the nature of the law.

So we can see that trying to create righteousness or merit favor from what we do externally does not work. Yet God has provided a way that does work. And this is why some prayers are answered and some are not. The truth is that all these prayers are answered, but the promise can only be fulfilled through the Spirit and not our human efforts. Overcoming arises from the inside and flows out.

This is why this book focuses on learning to walk in the Spirit. Human effort cannot produce righteousness. It cannot produce spiritual fruit. Human effort cannot please God in any way, for Jesus said that whatever is born of the flesh is flesh. It is the Spirit that

---

[3] Galatians 3:24
[4] Romans 3:19
[5] Romans 3:23

gives life.[6] The flesh cannot produce spiritual life or anything eternal. The flesh cannot change itself, nor can it change our spiritual position. Outward change cannot produce inner results. By inner I am referring to the inner man, the new spiritual nature we have been given through Christ. True change comes from the Spirit and flows into our lives.

It's time to stop trying to change yourself. You read that correctly. The best you can do is replace one fleshly way of thinking with another fleshly way of thinking. Let's look at a passage that helps to explain this. Look at **Micah 7:18-19**

[18] Who *is* a God like You, Pardoning iniquity And passing over the transgression of the remnant of His heritage? He does not retain His anger forever, Because He delights *in* mercy.

[19] He will again have compassion on us, And will subdue our iniquities. You will cast all our sins Into the depths of the sea.

This was written to the remnant of Israel during the time of their fall and was the hope of God's mercy, however, this principle applies to all. This passage is so rich, it's hard to comment on, for my words can never do justice to God's revelation of mercy. This passage is a glimpse into the Christian life and the door to walking in the Spirit.

When we have iniquities (or sins) how do we normally address them? We try to subdue them through the flesh. Some have limited success, but no matter how hard you try to subdue your flesh, you will sin. You may have sinful habits that you cannot break, and after years of trying you have given up hope. You may think you don't have sinful habits, but do you have a judgmental attitude, grumbling spirit, gossip, or act selfishly? This is woven into the flesh and is impossible to break free from by human effort.

Look closely at verse 19 again. Who subdues iniquities? You? No. It is God who subdues iniquities. This is not God's judgment against your sins. The context of this passage is God's mercies and His abundant pardoning of our sins. He is not angry, but is showing delight in mercy. This was completely fulfilled in Christ. In Christ all sin has been paid and taken out of the way. Yet we still struggle with sin in our lives. While our attitude is that we must try harder, God has

---

[6] John 3:6

shown the right way. Turn to Him, partake of His mercies and He will subdue our iniquities. Sin has no power over your life if you are in Christ. God has promised to subdue sin.

It is not your effort; it is God's work. True change comes from the inside and flows outward. It's the process of transformation. You were predestined to conform to the image of Christ.[7] God has already made the way. All you must do is walk in it. The average Christian spends years groveling in failure and mourning over their inability to overcome. Their Christian life has become a perpetual cycle of confessing their sins and praying for deliverance, only to see the same problems arise again and again.

Why doesn't God answer their prayers? Because the prayer has already been answered. The answer is found in Himself, but we are too focused on ourselves to see it. While we are wrestling with our flesh and being overcome by our iniquities, God is calling, "Come to Me and find rest for your souls."[8] Do you have rest? According to the Bible, the one who enters the promise of Christ has ceased from their labors and has entered the rest of God.[9]

This, my friend, is the secret of walking in the Spirit. We must cease from our labors and learn to look to Christ and believe in His finished work. When the people asked Jesus, "What must we do to work the works of God?" He answered, "This is the work of God, that you believe on Him whom He has sent."[10]

Let this be the theme of your spiritual life. The works you must do is this: believe on Christ. Period.

Sound too simple to be true? It should. The Apostle Paul warned the church, "I fear, lest somehow, as the serpent deceived Eve by his craftiness, so your minds may be corrupted from the simplicity that is in Christ."[11] If faith is complicated, it isn't the gospel. Just as Abraham believed God and it was accounted to him for righteousness, you must believe God to receive. We receive the gift of salvation by putting our faith in Christ, who died for our sins.

---

[7] Romans 8:29
[8] Matthew 11:29
[9] Hebrews 4:9-11
[10] John 6:28-29
[11] 2 Corinthians 11:3

Nothing changes after salvation. We live by the works of God – believe on Christ. Nothing more.

You are not right with God because of what you do. You are right with God because of what He has done. When you put your faith in Christ, the Bible promises that God places His Holy Spirit within you and gives you a new nature. That nature is born of God and is incorruptible. This makes you a child of God. As His child, you are right with God because of who you are. As you believe God, He has promised to subdue your iniquities.

It is God's job to transform your life. It is your job to look to Him. You'll find countless denominational and religious beliefs that present countless options, rules, regulations, and formulas. How do you know which way is right? Here is a simple test. Is spiritual success dependent upon man helping God to complete the work? If so, it isn't of God. The Bible said that God finished the work before the foundation of the world.[12] The Bible also says that we are complete in Christ.[13] The Bible also says that God, through His divine power, has given us all things that pertain to life and godliness.[14]

- The Bible says that you have been sanctified in Christ – past tense.[15]
- You have been justified.[16]
- You have been crucified with Christ and the body of sin (old man) has been done away with.[17]
- You have been made holy.[18]

Pick any spiritual attribute and look at how the Bible describes it in context to our spiritual lives. These are always listed as past tense. While we have been praying, "Lord make me righteous, holy, and sanctified," the Lord has already declared, "In Christ I have justified you, taken away your sin, sanctified you, made you holy,

---

[12] Hebrews 4:3
[13] Colossians 2:10
[14] 2 Peter 1:3
[15] 1 Corinthians 6:11
[16] 1 Corinthians 6:11
[17] Romans 6:6
[18] Ephesians 4:24

and done away with the body of sin that plagues you. Walk with Me and be transformed."

The prayer has already been answered, but like all the promises of God, they are received by faith. Just as Abraham believed and then received, we also must believe in order to receive. Does the sins and the weaknesses of your flesh overcome you? According to the scriptures, "Greater is He who is in you."[19] Do you believe? Do you believe the promise that you are forgiven once and for all? Look at **Romans 6:9-11**

[9] knowing that Christ, having been raised from the dead, dies no more. Death no longer has dominion over Him.

[10] For *the death* that He died, He died to sin once for all; but *the life* that He lives, He lives to God.

[11] Likewise you also, reckon yourselves to be dead indeed to sin, but alive to God in Christ Jesus our Lord.

Notice the term 'once for all'. Your sins were paid on the cross. The Bible says that we were crucified with Christ, we were buried with Christ, and we were raised with Christ. Jesus did not wait for you to believe and then go to the cross. He did not have to suffer many times from the beginning until the end of time. Jesus bore the sins of the whole world on His body. Past, present, and future sins have all been paid on the cross. Jesus did this once for all. Just as Jesus paid for your sin so you could receive salvation two-thousand years ago, Jesus also paid for your sin, period. What you did before knowing Him has been paid. In the same way, what you will do tomorrow has already been paid.

Keep in mind that God is not bound by time. He entered into time in order to reach mankind, but time is our limitation, not God's. If you spend a lifetime journaling your life's events in a book, at the end of life you'll have a snapshot of decades of events. You can go back 20 years and relive those memories. For you, time is in the book. You can go back to any point in time and see what you did. If you put the book in a bag and carry it with you, every event remains in the book. The book is not bound by time, but any moment can be viewed.

---

[19] 1 John 4:4

The Foundation of Grace

On a larger scale, God views the entirety of the world's existence as an object. Whether it was 6,000 years ago or sometime in the future, it is all the same to God. History is in His book as a singular event. Sin within the history of time is an object that was dealt with in one act of grace. God views sin in the singular. Consider **Romans 6:10** again,

For *the death* that He died, He died to sin once for all; but *the life* that He lives, He lives to God.

Sin is in the singular for a reason. Jesus is not paying for each sin individually. God took the account of sin, all sin, and nailed it with Him to the cross. The Bible describes our iniquities as a handwritten account against us. Revelation 20:12 describes two books opened at the Great White Throne judgment. This is not the judgment seat of Christ, where the Christian's works are tested to see if they are of God. (See 1 Corinthians 3:11-15 and 2 Corinthians 5:10) This is the judgment against sin. In one book is written the names of those found in the Book of Life. These are those who have received life from Christ. This is the judgment of God.

A second book is also opened and everyone is judged for their works. But an interesting thing happens to those who are in the Book of Life. They are never examined through the book of works. Nothing they have done are judged, for the works in this book are the things done in the flesh. According to the Bible, whatever is not of faith is sin.[20] This means that none of the works in this first book are considered good works.

This is proven true when the judgment comes to an end. They are condemned, not because their sins were found in the book of works, but because they were not found in the Book of Life.[21]

Why weren't those in the Book of Life judged according to what was written in the other book? The answer is found in **Colossians 2:13-14**

[13] And you, being dead in your trespasses and the uncircumcision of your flesh, He has made alive together with Him, having forgiven you all trespasses,

[14] having wiped out the handwriting of requirements that

---

[20] Romans 14:23
[21] Revelation 20:15

was against us, which was contrary to us. And He has taken it out of the way, having nailed it to the cross.

Do you see this wonderful truth? The works in Revelation's first book and all that is written against us has been taken out of the way. Why? Because it was nailed to the cross of Jesus Christ. And Jesus did this once and for all. This means that all your sin is paid. This is very significant as I'll explain shortly, but first let's look at this 'once and for all' phrase again. When Jesus repeated something twice, it was to emphasize its importance. This is why He said, "Truly, truly I say unto you," before making a very important point. The double use emphasized importance. This is also is why the rest of scripture repeats important principles. 'Once and for all' is repeated many times in regards to Jesus' sacrifice. It's repeated three times in Hebrews alone. Consider these passages:

Hebrews 7:27
who does not need daily, as those high priests, to offer up sacrifices, first for His own sins and then for the people's, for this He did once for all when He offered up Himself.

Hebrews 9:12
Not with the blood of goats and calves, but with His own blood He entered the Most Holy Place once for all, having obtained eternal redemption.

Hebrews 10:10
By that will we have been sanctified through the offering of the body of Jesus Christ once *for all.*

Why do you suppose the Bible repeats this truth three times in three chapters? Jesus is not being crucified each time you sin. Nor is He sprinkling the Holy of Holies with His blood each time you sin. In fact, the Bible is very emphatic when God states, "He entered the Most Holy Place once for all." If you read these three chapters, you will see that the priestly duties of atonement were the foreshadow of what Christ was to accomplish. They entered the holiest place of the temple once a year and sprinkled the altar with the blood of the animal sacrifice. It was a yearly reminder of sin, but the scriptures state, "The blood of goats and rams can never take away sin."

These were acts of faith in what was yet to be accomplished by Christ. Once Jesus came, the true debt was paid and He entered the true Holy of Holies and atoned for all sin, once and for all.

Here is where this is significant. Your debt has been paid through Christ's completed work on the cross. You need to do nothing. God's hand is already outstretched to offer this free gift to you. All you need to do is receive it by faith. The work has been completed. You were cleansed from your sin and the account against you was taken out of the way. That account is past and future. God looks at your life in the context of it all. He is not limited to here and now. God redeemed you and atoned for your sin, singular. It is an accomplished fact.

The body of sin, your flesh, has been done away with, for you have been crucified with Christ. You have been sanctified because you are in Christ. You are the righteousness of God in Christ.[22] It was never your righteousness, but God's righteousness credited to your account. Since it is not your righteousness, it is not dependent upon you. The Bible says that when we believe, we are like Abraham – we are credited with righteousness. Everything is past tense because it points back to the cross.

After being declared righteous in Genesis 15, Abraham acted without faith in Genesis 20 when he lied about his relationship with his wife and declared that she was only his sister. He did this to save his own skin. He was afraid the king of the land he visited would kill him to get his wife. Though he had the promise, his faithlessness nearly caused him to lose his wife to a king who wanted to marry her. Yet God intervened because of God's promise to Abraham, not Abraham's ability to measure up to a higher standard.

I know that many will raise their eyebrows at this idea, but consider the truth. Trying to merit righteousness never works. The best that human effort can provide is self-righteousness and pride. In fact the Bible says that those seeking to establish their own righteousness did not find the righteousness of God.[23] The Apostle Paul, who wrote two-thirds of the New Testament and launched the church revolution in the Gentile world made this statement, "That I

---

[22] 2 Corinthians 5:21
[23] Romans 10:3

may be found in Him [Christ], not having my own righteousness, but that which is from faith in Christ."[24]

There is only one way to be righteous. Faith in Christ. This is not only the call of salvation, but the call of daily life.

Many have rebelled against God's declaration of grace by faith alone because they fear that it leads to spiritual apathy. Some have gone so far as to declare that if grace is taught the way the Bible presents it, people will take it as a license to sin. We need rules in order to govern believers and keep them from turning the grace of God into justification to sin.

Nothing could be farther from the truth. First of all, is God so insufficient that He needs mankind to protect the way of faith? I once had a discussion with a church director who said that he was not willing to allow anything to be taught that didn't come through the denominational organization. "I know I can trust what they put out. It's safe and tows the line. I can't have that confidence unless it's first filtered through our organization."

So what is being said is that we need oversight in order to protect God's church. A watered down message is okay as long as it is safe. Though he acknowledged the lack of spiritual maturity among the believers after years of teaching this material, he still said it was better than risking something being taught that the denomination didn't agree with.

And we wonder why the church has no power. Does God need an oversight committee to protect the church? Certainly there should be guidance in the church and when false doctrine arises, it must be addressed. But to filter out everything except that which is considered safe does not allow the whole counsel of God to be taught. If teachers were being equipped as commanded in the scriptures, we would have mature believers we can trust to teach truth. Then we can fulfill the call that every part supplies what the church lacks. But we have said, "We believe God calls teachers, but we don't believe God can equip. And we don't believe that God has appointed members with gifts for the purpose of equipping the saints." Instead, we protect the church and snatch authority away from God and put our faith in man and manmade rules. Then we ask God to bless what has been taken from Him, and wonder why it doesn't work.

---

[24] Philippians 3:9

The Foundation of Grace

Every epistle in the New Testament addresses false teaching to some degree and how to handle this. Strangely missing is the call to restrict teaching to safe topics in order to prevent the possibility to a false teacher arising. It's not our responsibility to protect God. It's not our responsibility to protect the church. It's not our responsibility to protect members from sinning by setting up a new form of the law in order to keep people from going astray.

And this is the heart of Grace. Law teaches people how to act and what to think. Grace teaches people how to relate to God and trust in His completed work. Law cannot work. Grace is the only way the Christian life can work.

I say that law cannot work, but by this I mean that rules and regulations cannot lead people into walking by faith and experiencing God in the Spirit. Law can control people, but it cannot give freedom.

The second point I'd like to say to those who claim that grace is a license to sin is that they simply do not understand grace. Grace is God's unmerited and undeserved favor. It is God reaching out to those who cannot measure up to His perfect standard. And that includes every person who has walked this earth.

Grace is God's invitation to join Him in this walk through life. It's His call to fellowship, and once fellowship is established through Christ, relationship is born through learning to walk by grace. Grace is the never-ending favor of God. Because it is unmerited and undeserved, it is not based on performance or human righteousness. You are the righteousness of Christ in Him.[25] Let that truth sink deep into your heart. It is Christ's righteousness that has been given to you without merit. That means that God smiles when He looks at you.

When God looks upon you, He sees you in Christ. When you sin, because you have passed through the cross, God sees that sin as paid. No, God sees that sin as removed and cast into the sea. He sees Christ in you and you in Christ. When you fall short, God sees Christ in you and you in Christ.

Understanding this truth is critical, for as long as you think of yourself as the producer of righteousness, you will always fall short and will have the perception that God's anger is upon you. Then you will be like Adam, "I heard your voice and was afraid, so I hid myself."

---

[25] 2 Corinthians 5:21

We are no longer in Adam, we are in Christ. We are now among those who come confidently before the throne of grace. Let's put this into different terms to help understand. We are among those who come before the throne of favor. When you think of grace, think of the word favor. We come before the throne where God favors us. It's the place where God expresses complete acceptance, apart from anything found in the flesh. The flesh has been removed and you are before the throne as a new creation – created by God to have perfect fellowship with God.

We'll deal with what role sin has to play in another chapter, but first you must understand the perfection of grace. God's grace is not bound by human inability. That was the law. The weakness of the law is the flesh. Look at **Romans 8:3-4**

[3] For what the law could not do in that it was weak through the flesh, God *did* by sending His own Son in the likeness of sinful flesh, on account of sin: He condemned sin in the flesh,
[4] that the righteous requirement of the law might be fulfilled in us who do not walk according to the flesh but according to the Spirit.

Now let's look a few verses later in **Romans 8:9-10**
[9] But you are not in the flesh but in the Spirit, if indeed the Spirit of God dwells in you. Now if anyone does not have the Spirit of Christ, he is not His.
[10] And if Christ *is* in you, the body *is* dead because of sin, but the Spirit *is* life because of righteousness.

If you are in Christ, you are in the Spirit. You are not in the Spirit because you have worked sin out of your flesh. You are in the Spirit because you are in Christ.

The law was weak because of human weaknesses – the flesh. If you are viewing God's acceptance of you based on how good you are or what you have done, you are looking through the lens of the law. And you will always fall short. Just as the law could not make men righteous because of the weakness of the flesh, it still cannot make you acceptable because of the weakness of the flesh. If your acceptance is based on anything except Christ, you are trying to live out your faith under the law.

The Foundation of Grace

Grace has no weakness because the strength of grace is Christ. Law failed because it was dependent upon the flesh, but grace cannot fail because it is dependent on God alone. Since Christ cannot sin and God cannot lie, the covenant of grace cannot fail. Grace was the blood covenant of God and Christ sealed on the cross for us, and by the Holy Spirit within us. Grace cannot fail. The only thing that can thwart grace is the temptation to depart from grace and find another way.

Many Christians are imitating the failures of the Galatian church. They believed in Christ for salvation, but then thought they had to keep rules in order to complete the work of grace. Look at **Galatians 5:4-5**

> [4] You have become estranged from Christ, you who *attempt to* be justified by law; you have fallen from grace.
> [5] For we through the Spirit eagerly wait for the hope of righteousness by faith.

Once they started attempting to live the Christian life by human effort and works, they fell from grace and the Christian life became a jumble of confusion, failure, and fruitless toil. So what was the solution? It's found in **Galatians 5:18**

> But if you are led by the Spirit, you are not under the law.

It's interesting that immediately after condemning the church for trying to be made perfect through human effort, the Apostle Paul points to the Spirit as the means of escape and then launches into the works of the flesh verses the fruit of the Spirit.

And this is where the average Christian falls from grace. They see the works of the flesh in their lives, and according to the Bible, it's the natural flesh that produces these things, and the sins of the natural man are aroused by the law. Consider **Romans 7:5**

> For when we were in the flesh, the sinful passions which were aroused by the law were at work in our members to bear fruit to death.

Did you catch this vital truth? The law arouses the flesh, which then arouses sin. Can you see that we have it backwards? While legalistic teaching states that law is necessary in order to keep people from sinning, the opposite is true. Setting our minds on legalistic religions actually arouses the flesh, and the works of the flesh emerge. Look at **Galatians 5:19-21**

> [19] Now the works of the flesh are evident, which are: adultery, fornication, uncleanness, lewdness,
> [20] idolatry, sorcery, hatred, contentions, jealousies, outbursts of wrath, selfish ambitions, dissensions, heresies,
> [21] envy, murders, drunkenness, revelries, and the like; of which I tell you beforehand, just as I also told *you* in time past, that those who practice such things will not inherit the kingdom of God.

This is the fruit of the law, for the law is dependent upon the flesh. Instead of subduing the flesh, the law arouses the flesh. Once you put the flesh in charge of spiritual matters, it cannot do anything but produce works of the flesh. It will masquerade as righteousness for a time, but under the surface, these works are brewing.

The works of the flesh are explained in reference to the church trying to use human rules in order to obtain righteousness. But the promise is that if we are in the Spirit, we are freed from the law, and by default, the cords of sin that are tied to the flesh are also broken. Only then will we see the fruit of the Spirit. The Bible first contrasts the law, and then points to the works of the flesh, and then points to the Spirit and it's fruit. **Galatians 5:22-25**

> [22] But the fruit of the Spirit is love, joy, peace, longsuffering, kindness, goodness, faith,
> [23] gentleness, self-control. Against such there is no law.
> [24] And those *who are* Christ's have crucified the flesh with its passions and desires.
> [25] If we live in the Spirit, let us also walk in the Spirit.

There is no law to produce this fruit. Fruit of the Spirit is not bumped up against the law, but flows directly from the Spirit. This fruit is apart from the law – never by the law.

Do you see the great irony of how we view faith? When comparing our walk to keeping laws, the Bible warns against the works of the flesh. But when the law is taken out of the way, the fruit of the Spirit emerges.

So you should be able to see that while some claim that grace is the license to sin, the truth is that grace places our lives squarely into

The Foundation of Grace

the Spirit, and the opposite is true. Rather than sin, the fruit of the Spirit emerges and we are transformed into Christ's likeness.

Religion and its rules is the producer of sin, not grace. Rather than a license to sin, grace is our invitation to unite with God on a personal level, and as we grow in our relationship with God, we are changed into His likeness.

Law tries to make us into God's likeness by human effort so we can approach Him. Since man can never raise himself out of human nature, this cannot work. And since the law-keeper is empowering the flesh, sinful passions are ignited along with our human efforts of religion.

Grace calls us to abandon all and cease from our own labors and enter into His rest. Grace says that we can never attain to God's likeness by our own efforts. Therefore, because God loved us, He entered into our world, crucified our sins and fleshly passions with Himself, and now we have God's hand of invitation to enter into Christ and join the fellowship of redemption. He then changes us into His likeness through the Spirit as we grow closer to Him.

Law says we must become right before we can approach. Grace says that He approaches us and draws us into Himself so He can transform us by His power. Law says work. Grace says to rest in His works.

Until you understand this basic truth, you will never be satisfied in your spiritual life and never overcome sin in your flesh. Trust in Christ, enter His rest, and cease from your own works.[26]

This is the foundation of the Christian walk of faith.

Discussion questions:

How would you define grace in your own words?

Can we lose God's favor?

Is it possible to have God's favor and not experience it?

How would you define legalism?

---

[26] Hebrews 4:10

Can legalism make us acceptable to God?

Can legalism change us into Christ's likeness?

Can legalism produce spiritual maturity?

Why do people pray for holiness but never seem to have that prayer answered?

Why does the Bible say that we have spiritual attributes (righteousness, justification, holiness, sanctification, etc.) in the past tense?

Can someone who has fallen from grace still receive grace?

Beginning with Brokenness

As I stated in the first chapter, one thing I have observed in the faith is that those who truly understand grace have reached the point of brokenness. Each person that understands the depth of God's power has first come to the end of themselves. Until we reach the end of ourselves, we are bound by a mindset of human ability.

This is no wonder, for we are conditioned to think from the perspective of human achievement from birth. We are taught that we can do anything or become anything as long as we are persistent and work hard. If at first you don't succeed, try, try again. Quitters never win and winners never quit.

Sounds like good advice, and for the world, it is the right perspective, but God almost always goes counterculture. The Bible teaches that human wisdom is foolishness to God and God's wisdom is foolish to the world. **1 Corinthians 1:18-21, 27-31**

[18] For the message of the cross is foolishness to those who are perishing, but to us who are being saved it is the power of God.

[19] For it is written: "I will destroy the wisdom of the wise, And bring to nothing the understanding of the prudent."

[20] Where *is* the wise? Where *is* the scribe? Where *is* the disputer of this age? Has not God made foolish the wisdom of this world?

[21] For since, in the wisdom of God, the world through wisdom did not know God, it pleased God through the foolishness of the message preached to save those who believe.

. . .

[27] But God has chosen the foolish things of the world to put to shame the wise, and God has chosen the weak things of the world to put to shame the things which are mighty;

[28] and the base things of the world and the things which are despised God has chosen, and the things which are not, to bring to nothing the things that are,

[29] that no flesh should glory in His presence.

[30] But of Him you are in Christ Jesus, who became for us wisdom from God -- and righteousness and sanctification and

redemption --
[31] that, as it is written, "He who glories, let him glory in the LORD."

Take special note of verses 29 and 31. If your glory is not God Himself, it is in the flesh. God rejects the flesh and all its works. Even that which is done in the name of Jesus is rejected if it is human effort (See Matthew 7:22-23).

Until your life gets to the point where God is your strength and your efforts mean nothing, you are not in a position where God can use you. You are still in need of brokenness. What you do for God is mere human effort. Many Christians serve God in sincerity, but out of the works of the flesh.

Saul was such a man before God transformed him and changed his name to Paul. He served God with great zeal for the Lord, but he was sincerely wrong. All his education, self-sacrifice, life of service, and religious practices came to end in a sudden moment of revelation on the road to Damascus. That is where his religion ended, but it was only the first step in the process of brokenness.

At some point in his life, Paul developed a physical problem that affected his appearance. Some believe it was an eye-disease, but the Bible doesn't fully explain what the issue was. In Galatians 4, Paul said that he had a physical infirmity when he first came to the Galatian church, but he praised them for not rejecting him for this trial that affected his appearance in the flesh. They focused on the message he brought and not the appearance he struggled with.

This physical problem tormented Paul to the point where he pleaded repeatedly with God for deliverance. We don't know how long Paul wrestled with his infirmity, but at some point, brokenness finished its work in Paul's life. On three different occasions, Paul set everything aside to plead with the Lord for deliverance.

Place yourself in Paul's shoes. God has called you to ministry and you have to meet new people face-to-face as you start new churches and reach people who have never heard of Christ. Suddenly you develop a disfiguring infection that makes your appearance grotesque to look upon. How can you introduce yourself to new people knowing that the first thing they will see is your ugly appearance? You can't stand to look at yourself, so how can God expect you to face people who don't know you?

In your mind, this is a hindrance to the gospel. In the past, you walked confidently into a new area, met people in cultural centers, engaged them in conversation, and boldly proclaimed the truth of Christ. Years of training had refined your speech. Your education equipped you to deal with almost every argument you would encounter. God had prepared you well and now you were seeing success in ministry. But now all that seemed threatened by an unexpected infirmity.

You notice the second glances and uncomfortable looks people now give you. Each time you speak, you know people are distracted by your appearance. You feel distracted by your appearance, and even as you share with others about Christ, in the back of your mind you are thinking about how bad you look. You grow to hate the disease and become desperate for deliverance. You decide to set time aside to fast and pray for God to release you. Nothing happens.

Others agree to pray with you and you set time aside to plead harder with God. In your prayers, you promise everything you have to God. You even agree to take on a different infirmity. Just don't let this horrid look remain with you. Nothing happens.

After waiting without an answer, you again set time out to pour yourself out before God. You plead, promise, and beg. You even claim every promise in scripture that might apply to deliverance from this look.

This was the Apostle Paul's situation. Three times I begged God for deliverance. At last, God answered in an unmistakable way. Paul describes this in **2 Corinthians 12:9-10**

[9] And He said to me, "My grace is sufficient for you, for My strength is made perfect in weakness." Therefore most gladly I will rather boast in my infirmities, that the power of Christ may rest upon me.

[10] Therefore I take pleasure in infirmities, in reproaches, in needs, in persecutions, in distresses, for Christ's sake. For when I am weak, then I am strong.

This is brokenness. It's the point where you lose self-confidence and self-sufficiency, and become God-confident and rest in the sufficiency of Christ. A broken Christian has two important attributes. They have learned to reject the strength of their own abilities or reliance on the flesh, and have learned to look completely to the sufficiency of Christ.

Personal weaknesses and failures are irrelevant, for all sufficiency is of Christ. Personal abilities mean nothing, for if it is not of Christ and by Christ, it has no eternal significance or value. It is at this point where Paul can now say, "The things that were once gain, I count as loss. All things are garbage compared to the excellency of knowing Christ."[27]

It is only after we have come to the end of ourselves that we discover the beginning of the power of Christ. As long as you are confident in your abilities, you are limited to your abilities. What you bring to God means nothing. I know, that's a hard thing to accept, but until this truth becomes real, God must work in your life to bring about brokenness.

This is why Christians struggle with frustrations and failure. They don't recognize that God is breaking the confidence we have in ourselves so we can discover confidence in Him. Take to heart these two passages:

2 Timothy 2:1
> You therefore, my son, be strong in the grace that is in Christ Jesus.

Ephesians 6:10
> Finally, my brethren, be strong in the Lord and in the power of His might.

Where does our strength lie? If any of your strength is drawn from the flesh or human ability, you are not experiencing the power of God. And where does that power come from? It's foundation is in the grace of Jesus Christ.

Consider the truth of this for a moment. God is not waiting for you to attain to a certain level of maturity before giving you His power. It's already yours. It is unmerited and completely independent of human effort. But you can only be strong in the flesh, or in the Spirit - but not both. If you are strong in the Lord, you have the power of His might. If you are strong in yourself or confident in your abilities, you are limited to the strength of the flesh.

---

[27] Philippians 3

While it is true that the human spirit can be very strong, it is also true that the human spirit cannot have the strength of the Spirit. In fact, the strength of the human spirit is a liability to the Christian's life. It is our strength of will that creates a stubbornness that is determined to succeed. Our desire to overcome can cause us to go through much more hardship than God truly desires.

God will put you through as much hardship as it takes to break you. Some will tenaciously fight against what God is doing their entire lives. They are frustrated, exasperated, and exhausted, yet because they have been taught to never give up, they refuse to break. In error they believe that life is testing them or that if they endure long enough, they will scale the mountain. They often wonder why God does not deliver them, not knowing that this trial is from God.

I've heard people say, "God will never make me endure more than I can bear."

Wrong. God's purpose is to give you more than your flesh can bear, for once you come to the end of yourself, you cease relying on the flesh and begin looking to His Spirit of power. The passage people are quoting to encourage themselves is actually talking about temptation to sin. Even if it could be used for trials, the promise of a way of escape is through God's Spirit and not through the human spirit or efforts of the flesh. Let's look at that passage and discuss its context. **1 Corinthians 10:12-14**

[12] Therefore let him who thinks he stands take heed lest he fall.

[13] No temptation has overtaken you except such as is common to man; but God *is* faithful, who will not allow you to be tempted beyond what you are able, but with the temptation will also make the way of escape, that you may be able to bear *it.*

[14] Therefore, my beloved, flee from idolatry.

If you read back a few verses, you'll see that our example comes from those who committed idolatry and committed sexual immorality with the Moabite women as they turned to other gods. Then we are warned that any who think they stand should take heed. Then there is the promise of deliverance from sin and the admonition to flee from idolatry.

Let's be clear on this. God will not prevent you from being tested above what you can bear. He will prevent those who trust in Him from being tempted above their ability to resist. God will test you above what you can bear. If you have the power of His might, your strength is unlimited. If you are relying on self, you'll buckle under the weight. Let's also take into consideration the words of Jesus in **Luke 20:17-18**

> [17] Then He looked at them and said, "What then is this that is written: 'The stone which the builders rejected Has become the chief cornerstone'?
> [18] "Whoever falls on that stone will be broken; but on whomever it falls, it will grind him to powder."

This is the goal of brokenness. Those who fall upon Christ are broken, but He becomes their cornerstone. Those who resist will feel the crushing weight of the Lord. The grinding weight is not punishment, but the removal of our confidence in anything but Him. Some of us have to be ground to powder before we give up. Some people are destroyed by bitterness and refuse to let go of the flesh. Why is it that people get so angry at God and never turn to His power – a power that guarantees victory?

Do Christians have trials – even though they have come to the place of rest? Certainly. God uses trials to refine us, prune us, or to show His power to overcome what seems insurmountable. How then do I know the difference between God breaking me and God trying me?

This is a question that is often revealed in my attitude. If I find myself resisting, I am probably in need of brokenness. If I rest in Him, then I can be refined while I'm drawing near to Him. Does the pressure I feel cause me to try harder, or to look to Christ and rely on His might? Do I feel rest in my spirit? This is something I hope you'll understand as this book progresses. There is a peace that surpasses all human understanding, and even though I am pressed from the outside, there is a peacefulness within that allows me to rest fully on Christ regardless of circumstances.

The apostles stated, "We are pressed, but not crushed. Persecuted, but not forsaken. Always bearing about in our bodies the dying of the Lord Jesus."[28] The flesh and human nature have been put to death through Christ, but the Spirit makes us alive. If you feel forsaken, chances are you are being broken. If you are crushed, surrender to the Lord's breaking.

Sometimes we need to be broken more than once. That is because we have begun to rely on ourselves instead of looking to Christ.

In 1998 I came to the end of myself. My sins ruled my life and I could not overcome. I tried for 20 years to become a godly man, but the only thing I found was frustration. I gave up, but discovered that the only thing worse than trying in vain to live the Christian life was not living the Christian life at all.

Many times I cried out, "I just can't do it." But in April of 1998, I fully understood that my best efforts couldn't achieve the least of God's requirements. I finally understood that in me (that is in my flesh), nothing good dwells, and if anything good was to come of my life, God had to do it.

When I fully realized this, my life changed in an instant. God poured His life into my barren soul and I discovered what it meant to live for the first time. I discovered God's power to deliver me from sin and to empower me to live by faith. That was my first breaking. In a later chapter I'll share an amazing story of how God revealed His hand in my life, and then called me to rest in faith. I was not prepared to step into a deeper maturity, so the flesh had to be broken again.

If you are feeling the weight of the world, it's time to fall upon Christ. Whoever falls upon this Rock will be broken. Once the flesh has been broken, the power of the Spirit will flow freely through you. From a position of brokenness, Christ becomes real and life sweeter.

Stop praying for deliverance and begin praying for brokenness. Cease from asking God why, and begin asking God what He is trying to do. Surrender and allow Him to break you so He can establish you firmly on the rock of Christ. The power of the flesh being ground to powder is bitter, but brokenness is sweet.

Never resist brokenness. Experience grace!

Let me impose a few questions upon the reader. So brokenness teaches me the need to rely solely upon God's grace. The scriptures

---

[28] 2 Corinthians 4:8-11

teach that following the law stirs the flesh and entices sin. How then does grace lead me out of sin? How can just believing in Christ's work make me a godly person?

Well, how does just believing in Jesus provide salvation? I believed God and He credited me with righteousness. He then entered into my life, crucified the old man, and made me into a new creation, born of God and by the Spirit. He then made me into the temple of the Holy Spirit.[29]

The Holy Spirit is within you. Why? Because God revealed the truth of Christ to you, you believed Him, and because you received His gift by faith, God entered your life and transformed you into a new creation. How does our life become godly? How do we conform to the image of Christ? Let's let the Apostle Paul answer this question with a question. Look at **Galatians 3:1-3**

> [1] O foolish Galatians! Who has bewitched you that you should not obey the truth, before whose eyes Jesus Christ was clearly portrayed among you as crucified?
> [2] This only I want to learn from you: Did you receive the Spirit by the works of the law, or by the hearing of faith?
> [3] Are you so foolish? Having begun in the Spirit, are you now being made perfect by the flesh?

This was a church that Paul planted. They were Gentiles – or non-Jews. The Jewish believers were stuck in the Old Testament mindset and having trouble believing that Christ fulfilled the law and it was not necessary for salvation. These well-intentioned but misguided Jews entered the church and persuaded these immature believers that they needed to keep rules and regulations in order to complete the work of sanctification. In their situation, it was circumcision, but the same principle applies to any attempt to make ourselves perfect through human effort.

Are we so foolish, having begun by faith, do we think we now are made perfect by human effort? No. We are made perfect the same way we are redeemed – by faith in Christ. What is faith? Faith is believing God. Not merely a head knowledge. Saying "Yeah, I believe Jesus died for my sins," does not change anyone. But recognizing the gift of God and putting our trust in Jesus is the act of

---

[29] 1 Corinthians 6:19

faith. It is believing that He accomplished the work that I had no hope of accomplishing. I see my incapable efforts, my need for redemption, and His free gift. I believe, surrender, and God enters into my life to do His work.

Though the work was actually accomplished two-thousand years ago, it does not benefit me until I receive it by faith.

What changes after salvation? Nothing. The work of sanctification, holiness, forgiveness, justification, and any other spiritual work was accomplished two-thousand years ago. Are you so foolish, having begun in the faith, do you now think you must complete the process by human effort?

Sadly, most Christians are taught yes. But the answer is no. The work has been done, but it does not benefit you until you receive it by faith. And faith must be part of our daily walk. This is also how we are transformed from the inside out.

The Holy Spirit is within us, revealing righteousness to us, conforming us to the image of Christ, and opening our eyes of faith through the word. But we are distracted by various doctrines, opinions, and religious practices that profit nothing. If keeping rules accomplished the work of God, the church should be perfect by now. Yet I've heard countless testimonies of believers trying to do better but falling short. I was one of those believers. My past was filled with heartache and frustration as I tried to overcome my own flesh, but just as I felt like I was making headway, I'd blow it and lose all my hard-earned efforts. I had not ceased from my own works; therefore, I could not enter the rest of Christ.

It is when I believe I am sanctified that I learn to walk as the person God has made me. It is when I believe I have been made holy that I learn to walk in holiness. It's when I recognize God's abundant mercies that I learn to walk as His child. It is when I believe that God subdues my iniquities that I look expectantly to Him and allow the Holy Spirit to begin His transforming work in my life.

Understanding these things is the foundation of walking in the Spirit. I once worked as an IT professional. I was hired to resolve a technical issue for someone who had tried and failed to resolve a major issue. I diagnosed the problem and began working to fix it. The business owner watched over my shoulder while I worked. Just as I started working on the problem, he said, "No, that's not right. You should do this." I explained why that wouldn't fix the issue and began working again. "No, no. You should have done that differently," he interrupted me again. A few minutes later he said, "I have a friend who knows a lot about this and he said it should be done a different way."

Frustrated, I turned to him and said, "Was your friend able to resolve the problem?"

"No," he said.

"Have the solutions you are talking about worked?"

"No."

"Why don't you take a break and let me have a go at it. I'm very experienced in this type of problem." In a few minutes, his issue was resolved and the system was up and running.

You may have a friend, leader, or expert who knows a lot about religion. You may feel you have a lot of answers, but I assure you, you cannot fix yourself. Nor can those around you. It's time to step out of the way and let God do His work. Your best human effort can do nothing more than interfere with the work of Christ.

God has promised, "Walk in the Spirit and you will not fulfill the lust of the flesh."[30] Walk in the Spirit, not work to be in the Spirit. To walk in the Spirit you simply believe God and walk where He leads. That is when your life will begin to transform into His image. It is the patient leading and working of God to remove the things that hinder as we trust Him enough to obey. And obedience is fulfilled in this, "This is the work of God, that you believe on Him whom He sent."

Where you are looking is where you will walk. If you look at sin – even in an effort to overcome it – you will fall into the flesh. If you look to Christ, you will follow Him. Why do drunk drivers hit other cars? Their judgment is impaired and they always drift where they are looking. They look at something on the side of the road and drift towards it. They see oncoming headlights and drift towards it. If they don't recognize the danger in time, they can't swerve to avoid it. We all have the tendency to drift to where we are looking. This is true in driving, walking, or in our spiritual lives.

If you look to yourself, you'll drift into a fleshly way of thinking. If you try to resist sin, you are still focused on it and will drift towards it. If you are looking to Christ, your life will begin

---

[30] Galatians 5:16

following Him. It takes time to learn to quit looking at all the distractions of life and temptations of the flesh, but victory will come to those who look to Christ. Looking to rules leads into legalism. It never leads to righteousness. The truth is, we need to look to what God has given instead of to what we need to change. Let me share one last passage to clarify the goal of walking in the Spirit. Look at **Romans 2:14**

> For when Gentiles, who do not have the law, by nature do the things in the law, these, although not having the law, are a law to themselves,

The Apostle Paul is making a comparison between the Jews who were trying in vain to become righteous through the law with the Gentiles who knew nothing about the Old Testament Law. Notice, the Gentiles did not make up their own law, they kept the law by nature.

You and anyone who is in Christ, have been given a new nature. That new nature is born of God and is empowered by the Holy Spirit. We'll explore this in detail later, but our new nature is by God's Spirit. It is our new man, or new spirit. It is born of God and is by God. It has an incorruptible nature that cannot sin.[31] It serves God by nature because it is born of God. The Gentile Christians, who knew nothing about the law, had something within them that caused them to act according to the righteousness of God. They kept the law, not because of rules, but because they were living according to a new nature.

If you have been born into Christ, you also have a new nature. That nature has one desire – to abide in Christ and do God's will. Your flesh has one desire – to serve the law of sin. This is why you cannot overcome through human effort, for the flesh must serve sin. The secret to overcoming is to learn to walk according to your nature, not according to the flesh. And this is what walking in the Spirit is all about.

The work was completed through Christ. Now it's time to learn how to walk in Him. May God open our eyes to see the truth of what God has done and teach us how to walk in Him.

---

[31] 1 Peter 1:23, 1 John 3:9

Discussion questions:

Why did God refuse to remove Paul's thorn in the flesh?

Why didn't God just perfect Paul without making him suffer?

What does the Bible mean by, "Be strong in the grace that is in Christ?" (2 Timothy 2:1)

Will God allow you to have a burden too great for you to bear? Why or why not?

Have you ever said, "Why God?" If so, does the principle of brokenness affect your perspective of troubles?

Can hardship or stress teach us to receive grace?

Will Christians become stressed, or fall into despair?

Does God care?

How do troubles play into God's plan for your life?

Keystone Christians

You may have noticed the decorative keystones set into the middle of magnificent works of stone. In the center of a stone archway, there will always be a large, wedge shaped stone. It's normally larger than the other stones and made to look as if it were a decoration. Though it may be the crowning piece of art, without it an archway made of pure stone could not stand. Every stone in the arch relies on the keystone. Until the keystone is in place, the archway is dependent upon the builder. Once in place, the archway becomes the support for anything leaning upon it. Many Roman-built archways have survived for thousands of years.

When you think of Christianity, think of the archway. Do you support the tenants of the faith, or do they support you? The Bible says that faith is the shield that protects us from the fiery darts of the devil. Yet if you look at the lives of most Christians, they stand as a shield to protect their faith from attack. Our faith is rattled when an attack comes unless we can protect our beliefs from criticism, doubts, and other challenges of life.

Most Christians are like builders without a keystone. They have all the doctrines in place, religious practices in order, methods in motion, and they stand under the arch trying to hold it all together. What's worse, the Christian has to protect the arch from the storms of life, mockery of others, and the weariness of the flesh. When they grow tired and falter, the stones drop to the ground. The Christian duty has become the process of holding religion up while trying to pick up the pieces that fall when they stumble.

Such a one was I before God opened my eyes to the errors of my thinking. Is this what God wants from you? Jesus said, "You who are weary, come to Me and I'll give you rest. My burden is easy and my yoke is light." Why is Jesus' yoke light? A yoke is a wooden harness that connects two oxen together so they can plow a field in unison. We are called to be yoked to Christ, but unlike the oxen, we are not called to bear the weight of the mission. We are only called to walk with Christ as He bears the weight. Rest while laboring. That is the message. Jesus' promise is that He gives us rest while we are in the fields of labor. What a marvelous paradox!

The Christian supporting their own foundation cannot have rest. The Christian will never find rest for their souls until the keystone is in place. Once the keystone is in its proper place, the arch no longer needs to be held up. It becomes the support of everything leaning upon it. That is what your faith should be.

The keystone of faith is grace. Consider a passage many Christians can recite by heart, **Ephesians 2:8-10**

[8] For by grace you have been saved through faith, and that not of yourselves; *it is* the gift of God,

[9] not of works, lest anyone should boast.

[10] For we are His workmanship, created in Christ Jesus for good works, which God prepared beforehand that we should walk in them.

Do you see Jesus' promise of rest in this passage? "I will give you rest. My yoke is easy." Is that not the message of this passage, summed up in verse 10? We are not creating the work. Nor are we bearing the burden of doing something for God. We are called to walk in God's works that were prepared beforehand. We are yoked to Christ and walk in sweet fellowship as we walk through the field of labors. It is His work and we are yoked to Him in fellowship. The heavy burden is the result of us pulling against the yoke of faith, not when we are doing the work of God's will.

But let's drop back to verse 8. Grace through faith. Not merely faith. Grace is God's invitation of fellowship. We see that invitation, believe in His works, and receive it by faith. Nothing is dependent upon you. If grace is removed, what happens to faith? What happens to works? Suddenly it becomes dependent upon us. Instead of faith being a picture of God's unmerited favor, faith becomes a corrupted form of religion that is dependent upon man. A false faith says, I must believe. I must work. I must please God.

Perhaps you have heard it said, "You just don't have enough faith to cause God to act." Or maybe something like this common saying, "Faith spurs God into action. Doubt spurs the devil." There are many variations, but the general idea is that faith empowers God and doubt empowers the devil.

Friend, nothing could be farther from the truth. Is God dependent upon man? Does God need our faith in order to work? If this is what you believe, I challenge you to read the scriptures all the way through and note each time God declares that He acts according to His own will or indicates His foreordained purposes. Then note each time God was forced into action because of man's faith. In column one, you'll have many checkmarks. In column two, you'll have none.

God calls man to respond to the faith He has given, but God never is forced to act because of manmade faith. Manmade faith is mere superstition.

Faith is the revelation of God's will as He imparts into our spirit the power to believe, and grace is God's invitation to be part of His plan. God reveals what He is doing through the word, and because He loves us, God invites us to yoke together with Him as He unveils His will and brings His purposes to pass.

Grace is the keystone of understanding, for the heart of the gospel is the revelation of God's love for you. God so loved that He gave. The gospel is not that God loved those who were willing to give to Him, but that He first loved us. While we were sinners and enemies with God, Jesus died for the ungodly.[32] God did not save the righteous, for there were none righteous, no not one.[33]

Grace is the declaration of God's favor to you. Everything in our faith is an expression of God's favor. God favored you, so He dealt you, and each person, a measure of faith.[34] Faith is not man's ability to believe, for nothing of the flesh can please God. Faith is a gift of the Spirit[35] and faith is the fruit produced by the Spirit.[36]

Do you realize that everything God requires of you is a gift He has given you? God calls you to walk by faith because He has given you faith. He is merely asking you to receive what His Spirit has provided. Doubt and unbelief are works of the flesh, but faith is by the Spirit. The flesh provides doubt, but God provides faith. Faith is when God reveals Himself to you and then asks you to trust Him by walking where He is leading. The flesh rises up and questions God. Do you put your trust in the flesh, or in God? That is the difference

---

[32] Romans 5:6-10
[33] Romans 3:10
[34] Romans 12:3
[35] 1 Corinthians 12:9
[36] Galatians 5:22

between faith and doubt. Doubt may exist, but faith empowers you to overcome doubt. God calls you to trust Him in spite of your doubts.

Do not concern yourself with doubt, but turn to Christ and receive faith. Don't concern yourself with the weakness of the flesh, but turn to Christ and receive the power of His Spirit. Don't focus on the fear of judgment, but the favor of His love. His love is a gift that overcomes our inabilities. God's love empowers you to love God (because He first loved you) and also empowers you to love others. It's not your love, but His.

The Bible commands us to love one another. We are even commanded to love our enemies. In my flesh, I love what benefits me, but God has given me the power to love what my flesh cannot because of the gift of His love. Consider the words of **Romans 5:5**

> Now hope does not disappoint, because the love of God has been poured out in our hearts by the Holy Spirit who was given to us.

Why does God require us to love? It's an act of faith in God's grace. He has poured His love into our hearts and now asks us to trust Him with this gift by directing it outward to others. The flesh rejects those who take from us and despises those who harm or threaten us. But the Spirit provides the love of God and asks us to trust in the Spirit in order to overcome the natural weaknesses of our flesh.

Think about all the requirements of God's commandments. How hard it is to measure up to the standard of God. How hard it is to keep myself in perfect obedience. It's hard to do the things God commands. Or is it? Perhaps the problem is not by abilities or lack thereof, but my focus. Look at **Galatians 5:22-25**

> [22] But the fruit of the Spirit is love, joy, peace, longsuffering, kindness, goodness, faith,
> [23] gentleness, self-control. Against such there is no law.
> [24] And those *who are* Christ's have crucified the flesh with its passions and desires.
> [25] If we live in the Spirit, let us also walk in the Spirit.

Now think about all the things you want to become as a person. Think about all the commands of scripture. Think about the high standard Jesus placed on our lives. Do you realize that everything we need is found in this short passage? Do you realize that none of this is dependent upon you?

God is asking nothing of you except to walk in the Spirit as He has empowered you to do. These things are the natural outflow of the life walking in the Spirit. You don't need to learn patience. Patience is a gift of God's grace. You don't need to acquire faith, for it is the natural fruit of God's Spirit within you. Everything we need is waiting on us to turn to Him to receive.

Think about the power of this truth. How many times have you prayed for patience? Or if you are like many Christians, you fear to pray for patience. I was visiting a church and in Sunday School someone said, "I'm so impatient with my children. Please pray for God to give me patience."

The class shrieked in horror. "Don't ever pray that!" several people said in unison. It was explained that those who pray for patience will be tested. Oh the horror!

The truth is that we have already been given patience. The problem is that we don't walk in the Spirit. Most of us think we have to do something to chip away our impatient attitudes and labor to obtain patience.

What about the harsh spirit? God has promised gentleness. Those who fear have been given peace. Those who sorrow have been given joy. Everything we want to become is found in the fruit of the Spirit. Notice that it is the fruit of the Spirit, not the efforts of the Christian. Those who have entered Christ's rest have ceased from their own labors.[37] And we already have seen that mankind's labors are fruitless.

So how do we obtain these promises? By believing harder? Is it possible to believe harder? Can man muster up his own faith and force God into action? No. The works of God were prepared before the foundation of the world and you are called to walk in it. That is walking in the Spirit.

The command is, "If we live in the Spirit, let us also walk in the Spirit." Herein lies the breakdown of most Christian's lives. Who lives in the Spirit? Anyone born into God's kingdom by faith in Christ lives in the Spirit. Your inner man is a new creation, born of God and it finds its life in the Spirit of God. If you are in Christ, not

---

[37] Hebrews 4:10

only are you a new spiritual creation, but you have God's Spirit within you. By birth, you are in the Spirit according to the inward man. Now it's time to learn how to walk according to who we are in Christ.

Wherever you go, you are with God. Regardless of your outward actions, you live in the Spirit. The new man can never be outside of the Spirit. It's impossible, for your spirit is the life of God and is a partaker of God's divine nature.[38] You may have wandered far off course and God may seem like a million miles away, but you still live in the Spirit. You might have the weight of your flesh bearing down on you, but because you are in Christ, you live in the Spirit.

Regardless of how you feel, you are always the temple of the Holy Spirit because you are in Christ and He is in you. Walking in the Spirit may or may not stir happy feelings, but feelings do not determine whether we live in the Spirit. If you are in Christ, your life is in the Spirit.

Walking in the Spirit means we are walking in the will of God. We are either walking according to the flesh, focused on this life and ourselves, or we are walking in the Spirit, focusing on Christ. This is explained in **Romans 8:5-6**

> [5] For those who live according to the flesh set their minds on the things of the flesh, but those *who live* according to the Spirit, the things of the Spirit.
> [6] For to be carnally minded *is* death, but to be spiritually minded *is* life and peace.

Outwardly, it's not possible to tell if someone's actions are through the Spirit or of the flesh. We can do the things written in scripture and still be walking according to the flesh. When people came to Jesus to present good works done through human effort, He said, "You are a worker of lawlessness."[39] They presented the very works that the Bible says that His people should do. They worked and did many wonderful things in Jesus name. But He called them workers of lawlessness and rejected them and their good deeds.

---

[38] 2 Peter 1:4
[39] Matthew 7:21-23

What is the difference between the one Jesus declares as a good and faithful servant and the one He declares as a worker of sin? The answer is found in Romans 14:23, "Whatever is not of faith is sin."

How can good works be sin? Whatever is of the flesh is flesh. If you put lipstick on a pig, it's still a pig. If you put nice clothing on a corpse, it's still a corpse. What is dead remains dead, regardless of what setting you place it into. To be spiritually minded is life and peace. Anything else is of the flesh.

So what does it mean to be spiritually minded? Look at **Colossians 3:2-4**

> 2 Set your mind on things above, not on things on the earth.
> 3 For you died, and your life is hidden with Christ in God.
> 4 When Christ *who is* our life appears, then you also will appear with Him in glory.

Is Christ the focus of your life? I'm not saying, "Is Christ the reason for your life." Christ was the reason those who were rejected did their good works and wonderful things in His name. This may come as a shock to you, but God has not asked you to do anything for Him. God cares nothing about what you do for Him, nor does He care what you do in Jesus' name. God cares about this: do you know Him and are you walking in the works He prepared beforehand.

Are you making efforts for Him, or are you trusting in Him to do His work through you? Outwardly, there appears to be no difference, but the inward man is either walking as one yoked to Christ, or as one pulling his own plow.

Let me give an illustration from the Old Testament.

The Law Passed Before Grace Received the Promise

Moses was the law giver. He is the representative of the law. Through him, God delivered the Ten Commandments and all the law that governed the people. There weren't only ten commands. There were hundreds of commands and an entire legal system that came through Moses.

Once Moses received the law, he lived upright and perfect. He came before God, interceded for the people, communicated the law to Israel, and led the people to the promise. But he made one mistake. As he tried to keep the nation in line, he grew frustrated with the people. They complained, grumbled, and murmured. At one point, the people complained about the lack of water and Moses petitioned God. "Touch the rock," God said, "and water will spring forth.

Moses was at the end of himself and he took his staff, swung it in anger, and struck the rock. According to the Bible, that rock was Christ.[40] Moses failed on a single point. Instead of touching the rock, in anger he struck the rock. One small mistake robbed Moses of the Promised Land he desired to receive. Look at **Deuteronomy 32:51-52**

> [51] "because you trespassed against Me among the children of Israel at the waters of Meribah Kadesh, in the Wilderness of Zin, because you did not hallow Me in the midst of the children of Israel.
> [52] "Yet you shall see the land before *you,* though you shall not go there, into the land which I am giving to the children of Israel."

Deuteronomy 34:4

> Then the LORD said to him, "This *is* the land of which I swore to give Abraham, Isaac, and Jacob, saying, 'I will give it to your descendants.' I have caused you to see *it* with your eyes, but you shall not cross over there."

Welcome to the law. One mistake was all God pointed out. Instead of touching the rock, Moses struck the rock. But technically, didn't Moses still fulfill God's word? He accomplished the purpose of God. Water came out of the rock and that was the goal, right?

No, the goal was to honor Christ.

The Law Moses walked in required him to keep the law with absolute perfection. Yet Moses failed – though only partly. So you can see that the Law led the people to the Promise. The law got the people within eyesight of the promise, but the law could not enter into the promise.

---

[40] 1 Corinthians 10:4

Instead, God raised up Joshua to lead the people into the promise. Do you know what the name Joshua means? It means, "God is salvation." Joshua in the Hebrew is the same name as Jesus in the Greek. Joshua is a picture of Christ. Moses is the picture of the law. The law took the people to the promise but could not enter in. Jesus led the people into the promise. The law only took mankind to the point where they could see Jesus, and then the law passed away and Jesus took the people into His rest.

The land was by promise. The Law only makes allowances for those with absolute perfection. The Law never gives the promise; it only prevents offenders from qualifying for the promise.

That is the Christian life in a nutshell. The purpose of the law is to reveal man's incapability to measure up to the perfection of God's character. The law is the revelation of God's nature and character. The law revealed that character. The law led mankind through the desert of the world in order to show his inability to measure up to God's perfect standard so they would look to Christ. Then God fulfilled the law through Christ, who was perfect, and then led the people in by His own merit. The people entered by following Christ, not because of their ability to measure up. That is grace. Those who tried to enter into the promise without Joshua were driven out.[41]

The only thing required of those who entered the promise was to follow Joshua/Jesus. Even the battles they faced were fought by the Lord. The people merely walked where they were led to go, with the promise of God, "I will fight for you."

What then is works? Works are the process of following Christ where He leads and doing what He reveals, knowing this:
Philippians 2:13
> For it is God who works in you both to will and to do for *His* good pleasure.

The life of faith is not passive, for we are walking where He leads and doing what God reveals for us to do. God working in you is good works. But if you are working *for* God, your works are worthless. You are still on the desert side of the promise.

If your purpose is to look to Christ and just walk with Him, your character will be transformed into His likeness and you'll walk

---

[41] Numbers 14:40-45

where He leads. Then you'll discover the works God has prepared beforehand that you should walk in them.

Your goal is to follow Jesus. If He leads you to quiet pastures, rejoice in His refreshing. If He leads you into the valley of the shadow of death, trust in His rod of protection and staff of guidance. If He leads you to the work, don't pull the plow, but make sure you are yoked to Christ and walk with Him.

Many people get so caught up in their ministries that they lose sight of Christ. Hard work is not what pleases God. Being yoked with Christ and trusting in His works pleases Christ. I use this passage in other books, but it so beautifully illustrates the truth of human works. Look at **Luke 10:38-42**

[38] Now it happened as they went that He entered a certain village; and a certain woman named Martha welcomed Him into her house.

[39] And she had a sister called Mary, who also sat at Jesus' feet and heard His word.

[40] But Martha was distracted with much serving, and she approached Him and said, "Lord, do You not care that my sister has left me to serve alone? Therefore tell her to help me."

[41] And Jesus answered and said to her, "Martha, Martha, you are worried and troubled about many things.

[42] "But one thing is needed, and Mary has chosen that good part, which will not be taken away from her."

Was Martha's works commendable? By human standards, yes. But in reality, her good works were a distraction from what was truly important. Scripture states that she was distracted by serving. Then Jesus said, "You are worried and troubled about many things, but one thing is needed."

What was that one thing? It was for Martha to focus on Christ. Mary had that focus. She was learning from Him, getting to know Him, and growing in her relationship with Christ. Martha was so busy serving others that she lost sight of the only thing that was important.

Does this represent your works? Are you in the ministry? Are you volunteering in the church? These can be good works, but only if they don't become a distraction from the one thing that is important. When Jesus rejected the works of those who came to Him, He said, "I

Keystone Christians

never knew you." They presented works, but Jesus pointed at their lack of relationship with Himself.

If ministry distracts you from the relationship, it is mere human effort and is not commendable before God. If serving does not flow out of following Christ, it is an act of the flesh. Preaching can be an act of the flesh. Feeding the homeless can be an act of the flesh. All good works can be an act of the flesh if they are flowing from human effort instead of out of a relationship with Jesus Christ.

Mary was not working at the time she was criticized, but was still focused on Christ. She would have done anything Jesus asked. The relationship did not distract her from good works. It focused her on what was truly important. If Jesus had said, "Go and do," Mary was listening. Martha would never have heard God's call because she was too focused on her own ideas of service. Who pleased God? The one doing the most, or the one most focused? Who would have been in the right spiritual condition to do good works when Jesus gave the call?

Meaningless service fills most Christian's time, and they are so distracted by their own works that they miss the call of God. They miss the call because the relationship is absent. The relationship must be first, then works flow into our lives out of that relationship.

It's hard to maintain the right focus because the church praises busyness and frowns on those who refuse to be distracted. The church tends to be so busy on programs that they become the distraction from what is truly important. I've seen many people burned out over the years, but I have never witnessed someone focused on knowing Christ fall into this trap.

Our eyes must be turned away from Christ in order to be distracted, so this is the measure. If ministry is centered around knowing and following Christ, we are serving Him. If we can't go where He leads or must neglect the relationship, it is a work of the flesh.

Even those called by God have to work to keep their focus in the right place. When ministry flourishes, we become drawn to success. Then when God leads us to the works He is calling us to walk in, we are hesitant to move away from what we have made important and do what God has prepared for us. We can become more attached to the work than to Christ. This is a challenge for every believer, but it is summed up in these words spoken by the Apostle Paul in **Philippians 3:8-10**

> [8] Yet indeed I also count all things loss for the excellence of the knowledge of Christ Jesus my Lord, for whom I have suffered the loss of all things, and count them as rubbish, that I may gain Christ
>
> [9] and be found in Him, not having my own righteousness, which *is* from the law, but that which *is* through faith in Christ, the righteousness which is from God by faith;
>
> [10] that I may know Him and the power of His resurrection, and the fellowship of His sufferings, being conformed to His death,

Grace is God's invitation to know Him and walk in perfect fellowship. Christianity is not based on what you do, but who you are in Christ. God wants to have intimate fellowship with you. He has already brought us into the fellowship of grace, and now calls us to walk in that fellowship and enjoy intimacy with Him. Grace begins with forgiveness and redemption, where Jesus took the penalty of sin upon the cross and God declared you just and free from the law. That includes the law of works.

Grace does not end with forgiveness. Grace is God's invitation to walk with Him in the Spirit. Grace is the gift of Love God pours into your heart and the revelation of His purposes as He gives us faith – the spiritual power to believe and trust. Grace is God's power given to us and His invitation to step into eternity now and overcome the flesh that is bound to a temporal world.

This is the keystone of our Christian walk, because grace is what God has done for us and is doing through us. Rather than us upholding our efforts, Grace binds them together in Christ so we can rest in His works rather than laboring fruitlessly in our own works.

God is not limited by your failures, nor does He hold sins and weaknesses against you. Grace says, "Failure is a natural byproduct of human effort. Now that you have fallen in your efforts, taste of Me and experience victory." Stop worrying about how many times or in what ways you have failed God. Failure only proves the truth of grace. When you fail, it should be a call to accept the invitation of God's favor.

When you fall short, look up and see the invitation of Christ. Cease from your labors and enter His rest. You will fail when the flesh distracts you, but in Christ He gives you the victory. You become a partaker of Him, and then experience the easy yoke of walking with Christ, instead of carrying the burden of the law, which requires a perfection you cannot do.

If you have sinned and blown it, you are no worse off than someone who has dedicated their life to doing good works in Jesus name. Whatever is of the flesh is flesh. This is true whether it be an act of blatant sin, or the flesh masquerading as righteousness. The invitation is the same – come to Me and I will give you rest. That is the call of grace. That is the keystone of our Christian walk. The victorious Christian life is not dependent upon you, but on Him alone.

Discussion questions:

How important is understanding grace in the Christian life?

If we have all of our doctrines correct, but miss the message of grace, how does that affect our spiritual walk?

How does grace affect the way you look at God's commands?

How does grace affect the way you look at your own failures?

Explain in your own words the call of Christ, "My yoke is easy and My burden is light."

What does it mean to enter God's rest?

How can you do good works and yet rest from your own labors?

The Bible says, "When Christ who is our life appears." (Colossians 3:4). What does it mean to say Christ is our life?

Explain the law in your own words. How does this apply today?

What is God revealing by not allowing faithful Moses to enter the Promise?

Review Luke 10:38-42. Why did Jesus praise Mary as she rested and criticize the busyness of Martha?

Which of the two were more prepared for good works and why?

How does grace overcome our weaknesses and sins?

The Transformed Life

Let's begin this chapter with a short personal testimony. For most of my Christian life, I had no clue about the difference between walking according to the flesh and walking in the Spirit. For this reason I struggled for decades trying to live out my life in the flesh. I tried to make my flesh into a good Christian.

At times, I had just enough success to keep trying. Other times, I had so much failure that I gave up completely. I soon discovered that the only thing worse than trying to force my flesh to conform to a godly standard was living for the flesh with no attempt at a godly life.

Trying to live out my faith was frustrating, but allowing my flesh to rule my life was misery. If I tried to change the areas where I was weak, I might have success for a few weeks or months, but when something overcame my strength, I found myself right back where I began. It was like climbing a steep hill after a rain. Sometimes I'd make a lot of progress on my climb, but once I lost my footing, I didn't just fall down. I fell and slid all the way to the bottom.

Looking back I now realize how foolish I lived out the Christian life. I was trying to make my flesh do what it was not capable of doing. The Bible says that sin dwells in our flesh.[42] There are times when I could keep my flesh under control, but when it tired of this godly living, it rebelled and I could not bring it back under subjection. I was trying to force a holy standard upon something that is unholy by nature.

What happens when you wash a pig? You might be able to keep it clean for a while, but let it free on a hot day near a mud hole and what will happen? That pig is getting dirty. You can scold it all you want, but sooner or later the pig is going to seek relief.

This is the problem with the flesh. The flesh was born into a sin nature. By nature, the flesh is a sinner. It's not a sinner because it committed a sin. It commits sin because it is a sinner. It sins by nature and living for that nature is all it can do. Sooner or later, no matter how much you try to live by a godly standard, your flesh will crave sin, and you will not be able to force it into a godly mold.

---

[42] Romans 7:17-23

The flesh must be crucified. Not only must the flesh be put to death, but it must be replaced by something better. The good news is that these things have already been done through the death and resurrection of Christ. Forgiveness is offered through the cross, and life is offered to all who are in Christ. This is what God's plan of salvation is all about.

Let's stop for a moment and consider the gift of salvation. Salvation is not what you do for God, but what He has done for you. It's all about grace. Grace, by definition, is the unmerited, unearned favor of God.

Grace is the underlying foundation of the Christian life and is the underlying theme of this book. At no time should we view our spiritual life as what we are doing for God. Everything good in our lives and in our hope for the future is based on what God has done. God has dealt each person a measure of faith.[43] Believing God is an act of faith, and faith is a gift of God. He gives us the power to perceive the truth of Himself, and then calls us to stand upon the faith He has given us. And He rewards us for receiving what He has given.

Love is not what we develop for God. Love is first poured into our hearts by the Holy Spirit.[44] We are then called to love God with the love He has already given us. We love God because He has first loved us.[45] We see the amazing love of God, we find that His Spirit has poured that love into our hearts, and we then respond with the love we have been given. Then God rewards us for receiving what He has given.

In the same way, works are not what we do for God. Works are the purposes of God which He prepared beforehand.[46] God calls us to walk in the works He has prepared, and then rewards us for being a part of what He is doing.

Do you see a theme here? Everything is by grace. God calls us to walk in His unmerited favor, and then rewards us for being a part of what He is doing. It's all about the relationship – not the accomplishment. If I had only known this 35 years ago. I spent most of my life trying to earn God's approval, and never understood that

---

[43] Romans 12:3
[44] Romans 5:5
[45] 1 John 4:19
[46] Ephesians 2:10

He has already accomplished this on my behalf. My only call is to walk with Him in what He is doing. But this can't happen as long as I am living in the flesh and looking to myself as the source of righteousness or works.

A new nature must be in power before the flesh can be brought under subjection. Consider the words of scripture in **1 Thessalonians 5:23-24**

> [23] Now may the God of peace Himself sanctify you completely; and may your whole spirit, soul, and body be preserved blameless at the coming of our Lord Jesus Christ.
> [24] He who calls you *is* faithful, who also will do *it.*

The word 'sanctify' means to make something holy by separating it from what is profane. Sanctification is the work of God, not the work of man. He has set us apart for Himself, consecrated us for His Kingdom, and He does His complete work on our spirit, soul, and body. Once we understand that God has sanctified us,[47] we begin to trust in God's work and the process of transformation begins.

Transformation is when I begin living outwardly the work Christ completed on my behalf. As I believe, I release the areas of my life that are controlled by the flesh, and am transformed into the likeness of Christ.

I'm going to share the secret of victory few Christians understand. This isn't a secret God has hidden from us, but a secret we have hidden from our eyes. It is the eyes of the seeker that are veiled from this truth when they are covered by the law. Once the veil of the law is removed, transformation begins by looking at Christ. Carefully read this passage from **2 Corinthians 3:14-18**

> [14] But their minds were blinded. For until this day the same veil remains unlifted in the reading of the Old Testament, because the *veil* is taken away in Christ.
> [15] But even to this day, when Moses is read, a veil lies on their heart.
> [16] Nevertheless when one turns to the Lord, the veil is taken away.
> [17] Now the Lord is the Spirit; and where the Spirit of the Lord *is,* there *is* liberty.

---

[47] 2 Corinthians 11:3

¹⁸ But we all, with unveiled face, beholding as in a mirror the glory of the Lord, are being transformed into the same image from glory to glory, just as by the Spirit of the Lord.

The truth was stated plainly before their face, but the Jewish people could not see it because the Law of Moses veiled their eyes. The Gentiles, or non-Jews, have also created a law of legalism. When that law is before their face, they cannot see the transforming power of Christ. Legalism and law must be removed, and then the miracle of God begins.

How are we transformed? By what we do? By what we don't do? By trying harder, having more discipline, or making sacrifices? No. According to God's own word, transformation of our lives into the image of Christ begins when we place our eyes on Christ. We see Him through the mirror of His word. One day we will see Him face to face, but we don't have to wait for that day to be changed.

Remove the veil of human effort from your eyes, look to Christ, and the Holy Spirit performs the miracle of your life's transformation. It's a guaranteed promise! We all are being transformed into His image as we look at Christ. He is your life. He is your righteousness. He is your transformation.

As long as you are looking at anything or anyone else, transformation is not possible. Certainly people can change certain behaviors and experience some success. But there is only one way to overcome the flesh and be changed into the likeness of Christ, and that is to keep your eyes and trust on Christ.

It isn't the lack of completion of God's work that causes sin to dominate an area of my life. It is my act of choosing to walk in the flesh instead of the Spirit. By ignorance, I walk according to the deeds of the old dead nature, which has been crucified with Christ.[48] When I put my faith in the flesh over the Spirit, my desires are drawn from the old nature and I walk in the flesh. But when I believe God, I begin learning how to walk as Christ walked and am constantly being transformed into His likeness.

Overcoming the flesh is a daily process of looking at Christ and releasing what God is pruning away. Though the body of flesh has been crucified, our fleshly behavior and patterns of thinking are

---

[48] Galatians 2:20, Romans 6:6

woven into the fabric of our personality. We often don't even realize that we are borrowing from the flesh, but instead wonder why our ways aren't working.

As we grow closer to Christ, He will always reveal something fleshly in our life. These are often revealed when Christ leads us down the path of fellowship, but the flesh is tying us to the past. In order to move ahead, the cord must be cut. Sometimes the hindrance is the realization of something we gladly let go of, and we allow God to cut the cord. Other times it's so woven into our thinking that God has to surgically root it out of our lives. In other cases, we don't want to cut the cord because we find pleasure in the flesh. We like something in our flesh and cling to it.

In those cases, God allows the flesh to run its course. In fact, He brings circumstances into our lives that reveal the bondage of the flesh. The flesh then begins to weigh us down and bind us until we are broken under its weight and turn to the Lord. He then lifts or bears the burden and begins rooting what we have submitted to Him out of our lives.

The Lord will never force us down the road of spiritual maturity. Nor will He force us to abandon the flesh. He will show us the truth that the flesh is a burden and not an asset. Often, the only way to reveal the truth of the flesh is to allow it to have its power over our lives. When we realize its power over us, that is when we become willing to release ourselves into God's hands.

It is the lack of faith that prevents us from becoming the reflection of God's character. This is why the Bible warns, "Beware lest there be in you an evil heart of unbelief, departing from the living God." It isn't your lack of spiritual ability, but your inability to believe in the finished work of Christ and the value of God's kingdom. There is nothing between you and spiritual maturity but unbelief. Yet God has given you the faith to believe. All you must do is learn how to look to Christ.

The real process of maturity is learning to walk in what He has already done. The topic of sanctification can be confusing unless you recognize the work of Christ as the finished work of sanctification. The natural question that many ask is this, "Doesn't the Bible tell us to be sanctified? How can this be if it's already accomplished?"

Let's dig into the scriptures and get a clearer picture. First look at **1 Corinthians 6:11**

> And such were some of you. But you were washed, but you were sanctified, but you were justified in the name of the Lord Jesus and by the Spirit of our God.

This passage follows the Bible's warning that those who practice unrighteousness will not inherit the Kingdom of God. The Bible then goes on to name many of these unholy practices, then follows up by saying, "Such were some of you." Notice what follows next. "You were washed. You were sanctified. You were justified." All of this is an accomplished fact. It was accomplished through Christ.

It is past tense. In fact, realizing the past tense of God's work was the key that opened my eyes and changed my life. In the past, I tried to accomplish something that had already been done. Sin continued to rise up and take control of my life, and try as I might, I could not sanctify myself and overcome my sin. I could not set my life apart from the profane, and I could not make myself holy. Sin always defeated me.

I tried to crucify myself, but could not accomplish this. The reason is made plain through the words of Christ, "The flesh profits nothing. It is the Spirit who gives life."[49] The reality of life is that my human efforts are born of the flesh and the flesh can never produce anything acceptable to God.

Life changed when I understood the words, "You were crucified with Christ." "The body of sin has been done away with."[50] Past tense. Everything I was trying to accomplish has already been accomplished and the Bible always presents these in past tense. They were accomplished through the finished work of Christ.

Past tense must be the lens by which we view every spiritual gift and accomplishment. God has declared that no flesh will glory in His presence.[51] Our glory is the glory of God through Christ. Anything outside of Christ is human effort and the glory of the flesh.

Aren't we called to do something? In a manner, yes. What we do is believe God, let go of our own efforts, and walk in His works.[52]

---

[49] John 6:63
[50] Romans 6:6
[51] 1 Corinthians 1:29
[52] Ephesians 2:10

The Transformed Life

It is the work of God done in us and through us; not the work of us for God. This must be the foundation of our understanding. Otherwise, human effort corrupts the work of God. Now let us consider **2 Timothy 2:19-21**

> [19] Nevertheless the solid foundation of God stands, having this seal: "The Lord knows those who are His," and, "Let everyone who names the name of Christ depart from iniquity."
>
> [20] But in a great house there are not only vessels of gold and silver, but also of wood and clay, some for honor and some for dishonor.
>
> [21] Therefore if anyone cleanses himself from the latter, he will be a vessel for honor, sanctified and useful for the Master, prepared for every good work.

What is the doing on our part? It is to depart from iniquity and to remove the things from our life that produce dishonor. Are we sanctified? Yes. We have the seal that the Lord knows who are His, yet we are also called to depart from iniquity and remove from our lives the things that are contrary to our sanctification. I say to remove, but a better picture might be to release. God is removing the things that are contrary to Him. I either cling to sin or release it into God's hands.

We tend to look at our failures and sinful behavior and think that God seethes with anger. But the opposite is true. Anger against sin was poured out on the cross. Now God works with patience to remove the things that are contrary because He loves us. I mentioned this passage in the first chapter, but let's review it again. It is not you who removes sin from your life. It is God. All you must do is allow Him to take it. Release is the key word. Look at **Micah 7:18-19**

> [18] Who *is* a God like You, Pardoning iniquity And passing over the transgression of the remnant of His heritage? He does not retain His anger forever, Because He delights *in* mercy.
>
> [19] He will again have compassion on us, And will subdue our iniquities. You will cast all our sins Into the depths of the sea.

God does not delight in judgment. He delights in mercy, and it is also His delight to show compassion and subdue the sins that dominate our lives. He is our defender against the sins of the flesh. We have a tendency to view God as lashing out at us, but in reality He stands between us and the iniquity that seeks to overcome us. When we look expectantly to Him, iniquity falls. Sin seeks to overcome us, but the Lord subdues it and makes us into the overcomer.

Can I walk in grace while serving sin? No. Does God's favor depart because I served my flesh? No. Grace is unmerited favor, not favor that is merited when we act a certain way. Have faith in God's promise of grace. The goal of faith is our relationship with God. God has given me the hand of fellowship. When I take His hand I enjoy the relationship. If I am serving sin, where is the relationship now? I would be taking the hand of the flesh and submitting myself to it as my master (See Romans 6:15-16).

Anyone who thinks that grace is a license to sin does not understand grace. Grace delivers us from our body of sin so we can have fellowship with God. Grace is the love of God welcoming us into an intimate relationship, even though we were once bound to judgment against sin. Jesus bore the judgment of sin so we could receive the love of God. These topics will be fully explored as this book progresses, but before we move on, also consider **Jude 1:1**

> Jude, a bondservant of Jesus Christ, and brother of James, To those who are called, sanctified by God the Father, and preserved in Jesus Christ:

If you are in Christ, you are sanctified. The process of sanctification is not you learning how to become holy. You are a partaker of God's divine nature. Take to heart **2 Peter 1:3-4**

> [3] as His divine power has given to us all things that *pertain* to life and godliness, through the knowledge of Him who called us by glory and virtue,
> [4] by which have been given to us exceedingly great and precious promises, that through these you may be partakers of the divine nature, having escaped the corruption *that is* in the world through lust.

This should shed light on the question, how do we escape corruption? By becoming a partaker of God's divine nature. Religion teaches that we must rise to the level of God's nature in order to be sanctified. God has declared that we partake of His nature and through Him we escape corruption. We can never rise to God's standard; therefore, God reached down to us while we were still in our sins, and through His nature, we have been given all things that pertain to life and godliness.[53]

How do you view the phrase, "[He] has given to us all things that pertain to life and godliness?" Does all mean some? Are there exceptions, and what God really meant is 'some things'? No. You lack nothing. All you must do is believe God and receive His promises and partake of His nature.

So then sanctification is not me perfecting myself in obedience. Sanctification is an accomplished fact. It is what Jesus has already done for us through the cross. By faith, we receive what He has done and as we learn who we are in Christ, we also learn how to escape the corruption of our flesh and the corruption of the world.

My life testifies to this truth. What I could not do through more than thirty years of my best efforts, God accomplished through me. All I had to do was believe what God was revealing and walk as a partaker. The sins that dominated my life began to lose their grip because I began loving the nature of God more than the sin. Escape came by believing God and recognizing that He wanted me as a son, regardless of my ability to achieve a godly standard. Then it became His power to deliver me, not my power to defeat my own flesh.

The below passage is lengthy, but it speaks beautifully to what we are discussing here. Look at **1 Corinthians 1:2-8**

> [2] To the church of God which is at Corinth, to those who are sanctified in Christ Jesus, called *to be* saints, with all who in every place call on the name of Jesus Christ our Lord, both theirs and ours:
> [3] Grace to you and peace from God our Father and the Lord Jesus Christ.
> [4] I thank my God always concerning you for the grace of God which was given to you by Christ Jesus,
> [5] that you were enriched in everything by Him in all utterance and all knowledge,
> [6] even as the testimony of Christ was confirmed in you,
> [7] so that you come short in no gift, eagerly waiting for the

---

[53] 2 Peter 1:3

revelation of our Lord Jesus Christ,

[8] who will also confirm you to the end, *that you may be* blameless in the day of our Lord Jesus Christ.

Once again, what is the timing of this passage? Past tense. This is written to, "Those who are sanctified in Christ Jesus." Because they are sanctified, they overcome through the grace of God and the peace that flows from abiding in God's grace. The Apostle Paul explained his reason for expressing this in verse 7, "That you come short in no gift."

Understanding God's gift was presented to the church so that they did not come short in any gift. Many Christians miss the gifts given because they don't have knowledge of Christ's work. He is giving the gifts that enrich our lives, points to our inheritance, and shows us how to live the abundant life. Yet we are so distracted by religion and legalism that we never look to receive the gifts and promises extended to us by God's favor.

It's important to understand this truth, so let me reiterate it again. According to scripture, who does the sanctifying? Not you. It is the work of God on your behalf. And herein lies the failure of most Christians. We are trying to sanctify ourselves, but this is not possible. The thing which is profane – our flesh – cannot sanctify itself. Nor can the flesh be sanctified at all.

Our flesh is profane. It is so because the driving force behind it is a desire that was born into a sinful nature. Each person acts according to their nature. Consider wild animals. Some are tamed by man, put into shows, and are taught to perform. But what happens when one of these animals become stressed? They revert back to their wild nature. By nature, they fall back to who they are and act upon what is naturally in them.

Wild animals are kept in check by cages, whips, and other forces. However, when the forces keeping them in check have less effect on them than their natural tendency, the results can be tragic. We've seen news stories where elephants have gone on rampages, lions and tigers turn on their trainers, and chimpanzees attack their masters. The force of their nature has become greater than the force restraining them. Even while under control, the animal is not acting by choice. Their desire is to roam free and act according to their nature. Outwardly, it may appear as if they have changed, but they are not tame, and forced obedience is the only thing restraining these beasts of the earth.

Our flesh is the same way. If we are attempting to live a godly life by forcing our flesh to act within a Christian standard, it is operating under controlled frustration. You will be constantly acting contrary to your desires. By sheer force, you are taming the beast of your flesh. You are forcing it to resist what it craves, and to do what it despises. It's no wonder that so many Christians are frustrated!

The moment an opportunity to escape presents itself, restraint is cast off and good is rejected. Your temper will break free. What's more, it has a lot of pent up frustration to release. Your lusts will pursue its desires. Your greed will consume its prey. Whatever your flesh craves it will pursue, whether that be wreaking havoc internally, or pursuing sin externally.

You cannot turn the flesh against its nature. You can't take sinful flesh and turn it into a holy creation. There must be a change of natures. In Christ, we have obtained a new nature, but the flesh remains corrupted by sin and bound to the world. We must allow God to take away what is corrupt and replace it with what is incorruptible. Let's look at two passages that help explain this.

Colossians 3:9-10
> [9] Do not lie to one another, since you have put off the old man with his deeds,
> [10] and have put on the new *man* who is renewed in knowledge according to the image of Him who created him,

Ephesians 4:21-24
> [21] if indeed you have heard Him and have been taught by Him, as the truth is in Jesus:
> [22] that you put off, concerning your former conduct, the old man which grows corrupt according to the deceitful lusts,
> [23] and be renewed in the spirit of your mind,
> [24] and that you put on the new man which was created according to God, in true righteousness and holiness.

When we put our faith in Christ, God makes us into a new creation by giving us a new spirit – one that is incorruptible. This is the new man. The old man was crucified with Christ. Yet we are called to do two things in these passages. First look at Colossians. You *have* put off the old man with his deeds. That is the untamable nature of the flesh we have been talking about. We *have* put on the new man, which is the new life given to us in Christ. We aren't taming the flesh, but putting it off while putting on God's gift of new life.

Look at the above passage from Ephesians. Now we must put off the former conduct, which is the old man. Before Christ, we only had one nature – the sinful nature born through Adam. That nature was bound to our bodies and we acted upon it. We had nothing but the old nature. It is corrupted and dying. It is destined for condemnation, and to consume what is under condemnation. It can do nothing but what is allowed by its nature. Can the old man do things that appear good? Certainly – as long as there is a self-serving motive behind it.

The new man is given when God breaks the cords of the old man and crucifies it with Christ. Yet its deeds remain in the body. The nature is dead with Christ, but the body remains corrupted with his old deeds. Because we still live in a body of flesh, those deeds crave to be served. Yet we must be vigilant to put them off *by* putting on the deeds of the new man. We must learn to draw our volition from the Spirit and not from the flesh.

Godly living is not forcing yourself to do what you don't want to do. Nor is it resisting what you crave. Godliness is found in the new man. By nature, our desires will change.

Legalism is trying to force ourselves to serve God by human effort and attempting to use the flesh to overcome sinful deeds rooted in our old nature. We cannot use a crucified nature to overcome the flesh that still craves that nature. Jesus said, "A house divided cannot stand;" therefore, trying to use the flesh to overcome itself is a religion that cannot succeed. Grace is the power of God given to us and the invitation to join God in an eternal walk of life.

When speaking of human nature or the flesh, I am referring to the deeds of the old life. We do not have two natures. It can appear that way because the flesh acts according to the old ways of life, but according to scripture, the old nature is buried in Christ. It has no power over us, yet sinful deeds remain in our bodies of flesh and draw us into a fleshly way of thinking.

Legalism is man-dependent. Grace is God-dependent. Legalism bears the weight of our failure and then tries to beat us into submission with guilt, but grace carries us when we cannot stand. Grace calls us to be strong in the Lord and through the power of God's might.[54] Legalism demands more strength than our flesh can provide. The legalist then is either blinded from seeing their failures by human pride, or defeated by human guilt – or a combination of the two.

Sadly, legalism has no eternal value. Anything accomplished is of the flesh and the flesh cannot inherit the kingdom of God.[55] The flesh can do nothing but demand our submission and attempt to rule our life. It will rule us through lusts, and sometimes that lust masquerades as religion and good works. Whether it is open sin or the pride of religion, the life ruled by the flesh misses the promises of God.

This is where the struggle of the Christian life is found. Our entire life has been centered upon the flesh – where the old man once reigned. Now we must learn how to put off the flesh and draw our nature from the inner man. This is what it means to walk in the Spirit.

I grew up in church and have never been taught what it means to walk in the spirit, and this has created a barrier to understanding the inner workings of God in my heart. Once my eyes were opened to the call to walk in the Spirit, everything changed. The flesh lost its grip and the sins and weaknesses I thought I would never overcome became powerless. Consider Jesus' words to the woman at the well in **John 4:**

[13] Jesus answered and said to her, "Whoever drinks of this water will thirst again,

[14] "but whoever drinks of the water that I shall give him will never thirst. But the water that I shall give him will become in him a fountain of water springing up into everlasting life."

If what Jesus said is true, how can any Christian be dry in their soul? Why don't we all have this fountain springing up that constantly quenches our thirst and gives us life eternal? Why don't more Christians experience what Jesus promised?

---

[54] Ephesians 6:10
[55] 1 Corinthians 15:50

The truth is that if you are in Christ, you have this fountain, for it is the outflow of the Holy Spirit.

For many years I read this passage and wondered at it. I often thought, why do I not feel this way? I knew I was a Christian, but also knew that I was not experiencing this fountain springing up and flowing through me. For the first thirty years of my Christian life I lacked this experience. Then I discovered what it truly meant to walk in the Spirit, and everything changed. Not only do I see the broken chains of my past and the victory of freedom, but I also am refreshed by the Spirit as often as I will drink.

This refreshment isn't dependent upon circumstances. It is not dependent on human effort at all. Human effort interferes with the expression of God's grace and power. It is our self-efforts and self-filled lives that clog the flow and prevent us from experiencing what God has given us. You *have been* given all things. That means everything you are seeking for in your spiritual life has already been provided. If you aren't experiencing this, something is in the way. You.

"But you don't know how sinful I have been," you might say. "Can God flow through someone as corrupt as me?"

When the Children of Israel wandered through the barren desert, they asked, "Can God provide?" They looked around the barren land. No water. No food. No provisions. Can God provide a table in this wilderness? Impossible. He would have to open the windows of heaven and make water come out of the rocks. And do you know what He did? He sent manna from heaven and made water gush out of a rock.

Can God make the rivers of living water flow from a barren soul? Can God feed the famished spirit? Don't be faithless! God delights in bringing life out of the barren heart and making the dry soul bloom like a rose. That's the life ready to receive. The Lord does not need a way. He makes the way. He doesn't need the sinless life. He makes the life sinless. He wants the sinner, the failure, the weak, and the hungry.

It does not matter how bad you've blown it. It's God's glory to turn our shame into a trophy of grace. Your sins are not God's barrier. The only barrier God has established for Himself is unbelief. He reveals His goodness and then calls for you to trust in Him. Trust Him and discover what He can really do.

My hope is that you will experience this victory. It's already yours.

Discussion questions:

The Bible says, "May God sanctify you completely" (1 Thessalonians 5:23-24). The Bible then says, "But you were sanctified" (1 Corinthians 6:11). Explain what is sanctified and what is being sanctified.

Why does legalism veil our eyes from the work of Christ?

How is that veil removed?

Review Micah 7:18-19. How are our sins/iniquities brought under control according to this passage?

Review 2 Peter 1:3-4. What is meant by 'all things'?

Is there anything we can add to Christ's work to make it more complete?

How do we receive all these things?

How is the flesh crucified?

What does it mean "since you have put off the old man with his deeds?"

How do we renew our minds? (Ephesians 4:21-24)

Jesus promised those who receive Him will have a fountain of life springing up. Why do many Christians not experience this?

Is spiritual maturity only for a select few?

Life in Abundance

John 10:10

> The thief does not come except to steal, and to kill, and to destroy. I have come that they may have life, and that they may have *it* more abundantly.

Many miss the depth of this promise for two reasons. First, they never learn what it means to abide in Christ, so they remain blinded to the deeper life God has provided. Second, people confuse abundant life with abundant possessions. Jesus constantly warned against loving riches and even stated that things in our life have a tendency to choke the word and make us unfruitful. Jesus also made statements such as, "A person's life does not consist of the things he possesses," "It is hard for a rich man to enter the kingdom of heaven," and "Woe to those who are rich, for you have received your consolation."

While God does not forbid wealth, He does warn us not to strive for the riches of this world or allow ourselves to serve money. The abundant life is not a life filled with possessions, but a life filled with the Spirit. Keep in mind that the same message preached to you is also preached to the bushman who lives in a grass hut. If someone can't have the abundant life in the jungles outside of civilization, then it isn't the abundant life Jesus has promised.

Also consider how Jesus warned that we should *not* be treasuring up for ourselves things here on earth, but the things for heaven.[56]

If possessions were the abundant life, the wealthy should be satisfied, but this clearly is not the case. The attitude of the wealthiest man on earth was, "I need just a little bit more."[57] Things cannot satisfy. Jesus referred to money (or mammon) as something that tested our faithfulness, but the true riches were to those who were faithful.[58] Also consider the words of scripture in **Titus 3:4-7**

> [4] But when the kindness and the love of God our Savior toward man appeared,

---

[56] Matthew 6:19-20

[57] http://www.newworldencyclopedia.org/entry/John_D._Rockefeller

[58] Luke 16:11

^{5} not by works of righteousness which we have done, but according to His mercy He saved us, through the washing of regeneration and renewing of the Holy Spirit,
^{6} whom He poured out on us abundantly through Jesus Christ our Savior,
^{7} that having been justified by His grace we should become heirs according to the hope of eternal life.

The true abundance comes through the Spirit. One day this promise will be visible, but even now we have this given abundantly through Christ by the Spirit. Are you living life more abundantly?

In the passage that introduced this chapter, Jesus is making a contrast. Thieves kill and steal, but He leads His sheep into the abundant life. So what is the abundant life? Do your religious beliefs rob you of joy? Does your spiritual life provide the peace of God, or the grief of your shortcomings? Peace and joy – or the lack thereof – reveals whether Jesus is leading or the false shepherd is robbing. Let's look at **1 Timothy 6:6-11**

^{6} Now godliness with contentment is great gain.
^{7} For we brought nothing into *this* world, *and it is* certain we can carry nothing out.
^{8} And having food and clothing, with these we shall be content.
^{9} But those who desire to be rich fall into temptation and a snare, and *into* many foolish and harmful lusts which drown men in destruction and perdition.
^{10} For the love of money is a root of all *kinds of* evil, for which some have strayed from the faith in their greediness, and pierced themselves through with many sorrows.
^{11} But you, O man of God, flee these things and pursue righteousness, godliness, faith, love, patience, gentleness.

Notice one key point – what was pursued is what came to fruition. Those who pursued the things of this life did not find contentment. They found sorrows. Things satisfy for a moment, but when the moment has passed, there is no contentment. People who pursue satisfaction through things will sorrow in the end. The true gain is godliness with contentment.

Also note that we are called to pursue righteousness, godliness, faith, love, patience, and gentleness. We are not called to produce these things, but to pursue them. We pursue these by pursuing our relationship with our Heavenly Father, for we are partakers of His divine nature. These are ours for the taking, but we must believe God and receive them by faith. Read Galatians 5:22-23. In this passage you will discover that each of these are by the fruit of the Spirit. A life partaking of the Spirit will see these things emerging. This is the normal outflow of spiritual maturity. It's not something you accomplish, but something God produces in you when you walk in the Spirit.

What the natural minded man or woman does not realize is that it is impossible to find contentment through human effort. Contentment cannot be found through romance, friendship, a successful career, money, hobbies, or any other human endeavor. Why do people go through a midlife crisis? Just listen to the words of those going through this struggle. There are generally two mindsets of a midlife crisis, and both prove the truth of the real source of abundant life.

One mindset comes from those who feel as though they have missed out on life. They were always well behaved and kept their life on the straight and narrow. Yet now they look back and feel as though they missed experiencing the world. Now that life is half over, they want to go back and reclaim what was missed in their youth. The symptom of this mindset comes out in many ways, but the end result is almost always heartache.

The second mindset is found in those people who have invested their entire lives in building a career and establishing their financial security. They have all the possessions that the world promised would make them feel successful and satisfied, yet they feel incomplete. It is as if they have invested their lives in climbing the mountain of success only to find that nothing of value is up there. When they finally stop and look at what they have gained, it all appears worthless. If they die with all this stuff, what does it matter? Is this all life has to offer?

Both of these crises have something in common. They are focused on what is passing away and loving what cannot satisfy. Possessions can't satisfy. Experiencing the world cannot satisfy. I've seen many religious and non-religious people come to the point of realizing that all their work is in vain. I have not seen someone who understood what it means to walk with God come to this point. The reason is this – He alone can satisfy. He is our exceedingly great reward.

Let's clarify what it means to walk with God. Walking with God doesn't mean you read your Bible, pray, go to church, and do religious activities. It is possible to do all these things and still never know what it means to have an intimate relationship with God. Walking with the Lord does indeed draw our hearts to prayer, give us the desire to seek Him through the word, and we will do good works and desire fellowship with other Christians. But doing these things does not equate to knowing God. There is a difference between knowing about God and knowing God.

Discovering intimacy with God is what puts life into perspective. Seeking to satisfy ourselves always falls short because we make ourselves the focus of our efforts. We are the source of our satisfaction. But when God opens our eyes to see what it truly means to walk in the Spirit, nothing in this life can satisfy us, *and* yet we are completely satisfied in Him.

This is why the spiritually minded man or woman can't fall into the crisis of living for the world. They already have discovered that a career cannot satisfy. They work, but with the mindset of doing all things for the glory of Christ. They have already discovered that the world cannot satisfy, so the overwhelming urge to regain what was missed is absent. Why should I care that I missed out on the parties, pleasures, and experiences I missed in my youth? Even if they could have a semblance of pleasure, it pales in comparison to the greatness of knowing Christ.

The person who truly discovers what it means to know and walk with Christ will echo the words of **Philippians 3:8-10**

   8 Yet indeed I also count all things loss for the excellence of
   the knowledge of Christ Jesus my Lord, for whom I have
   suffered the loss of all things, and count them as rubbish, that
   I may gain Christ
   9 and be found in Him, not having my own righteousness,
   which *is* from the law, but that which *is* through faith in
   Christ, the righteousness which is from God by faith;
   10 that I may know Him and the power of His resurrection,

and the fellowship of His sufferings, being conformed to His death.

I pray you will discover this truth and count all things of this life as a loss. What I missed out on doesn't matter, because all things are a loss in this life anyway. If I'm cheated or deprived, what does it matter? All things are a loss, for everything is garbage in comparison to the richness of this abundant life I have found.

A destitute man will pick through the stench of a dumpster and rejoice when he finds something he counts as valuable. Yet someone wealthier than him has tossed it away as garbage.

The Christian who lives for the world is the person digging through the dumpster. For a brief moment they rejoice when they find something that has a hint of value, and when the thrill fades, they begin rummaging through the garbage for more. They don't realize that they are digging through garbage because the garbage is all they have ever known. The world appears to have value because they have never glimpsed the excellence of knowing Christ.

We all claim to have this knowledge, but if this were true, the church would be living by a different standard than the world. The Bible warns that many will be ever learning but never able to come to the knowledge of the truth. This is you and I without God's revelation. Bible study and church become places where we gather information, but information alone is just words on a page. We can become databases of knowledge without becoming living people of understanding.

True understanding comes by revelation from God. We are the receivers of knowledge, but we must also become the receivers of God's revelation. Consider the words of **Proverbs 2:1-9**

¹ My son, if you receive my words, And treasure my commands within you,

² So that you incline your ear to wisdom, *And* apply your heart to understanding;

³ Yes, if you cry out for discernment, *And* lift up your voice for understanding,

⁴ If you seek her as silver, And search for her as *for* hidden treasures;

⁵ Then you will understand the fear of the LORD, And find the knowledge of God.

^{6} For the LORD gives wisdom; From His mouth *come* knowledge and understanding;

^{7} He stores up sound wisdom for the upright; *He is* a shield to those who walk uprightly;

^{8} He guards the paths of justice, And preserves the way of His saints.

^{9} Then you will understand righteousness and justice, Equity *and* every good path.

Notice the progression of this passage. Is knowledge important? It certainly is, for unless we receive God's word, we have nothing to understand. But the road doesn't end with the acquisition of knowledge. There must be revelation, and before revelation there is a hunger for understanding. Once we treasure what God has given, we set our hearts to cry out to Him for understanding.

Jesus said, "Blessed are those who hunger and thirst for righteousness, for they shall be filled." But what if there is no hunger. Or no thirst? Where there is no recognized need, there is no vision of God's provision.

Consider the teachings of Jesus. There were times when He taught thousands. They listened to His words, were amazed at His understanding, and then went their way. They took knowledge away, but it was soon lost from their hearts. Jesus likened it to a raven snatching up the seeds on the wayside. They received it with joy, but it was soon taken from their hearts because it never took root.

Jesus taught the multitudes and sent them away, but those who became His disciples came to Him and asked the meaning of what was taught. This was not only Jesus' twelve soon-to-be apostles, but it was both men and women who sought to know His truth. On one occasion, Jesus sent seventy of them out in pairs.[59] In the upper room at Pentecost, there were one-hundred and twenty.[60] Many disciples abandon Jesus when His teachings became too hard to accept.[61] The point to understand is that Jesus did not only teach the inner twelve, but all who would follow Him.

---

[59] Luke 10:1
[60] Acts 1:15
[61] John 6:66

This hasn't changed. Those who seek find. Those who walk away, even though they may receive the word and feel inspired, will lose what they have received. Until there is a hunger to know Him and a thirst to be quenched with the Spirit, a believer's state remains in the flesh. That person lives like a pauper and never discovers the richness of the abundant life. We are heirs to the kingdom, not beggars of this world.

Let me clarify something about the source of hunger. Jesus said that no one can come to Him unless he is first drawn by God. I believe our hunger is the drawing of God's Spirit. Every person in Christ is being constantly drawn to the word and to God, for this is one of the roles of the Holy Spirit. Hunger is the response to God's drawing. People don't feel hunger because they are filling up on other things. Jesus said that the word will be choked out of the life of many because of the cares of this life and other things coming in. God's call is the quiet voice that is heard by those who listen. If other things coming in crowds out the word, we will be filled on junk and miss the hunger God provides.

Few will find the abundant life, even though it has already been given to them through Christ. You *have been* crucified with Christ that the body of sin might be done away with. You *have been* raised with Christ in the newness of life. You *have been* given all things that pertain to life and godliness through Christ. These are all promises in the past tense – not future.

We don't need to pray for our sinful desires to be taken away – that body of sin, where ungodly desires dwell. It has already been done away with.[62] We don't have to ask God to give us a godly mind; we have already been given the mind of Christ.[63] We don't need to ask for these things, we need to ask for God to reveal to us the reality of who we are and what He has given. You have been raised with Christ if you have died with Him.[64]

None of the things written in this book are revolutionary. At one time I thought I was being radical until I started reading and discovering how many others also taught these truths in past generations. This has been taught by the apostles in the scripture, and

---

[62] Romans 6:6
[63] 1 Corinthians 2:16
[64] Romans 6:4

preachers of the word since the beginning. Yet somehow these things are absent from the understanding of the modern church. I say 'modern church', but this problem has been consistent from generation to generation. It seems that only a few truly learn what it means to seek and find in each generation, yet this has been given to all.

It has caused me to ask this question. If growing in fellowship with God has revealed deeper truths of scripture that I was never taught, yet I have come to the same conclusion as others from previous generations and those who recognize it today, why don't more people see these things?

Mere religion doesn't fulfill – even that which is wrapped in a Christian veneer. When people take off the mask and share honestly, few actually say they are abundantly satisfied. They are dependent on circumstances, and more often than not, they have fear, doubt, and uncertainty in their faith. Why aren't Christians more satisfied? Living as a Christian according to what God has revealed satisfies the hungry soul, but living a Christianized religion does not.

Varying beliefs and practices have always come into the church and distracted God's people from the depth of understanding He has intended. It is much easier to teach people how to practice religion than it is to give understanding of the things of the Spirit. The Spirit comes by revelation, and that can't be taught. Principles can be taught, which can show the need for revelation, but ultimately, the abundant life can only be found by the seeking heart that is grounded in the word. By seeking, I mean a heart that seeks to know God and glorify Christ. A heart that seeks its own self-interest remains blind.

It's not possible to teach someone to hunger and thirst for righteousness. It isn't possible to teach someone how to have a heart that cries out for discernment, wisdom, and understanding. Until there is a realization that life must be of Christ or it is worthless, there cannot be a hunger for Him. And since this can't be taught, churches fall back to merely teaching religious practices, and over time the deeper things are forgotten. Then religion and denominationalism take the place of what should only be reserved for Christ.

Knowing this to be true makes a book like this all the more difficult to write. Yet it must be done, for when the heart begins to yearn for something greater than status-quo Christianity, believers need to know where to point their hearts.

Many stand by the wayside with selfish gospels that promise fulfillment. Many claim to have secret knowledge and distract people with hidden meanings, secret Bible codes, personal revelations, and other distractions that give a false pretense of spiritual knowledge. Why is it so appealing to find secret knowledge but we are not excited when someone unveils the plainly stated truth? None of these things are hidden truths. They are hidden only from the fleshly mind, for the things of the Spirit can only be understood through the Holy Spirit. See 1 Corinthians 2:14.

We are only blind to these truths because we don't understand God's call. We are called out of the flesh and into the Spirit. Then we have the promise that God's Spirit teaches us all things and nothing is hidden from us.

Perhaps our first prayer should be to break us so we see our need, and reveal in us the hunger for Him. That alone is the heart God promises to satisfy. When we are dissatisfied with pursuing religion through the flesh we will be open to seeking God through the Spirit. Then we have the promise, "Seek and you shall find."

God wants you to find Him. The urge to seek is the call of God. Answer that call and you will find Him. Yet don't forget that we serve an infinite God. The call to seek never fades. Each truth you discover is the building block for the next thing God is about to reveal. Never stop seeking and you'll never stop discovering. Intimacy with God grows as you learn more about Him as He invites you to walk with Him. It's a never-ending journey.

As we move through the truths of scripture, I pray that you learn how to discern the difference between emotionalism from the Spirit and learning how to discover God's desire to reveal Himself without dependency on a teacher. You already have the anointing of God. Walk in it.

Discussion questions:

What is the abundant life?

Can someone be in poverty and still have the abundant life?

What about someone in prison for their faith?

Life in Abundance

Can we have money and be in God's will?

Can we be in need and be in God's will?

How does our attitude towards the world reveal the affections of our heart?

Can financial stability or success in a career make someone content? Why or why not?

Is financial prosperity the evidence of God's favor? Is poverty the evidence God does not favor someone?

When Jesus taught the masses, why did only a few come to Him afterward?

What happened in the lives of those who thirsted for more?

Can you know God without knowing the Bible?

Can you know the Bible without knowing God?

Review Proverbs 2:1-9. Who has the promises of God's revelation?

Brokenness leads to Spiritual Maturity

Why am I going through this?

You may have heard someone say this. Chances are, you have said it a time or two yourself. It's the natural human reaction to stress or hardship. What few people realize is that God's plan is not to make you happy. Certainly He wants to bless our lives, but God also knows that the greater blessing is not found in the flesh. The flesh becomes addicted to pleasure. We want happiness. We want affirmation. We want to feel God and become addicted to our feelings instead of trusting in faith.

Many times in life will be filled with joy, happiness, peace, and good feelings, but these are not the measure of faith. In fact, the Lord will break us of all dependence on the flesh. Look at the words of **Philippians 3:3**

For we are the circumcision, who worship God in the Spirit, rejoice in Christ Jesus, and have no confidence in the flesh,

The Bible is specifically addressing those who try to become righteous by human effort – namely the Old Testament law of circumcision. But this equally applies to any confidence in the flesh. Feelings are of the flesh. When I say 'of the flesh' I am speaking of our natural personality. Feelings are not evil or good. But they can be either evil or good. There are times when feelings betray us.

The Apostle John said, "Though our hearts condemn us, God is greater than our hearts."[65] There will be times when your feelings will condemn you with irrational fears, guilt, and negative feelings. If your trust is in your feelings, it is not in God. If you put your trust in anything but God, it is not true faith.

The Lord does not want you to be in bondage to the flesh – any part of the flesh. So He will break your dependency on feelings, your confidence in your abilities, or any other human foundation you stand upon.

---

[65] 1 John 3:21

When someone comes to Christ, most people have an overwhelming flood of emotions. This doesn't happen to everyone, but most express this joyful feeling. Yet in a few weeks the feelings begin to fade. Then they put their focus on getting that feeling back. The carnal Christian believes that if they feel good, God is pleased. If they don't, then there is something wrong.

Emotions are fickle. Why do people sin? They are doing what feels good. I've seen Christians act contrary to the Bible because 'It just feels right'. In the end, the feeling is gone and sorrow and shame take place of the feeling. God knows that one of the greatest tools of the devil is your feelings. If he can manipulate someone's feelings, he can manipulate the whole person. That is unless faith has taken its proper place. We can capture a glimpse of the Christian life in **Psalm 23:1-6**

[1] The LORD *is* my shepherd; I shall not want.

[2] He makes me to lie down in green pastures; He leads me beside the still waters.

[3] He restores my soul; He leads me in the paths of righteousness For His name's sake.

[4] Yea, though I walk through the valley of the shadow of death, I will fear no evil; For You *are* with me; Your rod and Your staff, they comfort me.

[5] You prepare a table before me in the presence of my enemies; You anoint my head with oil; My cup runs over.

[6] Surely goodness and mercy shall follow me All the days of my life; And I will dwell in the house of the LORD Forever.

The picture of the Lord being our shepherd shows our complete dependency on Christ and our need to follow wherever He leads. Most of us want to camp out in the green pastures, and we lament when we are taken into the valley. But what is the purpose of the valley? It is where we learn to trust completely on the Lord.

Anyone can have faith in the safety of the pasture, but most are trusting in the pasture and not the Lord. When the Lord becomes the focus, we are comforted by Him regardless of the circumstances.

Just before Jesus went to the cross, He took Peter, James, and John with Him to the top of a mountain. To their amazement, Moses and Elijah met them there and began talking with Jesus about the coming death He would face. As the men turned to leave, Peter stood up and said, "It's good for us to be here. Let us make a tabernacle for You, Moses, and Elijah."

Peter was clinging to the mountain top experience. He did not want it to end, so his idea was to build a camp up there and keep the experience going. But the experience wasn't the purpose. It was the time of encouragement to prepare Jesus for the deepest valley anyone will ever walk through.

This is the natural attitude of every Christian until their life is fully established in Christ. We want the mountain top. We want to build our home there and never leave. But what we don't realize is that we are putting our confidence in the emotions of the moment instead of in the Lord.

God leads us to the mountain of rest. We enjoy the green pastures and quiet waters. But that is not the goal. That is the rest for the journey. When we begin viewing the pasture as though it is the reward, we'll resent the valley of the shadow of death. Instead of saying, "Your rod and staff comfort me. Even though I'm surrounded by enemies, I enjoy fellowship at the table, for you are with me," we are dragging our heels and saying, "Why can't I go back to the pastures?"

God does not want you to trust in the green pastures. God wants you to trust Him. God doesn't want you to love His provisions as though they are your reward. Don't short change yourself. God is your exceedingly great reward. And everything He brings in your life breaks your dependency on anything but Him as it reveals to you the goodness that can only be found while looking to Him for all wants and needs.

Let me illustrate this with a personal testimony. If you've read my other books, you'll be familiar with this story, but I'm going to present it from a clearer perspective.

In 1998, God dramatically intervened in my life. My life was in shambles, and though I became a Christian at a young age, I tried to live out my faith through my own efforts. I failed miserably, but that is for another book. In 1998 my internal world collapsed. On the outside, few people knew what I was going through, but inside everything was falling apart. I completely abandoned the church and my faith. Since I couldn't measure up to Christianity, I would abandon it. Three years later, I realized that abandoning God didn't

Brokenness leads to Spiritual Maturity

work either. I was miserable trying to measure up to God. I was more miserable turning my back on God.

In April of 1998, I took off to walk in the woods and pray. For the next few days I poured my misery out. At last I said the words that summed up my journey, "I can't do it." When I gave up completely, the Lord flooded my life with His presence, broke the chains of my bondage to sin, and I walked out of the woods that day praising the Lord for my freedom. I ended my prayer by saying, "Lord, I know this isn't for me alone. I know you are calling me to study the word and teach it. I cannot pursue my career and you at the same time."

I worked in IT at the time, and because technology changes so fast, everything that is relevant today will be obsolete in a year. It requires dedication to stay certified and knowledgeable. I knew I couldn't serve God in the word and serve my career. So I prayed, "Lord, I put my career completely in your hands. I will focus on knowing Your word, and I leave my financial needs in Your trust."

I could write a hundred pages on the miracles God accomplished through my career. Though I was not faithful as I should be, God was more than faithful. I got raises I did not deserve. I had opportunities to serve in ministry during times when I was paid for projects that were on hold for months at a time. Then my company was bought by a large corporation. By this time I was on a team of eight people who were spread around the country. We were told that the merger was eliminating our positions and we were to find a job in the company or with another company.

It was stressful, but my job was preserved and eventually I was rolled into a department in my new company. As I walked in, they were having a massive layoff. I carried my box in, while hundreds of people were walking out.

Upon my arrival, I found that my new group was going to have a layoff in ninety days. A manager who didn't even know my name was going to decide my fate. Or was he? I found myself in a position where I knew nothing and had no help. The contractor supposed to help me was let go the next day, and I was responsible for converting the entire building to a new network setup. One I knew nothing about. Nor did my team. Nor did my manager.

I sat down and prayed, "Lord, I'm lost. I've asked for help, but no one can help me. I don't even know how to connect to the network of this new company, and I am falling flat on my face. Show me where to turn."

Before I finished speaking the words, a man named John Crawford walked by, saw my scattering of papers, and said, "Oh, I see you are on the migration team. I was the guy who worked out the process." I looked up with a gaping mouth as John told me all about the project and what they did to set it up. He told me about the tools and documentation he wrote. I never even asked him a question. I opened my mouth to say something, but he looked at his watch and said, "Oh goodness! I've got another meeting. It's not easy being indispensable." And with that, he was gone.

Suddenly I was off and running. Then another person came by. Steve. He was soon to be one of my coworkers. Steve was a geek in the truest sense of the word. He loved technology and he talked about some tools he found on our IT sight and how he was using it to automate some of his tasks. As he talked, I realized that I could use these for my project. I had more than a thousand people to convert and I was working solo.

A few weeks later, teams from other cities were calling my boss and asking how Atlanta was getting done so quickly. It wasn't long before I was training teams in across the country and before the ninety days was up, every person in upper management knew my name. And everything seemed to drop straight in my lap.

Then the layoff day arrived and my manager was let go. In fact, every person in our department was let go. Then managers would call and offer jobs to those they wanted on their team. The new IT manager was Jack Liggins. I had never met the man, but I was the first person he called. He offered me the position of team lead in his group. Again I stood in amazement. Three months ago, there was no hope that I would survive this lay off, but now my reputation had grown to the point where a manager who never met me was offering me his lead position.

I was in the green pastures. I thought this was the Christian life. Blessings built my confidence in the Lord, miracles showed His power to direct my paths, and I knew God was in control. I was pleased that my reputation was so highly regarded throughout the company. What I didn't realize is that God was showing me His power so that I would trust Him when hardship threatened me.

I was confident in my job. I was confident with my IT skills. I was confident that God had gifted me to be analytical and I was good at taking processes and improving them. I was confident in my reputation. Then the company had another reduction in staff. I survived the cut, but my manager did not. Two IT teams were combined into one, and I was under a new manager. This time I knew the manager and felt good about the move.

Within a few months, I realized I had a problem. The manager was very unethical and had favorite tech that were not required to even show up for work. Their timesheets were forged and even though all their tickets went past due, the reports always showed them on time. And it was the team lead's job to make sure the numbers were cooked. My job was to cover for those who weren't working, and hide the fact that our team wasn't fulfilling the company's requirements.

At first, I thought the manager wasn't aware of what was going on. The manager kept denying there was an issue and acted as if they were ignorant, so I took the true numbers to them and said, "Look at this. This tech is past due on everything. One problem ticket sat without any action for seven months, but it was changed on the reports to show that it was completed on time. I can't cover for these past due tickets."

That was the day the world turned upside down. The manager printed something out, came to my desk and threw a handful of reports at me and said, "This is the report I go by." The manager was shaking with rage and this reaction caught me completely by surprise. Up to this moment, we had a great working relationship. But now a condemning finger pointed at my face and I heard the words, "Eddie, when I write someone off, I never forgive, and I never go back!"

I was demoted from team lead, and the manager went on a campaign to remove me from the company. That's when I began to hear the stories that this had happened before. Twice. And both people who questioned this practice were let go by the company. Now I was in the gun sights.

Every time a ticket was about to go past due, it was assigned to me. I was given a forty-thousand mile coverage area for retail and office sites. The next highest coverage area was less than a hundred miles. I put in 60 – 80 hours a week to cover my workload. I tried to overcome this adversity with higher performance. Even though I had the highest production in the group, my reputation was being massacred.

When my work was surveyed, my customers gave me the highest possible ratings, but my manager gave me the lowest possible rating. Surely someone has to see a problem with this.

A few months earlier, managers were coming to town and taking me to lunch. I was being invited to be on important projects. I even led a management training class that was attended by managers and prospective managers all over the nation. Now I was hearing things like, "What happened to Eddie?" Why couldn't they see that this was slander? I had a review a couple of months earlier, and it had nothing but praise. A month later my quarterly review had nothing but failures. No one saw that the tickets were assigned to me after it was past due. Or that the project was given to me right before the deadline. Or that my projects were reassigned to other techs after the work was done.

I could go on and on, but I think you get the picture. I once counted on my reputation, and now it was gone. Though I counted on my high performance to prove my work ethic, no one noticed. I contested my review and disproved every allegation. The specifics were removed, but the law rating remained. Human Resources said they trusted the manager's evaluation of performance. I was called to attend a conference call a supposed failure where I was sent to one city and was supposed to be in another. I produced the email that sent me to the wrong place, but the director said, "Your manager explained to me that you were instructed that this email was incorrect and you knew what was expected of you."

Everything I depended upon was gone. My reputation was demolished. My integrity was trashed in the eyes of others. My performance was counted as worthless. My promotion had been taken away. Now my very job was in jeopardy. This had been going on for two years at this point.

"Lord, isn't my reputation important to you?" I prayed.

The truth is, God doesn't need my reputation. He gave it to me, and He has the right to take it away if that's within His purpose.

"Lord, what about my job? This person is going to make me lose my job. And I've done nothing but work my tail off."

It was as if the Lord said, "Have you learned nothing over the last several years? Weren't you told that your job was being eliminated? What did you have to do? Nothing. I told you to wait, and you saw My ability to make a place for you. And I exalted you when you didn't work for it. Do I now owe you because you are working for it now? Did I tell you to dedicate every waking hour to your job? Can man take away your job against My will? Who do you trust, your manager or Me? Your efforts or Me? Your reputation or Me? Your abilities or Me?

Then the Lord revealed the scripture, "Christ suffered, leaving us an example…when He was reviled, did not revile in return. When He suffered, He didn't threaten, but committed Himself to Him who judges righteously."

Now that will cut to the heart. God called me to take my notes where I was keeping a log to protect myself, and cast it away. He called me to forgive and pray for the one who was trying to harm me. Most of all, God called me to release all into His hands, and trust Him. He judges righteously and He will plead my cause or will sustain me in spite of hardships.

What God was doing is breaking me. He broke my confidence in the flesh. My reputation depended upon people. Gone. My performance depended upon myself. Worthless. My defense of myself also depended upon the flesh. Gone. It was easy to see God's hand in the green pasture and beside the quiet waters, but it took a long time to realize that the turbulent river of stress and the valley of struggle was also His blessing.

As long as I trusted in my abilities or anything of the flesh, I was not dependent upon the Lord. The flesh had become a crutch and now God was calling for me to walk by His power.

We all struggle with the flesh. We depend upon feelings, and God weans us off them as He reveals to us true faith in Him. We depend upon those around us, and tension strains relationships and God calls us to trust in Him and not men. We work in the church, do ministry, and perform in many ways because we are depending on the flesh. We are trying to earn the affirmation and praise of people, or are trying to feel self-worth by performance based religion. God will break these things.

For two years I fought against God's hand because I clung to the flesh thinking it was a blessing from God. I tried to protect the reputation He gave me. But God didn't ask me to defend my reputation. He called me to break my reliance on it and place my reliance on Him.

Once my understanding dawned, bitterness also dissipated. How can I be embittered against someone God was using to mature me into His grace? My manager didn't harm me. This person was a tool of God's compassion and love, used to show me what I could not have learned any other way. If anything, I should be grateful to God for bringing this person into my life.

Spiritual maturity cannot occur until we are weaned off the flesh and onto faith in Christ alone. God is not looking for self-reliant Christians. In fact, God rejects self-reliance completely. God does not help those who help themselves. God is the help. Christ is our life. Just as He made Himself of no reputation, now He asks us to follow that lead. My reputation means nothing. If God wants to exalt me in His time, He will do so. If God is better glorified by humbling me, I must trust in His will.

The spiritually mature are not those who have been Christians the longest. It is not those who are the oldest in the church. It is not those who serve more. Nor is it those who know the Bible the best. Faith is not based on how many scriptures you have memorized, but whether you are walking by faith. Faith is to have no confidence in the flesh, and complete confidence in Christ and all He provides.

God will break you. By breaking, I don't mean to destroy, but to break you away from the flesh so you cling to Him. A broken Christian is one who has released confidence in everything but God. We should be in a position to where we cannot be sustained unless God is holding us up.

Is your health failing? Release the hope in the flesh and trust completely in the Lord. Are your finances gasping for life? Release your trust in money and cling to the Lord. God has the right to take anything from our lives, and we trust in His decision because He has promised that everything is good to those who are called into His purpose.

Would I have had to endure three years of stress if I had learned to trust sooner? I don't know. I do know that God left me in that situation for another year after I released my confidence into His hands. Whether it would have been three years or six months, it doesn't matter. The burden was not mine to carry, and my stress was needless because I was bearing a burden God had reserved for

Himself. God allowed the burden to break me so that I would understand that I could not carry it.

One day when Jesus sat at a table for dinner, a woman came in with an alabaster box of precious ointment. Its value was equivalent of a year's wages. She broke the box and poured the ointment on Jesus' head. The room was filled with the fragrance. Many scoffed and called her act a waste. She could have used the box for a special occasion. She could have sold it for a year's wage and used it to feed the poor. Yet Jesus praised the woman for celebrating His burial.

This is the broken life in the flesh. While the flesh is strong, it's just a box that houses our pent up life. But when it is broken, the aroma spreads to the world around us. We have died, and the Spirit of God is free to do its work. Many will scoff, but God will rejoice. To celebrate the death of the flesh is to celebrate the life of the Spirit.

While you are holding on to your life, you remain alone. The Bible says that the Christian is the aroma of the world. To those who are lost, we are the aroma of death. To those who are being saved, they experience the aroma of life.[66]

I'm sure the woman treasured this box, but once she recognized the value of Christ's death, she was willing to pour out what she valued to receive His life.

Likewise, how did Jesus feed the masses? A young child brought a few fish and a loaf. Jesus broke them and used them for a work greater than what the unbroken items could have done on their own.

When you offer your life to God, He will break it. Don't view brokenness as the hand of scourging. It is God breaking what has no value in order to produce something of immeasurable value. The flesh is broken so you can experience the fullness of the Spirit. And you know what? The flesh is already dead. It's worthless. God is breaking what is worthless in order to reveal what is priceless.

To the woman with the alabaster box, she probably viewed the box and valuable. But the box itself was worthless. It was what was in the box that had value. Don't view your life in the flesh as valued. Let God break it and discover the true value of God's favor.

---

[66] 2 Corinthians 2:16

The process of breaking doesn't have to be difficult. It is only difficult because we are holding on to what must die. The tighter I cling to the flesh, the more I will experience the suffering of the flesh.

Once we let go, we may still have to endure, but we'll experience peace instead of frustration. We'll view our circumstance as God's hand of love instead of life's hardship. Instead of saying, "Why is this happening," we'll be rejoicing in what God is doing.

A Christian who recognizes God's love will willingly release what God is pruning away. A child who trusts experiences the joy of God's love.

I have several daughters. When my oldest daughter was very young, she was trusting of me. One day she got something in her eye that caused her pain. I took some eyewash and had her lay on a towel. Though she didn't like for me to mess with her eye, she allowed me to flush it and get the obstacle to the corner so I could pick it out. I couldn't leave the item in her eye, or it would have caused more problems. In a few minutes, she was up and relieved to have the debris out.

The almost identical thing happened to another daughter years later. She came in crying that something was in her eye. I wanted to flush it out, but she wouldn't let me. When she squinted her eye, the object caused her great pain. But when I tried to put drops in, she screamed and fought me. Though the object in her eye was causing her pain, she was unwilling to allow me to remove it or even put eyewash in her eye.

I gave up, but she was in such pain, I had to do something. If I took her to the hospital, they would just do the same thing I was trying to do. Finally I had to restrain her and put the flush in her eye. What should have taken a couple of minutes took more than an hour.

This is a picture of how we relate to God. If we put our trust in Him, God removes the things that prevent our life from blossoming in Christ. If we fight Him, we are only causing more pain. God is more interested in your benefit than your comfort. Sometimes He allows us to scream until we are too exhausted to resist. Sometimes God will force His will upon us for our good. Other times, He will allow our burden to become so heavy that we have no place to turn but Him.

But what if we learned to trust Him so we didn't have to suffer needlessly?

Brokenness leads to Spiritual Maturity

Don't misunderstand me. Suffering in this life is necessary. Shortly, we will look at the life of Job. He was faithful in all his ways, yet the Lord allowed him to be stripped of everything he valued. Job's faith was proven true, but Job was also pruned of his self-righteousness.

We'll also examine the life of Joseph. He too was faithful, but went through thirteen years of trials. Yet the suffering was necessary in order to strip away all self-confidence. As a youth, God revealed that Joseph would become great, and he boasted of this to his brothers on several occasions. Joseph thought he was special, and his calling was tainted by human pride. But when he stood before his brothers at the end, he fully understood God's hand and purposes.

It wasn't because Joseph was better than his brothers. It was because God wanted to show His own power through the weakness of Joseph and through many miraculous events, Joseph and his people were saved from a seven year famine.

Another example is Peter. Peter loved Jesus with all his heart. He was so dedicated to the faith that Jesus nicknamed him Cephas – a stone. Though Peter obeyed everything Jesus commanded, his confidence was in himself. When Jesus foretold that all would be offended and abandon Him, Peter said, "I will never abandon or deny you. I will die with you." 'Self' was his confidence.

Judas betrayed Christ and showed up with a detachment of soldiers. The word used in John 18:3 is the Greek word 'speira', which is a unit of 600 men. This means that Peter drew a sword, stepped between Jesus and went into battle against 600 warriors. Now that is courage.

But Jesus rebuked him. He thought he was doing God's work, and when rebuked, he went into an emotional tailspin. A few verses later, Peter is being accused by a servant girl. To put this into perspective, this girl's testimony was inadmissible in that era. Yet Peter coward in fear at her accusation and denied Christ – not once, but three times.

A few hours earlier, Peter was bulging with self-confidence, but now he was a broken man, weeping bitterly at his failure. But the truth is that Peter was not walking in faith until all his confidence was stripped away. Once his flesh was slain and his reputation laid in the dust, Jesus restored him and God used Peter mightily. But while in his own strength, Peter was a man of the flesh acting in the flesh.

In the same way, God will strip you of what is worthless in the flesh so that the life of the Spirit can be powerful in your life. God has said, "My strength is made perfect in weakness." As long as you are strong for the Lord, you are all the strength you have. But once all confidence in you has been removed, you'll discover true confidence – the strength of the Lord.

Let me say this again – spiritual maturity is when you learn to cease from trusting in yourself and rely completely on the Lord. Maturity is when you cease from your own labors, and trust in the work of Christ. When self-confidence is gone, Christ confidence emerges. That is your strength. Anything else is merely the flesh.

Are you frustrated? Exasperated? Stressed? Fearful? These are all signs that our hope is through the flesh. Have no confidence in the flesh. That is true spiritual maturity.

Set your minds on things above (eternal), not on things of the earth.[67] Once the flesh is broken and the eternal perspective becomes what you value, the things of the earth will lose their grip on your heart and mind.

Discussion questions:

Explain what brokenness means in your own words.

Why did Jesus rebuke Peter when he defended Christ?

Was God angry at Peter for denying Jesus?

Was Peter's denial part of God's plan?

Did Peter's failure benefit his spiritual life?

Read Luke 9:33-35. What can we learn from this to apply to our own lives?

When God takes you through trouble, what is God's purpose behind it?

---

[67] Colossians 3:2

Brokenness leads to Spiritual Maturity

Will trials ever be more than we can bear? Why or why not?

Why does God break the flesh?

If we get angry at God, does He stop the trials?

Is it possible for our reaction to cause a longer struggle?

If God is love, how does that affect our view of God's process of breaking the flesh?

Why does God want to break our strength?

Spirit, Soul, and Body

I was taught to scoff at the concept of anything but spirit and body. The concept of a separation between spirit and soul was considered error, but since the Bible clearly makes this distinction, it's not something we can reject. Plus, it's vital to know that we have an incorruptible spirit – even when our soul acts according to the flesh. Learning to discern between the desires of soul and the spirit helps us to also learn how to train our minds as to which source to accept direction from.

Rejecting these scriptures hindered my understanding of spiritual living. Of course, I would have never said that I rejected scripture, but anytime I have to explain away something that does not fit my belief system, I am rejecting scripture by choosing my beliefs over God's word.

Even the Old Testament draws a distinction between the soul and the spirit. In the example I'm about to use, Eli the priest saw Hannah in the temple, mouthing words as she poured her heart to God. He thought she was drunk and questioned her behavior. Look at **1 Samuel 1:15**

> And Hannah answered and said, "No, my lord, I *am* a woman of sorrowful spirit. I have drunk neither wine nor intoxicating drink, but have poured out my soul before the LORD.

The anguish of Hannah's soul was born out of a sorrowful spirit. As is the case with many spiritual truths, what is hinted at in the Old Testament is made plain in the New Testament. Consider this clear passage from **Hebrews 4:12**

> For the word of God *is* living and powerful, and sharper than any two-edged sword, piercing even to the division of soul and spirit, and of joints and marrow, and is a discerner of the thoughts and intents of the heart.

Why does the word of God divide the spirit from the soul? Why does the Bible make a distinction between the spirit and the soul? Because they are two parts of our being. This will be made even more clear as we examine more passages, but let's first talk about the differences between the body, soul, and spirit.

The body is our physical being. It's how we interact with the world and sense all that is around us. The soul is our personality. It's a combination of our emotions, intellect, and is subject to our will. It's the part of you that creates your individuality. The spirit is the inner being of man. It's the place where we interact with the spiritual realm.

Think back to Adam. God commanded, "Of every tree of the garden you may freely eat; but of the tree of the knowledge of good and evil you shall not eat, for in the day that you eat of it you shall surely die."[68] The law was presented, and what was man attracted to? The plethora of good things provided by God? Or the one thing he couldn't have? The law stirred man toward temptation and he ate of the only tree forbidden to him. Did Adam die the day he ate of the tree? Absolutely.

Death is the cessation of life. To be dead to God means that we no longer have life with Him. The wages of sin is death, and Adam died the moment he turned from God and sought fulfillment in his own soul.

Something in Adam died the moment he sinned. Once the spirit was cut off from God, man became self-focused instead of God-focused. While man was God-conscious, he had no consciousness of sin or his condition. But once spiritual death took place, man began looking to himself and his knowledge of good and evil. And what was the first thing he saw? We'll let Adam explain, "I heard Your voice [God's], I was afraid because I was naked, and I hid myself."

Who told Adam he was naked? His own soul testified against him with the new found knowledge of good and evil. Before the fall, good was found in the Lord and mankind enjoyed partaking of God's goodness. After the fall, separation occurred and man looked to himself for goodness. Instead of finding goodness, he saw nakedness and shame. This caused him to hide from God and seek to cover himself. And we still struggle with the knowledge of good and evil today.

In Christ, the death of Adam is reversed through the new life given to us by the Spirit. In spiritual maturity, we must wean our focus off our own souls and learn how to again become God focused and God-conscious. Because we were raised within human nature, we

---

[68] Genesis 2:16-17

naturally rely on our soul for knowledge and understanding. But our soul is focused upon itself and how it interacts with the world through our bodies. Yet we need to cease from looking at our soul for answers and begin looking to the Spirit.

In the spirit, we become God-focused. In the flesh, we become self-focused. In self, we see nakedness and shame. The more focused I am on my performance, self-confidence, and self-reliance on my own righteousness, I am more focused on where I fall short. It is the knowledge of good an evil.

Though we try to focus on our own goodness, that goodness is tied to a dead nature, and no matter how much self-improvement we accomplish or how many good deeds we perform, the knowledge of evil is always there. People practice self-deception and convince themselves that they are good, but in the back of every person's mind is a knowledge of our shortcomings.

Something unexpected happens when we become God-conscious. Our focus is taken off ourselves and our spirit blossoms into full growth. When our spirit thrives, it empowers our soul to live by a godly standard and this flows out to our actions in the body. Our soul rejoices in the Lord and this affects every area of our life. That's why the Bible says that we are changed into His likeness as we look at Christ.[69]

The naturally minded man takes the opposite approach. He starts with the body and tries to work toward the soul. The natural man tries to change who he is by what he does. While this might have limited short-lived success, what I do can never change who I am. However, who I am directly affects what I do.

Sin comes from the outside and works its way inward. Temptation comes from desiring something, receiving it into the mind, conceiving it in our heart, and then executing sin through our actions, attitudes, and behaviors. Righteousness comes from the Holy Spirit within us, through the new spirit we have been given, transforms our soul, and changes behavior, attitudes, and actions. That's why sanctification begins in our spirit. **1 Thessalonians 5:23-24**

> [23] Now may the God of peace Himself sanctify you
> completely; and may your whole spirit, soul, and body be

---

[69] 2 Corinthians 3:18

Spirit, Soul, and Body

preserved blameless at the coming of our Lord Jesus Christ. [24] He who calls you *is* faithful, who also will do *it*.

Notice the process. Sanctification begins in the spirit and flows to the soul and body. The reason is that the person we are in Christ has already been sanctified. And the process of transformation completes the process in our soul and body. Consider **1 Corinthians 6:11**

> And such were some of you. But you were washed, but you were sanctified, but you were justified in the name of the Lord Jesus and by the Spirit of our God.

In this passage, Paul is explaining how that the church should not be living by the standard of the world – those who cannot inherit the Kingdom of God. He lists the sinful behaviors in the world, and then says, "And such were some of you." In Christ, they were sanctified – past tense.

In Christ, you were sanctified – past tense. In Christ, you were justified – past tense. In Christ, you were crucified with Him and the body of sin has been done away with.[70] The result? We are no longer slaves of sin. Consider **2 Corinthians 5:17-18a**

> [17] Therefore, if anyone *is* in Christ, *he is* a new creation; old things have passed away; behold, all things have become new.
> [18] Now all things *are* of God, who has reconciled us to Himself through Jesus Christ,

You are not the sinner you were before Christ. The spirit that was alienated from God was crucified with Christ and you were born again by the Spirit. You have a new spirit and you are a new creation. Let's bring another passage into the discussion to help clarify. **1 John 3:9**

> Whoever has been born of God does not sin, for His seed remains in him; and he cannot sin, because he has been born of God.

---

[70] Romans 6:6

Spirit, Soul, and Body

Until I understood the difference between my spirit and soul, this passage used to disturb me. How can I be a child of God if I still sin? Rather than answering this with my words, let's let the Apostle Paul answer in **Romans 7:22-25**

> [22] For I delight in the law of God according to the inward man.
>
> [23] But I see another law in my members, warring against the law of my mind, and bringing me into captivity to the law of sin which is in my members.
>
> [24] O wretched man that I am! Who will deliver me from this body of death?
>
> [25] I thank God -- through Jesus Christ our Lord! So then, with the mind I myself serve the law of God, but with the flesh the law of sin.

Where does sin dwell? In our flesh. What part of us rejoices in the law of God? The inner man. The inner man is that new spirit. The old man has been put to death and the inner man is born of God. It cannot sin because its life is in God and intimately bound to the Holy Spirit. This is how Christ dwells in us and we in Him. Our inner man is in Christ. Christ is inside us through the Holy Spirit. This is why the Bible says, "Do you not know that you are the temple of the Holy Spirit who is within you?"[71]

You are not the sinful man or woman you were before Christ. If Christ is in you, that person is dead and gone. You are not that person anymore. Your body doesn't understand this truth. Your soul does not understand this truth – at least not at first.

In the past, your soul lived only to serve your body. Your spirit was dead to God and was made subject to the desires of your soul. But when the word came, so did faith. Faith comes by hearing the word of God. The word of God, when believed and received, does it's work. One work is to divide the soul from the spirit. The old spirit is put to death, and a new spirit is born when the Holy Spirit created new life within us.

But there is a problem we all must deal with. The soul still desires to live according to the flesh and through the flesh, sin seeks to overrule our spirit. Because most Christians don't understand the

---

[71] 1 Corinthians 6:19

power of the spirit, we subject ourselves to the desires of the flesh and allow it to again rule. As Paul put it, sin within my flesh wars against my mind, trying to bring it back into subjection to sin. The mind should be under the control of our spirit, but can be made subject to our soul. When the soul follows the desire of the flesh, we begin looking to the flesh for help, but find bondage. Yet most Christians try to live the Christian life through the flesh because that is all they have ever known. And the flesh's desire is to bring you under bondage to serve its desires.

That is when the Christian becomes carnally minded and lives according to the wages of sin instead of the promise of the Spirit.

I realize this is a lot to process, but understanding this is vital to walking in the Spirit. Our new spirit is in constant fellowship with God through His Holy Spirit. Through our spirit, the mind of Christ is revealed and we discover the will of God. The inner man rejoices in the law of God. We are not trying to connect to God through the law. We *are* connected to God, and through this fellowship the law naturally flows into our life. We aren't keeping the law, we are partakers of God's divine nature, and this is our natural delight.

Let's search out this truth from the word. This is a long passage, but carefully read it, for this is a vital part of living in the Spirit. **1 Corinthians 2:9-16**

^{9} But as it is written: "Eye has not seen, nor ear heard, Nor have entered into the heart of man The things which God has prepared for those who love Him."

^{10} But God has revealed *them* to us through His Spirit. For the Spirit searches all things, yes, the deep things of God.

^{11} For what man knows the things of a man except the spirit of the man which is in him? Even so no one knows the things of God except the Spirit of God.

^{12} Now we have received, not the spirit of the world, but the Spirit who is from God, that we might know the things that have been freely given to us by God.

^{13} These things we also speak, not in words which man's wisdom teaches but which the Holy Spirit teaches, comparing spiritual things with spiritual.

^{14} But the natural man does not receive the things of the Spirit of God, for they are foolishness to him; nor can he know *them,* because they are spiritually discerned.

^{15} But he who is spiritual judges all things, yet he himself is *rightly* judged by no one.
^{16} For "who has known the mind of the LORD that he may instruct Him?" But we have the mind of Christ.

What a wonderful treasure trove of truth we find in this passage! First take note of verse 10, God has revealed His truth to us by His Spirit. The passage goes on to explain that God's Spirit is communicating with the spirit of man to reveal the things the world cannot perceive.

Man's wisdom falls short. This includes wisdom from the world – those trying to influence you by human understanding, and the wisdom coming from your own soul. Wisdom born from our own intellect is not the wisdom of God. God did not remove our flesh, but instead gave us a new spirit that draws revelation directly from the Spirit of God. We have the mind of Christ because the Spirit of Christ has taken up residence within us.

God's Spirit is communing with our spirit and revealing the will of God and the mind of Christ. However, if we are drawing from our soul, we will be led by the flesh and never perceive the prompting of the Spirit. In fact, we can become so callous that we become unaware of our spirit and God's Spirit within us. We must lead our soul through the Spirit, and not allow the soul to be our leader.

Spiritual maturity comes as we learn how to perceive God through our spirit and learning how to discern between emotions and the prompting of God.

This can be very difficult because emotions can mimic affirmation. Even the cults know this. While talking to a Mormon he gave a request, "Just pray about the Book of Mormon and see if God affirms it to you."

Why pray about what God has already answered? I'm told to test the spirits to see if they are of God, not seek affirmation from the spirits. If you pray about something, you are putting yourself in the mindset to receive it. I've heard a Christian give a testimony that her adultery was of God. How did she come to that conclusion? Because when she prayed, she felt right about leaving her husband and going to her new found love. And because the thought made her happy, she was sure it was God's will.

Spirit, Soul, and Body

Emotions will deceive you. Prayer is the process of seeking the Lord – not seeking what we want. Certainly we pour out our needs and seek guidance. But prayer is not saying, "God bless what I'm doing." Prayer is saying, "God reveal yourself and your will to me."

Look at the example of Jesus in the garden just before He was arrested. He knew the crucifixion was at hand, but He prayed, "Father, if there is any other way, let this cup pass from Me. Even so, not My will, but Yours be done."

What did Jesus desire? He wanted to escape the cross. This was despite the fact that He testified, "It was for this purpose I came into the world." But what was the fruit of His prayer. His goal was to push His will (to escape suffering) out of the way and to submit to the will of the Father.

We follow the same model. I might want something, but I am not praying to receive what I want, but for God to reveal His will to me. If our will is in agreement with God, then that prayer will be affirmed in our spirit – not necessarily in our emotions. More times than not, we'll find ourselves submitting, not our will but Yours.

God planned His will into creation; therefore, only one purpose will stand. The question is, will I be standing in that purpose, or will I be standing upon human desire.

Even so, one thing is important. If your focus is to know Christ through His word and learn what it means to commune with God, the purposes of God will fall into place. It is not possible to seek God and walk with Him intimately, and miss His will or promises. God will not let the godly fall short of His goodness. And who is godly? Those who learn what it means to be a partaker of His nature. The godly are not those who force themselves to act according to a self-imposed standard, but rather it is those who delight according to the inward man. Those are the ones who walk in the understanding that comes from the mind of Christ.

You have the mind of Christ. You have an incorruptible nature. You have been sanctified, justified, crucified, and raised into a new life that is of God with eternal promises. That is why the Bible says, since we are in the Spirit, let us also walk in the Spirit. Walk in who you are, not what the flesh is or who you were.

Let me address one other thing before moving ahead. The passage we looked at earlier stated we have the hope that we would be sanctified completely, spirit, soul, and body. Yet we are also told that we have been sanctified through Christ.

Is this a contradiction? No. You have been sanctified, or set apart for God. Who are you? You are a new creation, born of God through the Spirit. You are a new man (or woman) that cannot sin from a spirit that is incorruptible. Our spirit has to be incorruptible because it is in Christ and is the life of the Holy Spirit. Your inner man is sanctified. Everything you need has already been accomplished by Christ and is given to any who are in Christ.

Your soul still desires the flesh. We can understand this better by looking at the words of Christ in **Luke 5:37-39**

> [37] "And no one puts new wine into old wineskins; or else the new wine will burst the wineskins and be spilled, and the wineskins will be ruined.
> [38] "But new wine must be put into new wineskins, and both are preserved.
> [39] "And no one, having drunk old *wine,* immediately desires new; for he says, 'The old is better.' "

Your old nature cannot contain the new wine of the Spirit. You become new, and the Spirit is contained in you. But your personality is confused. Your flesh still desires the old life because it things the old is better. That's why we sin. We are stuck in the old mindset and haven't learned how to taste the goodness of the Lord. To the flesh, the old is better, but to the inner man, who lives according to an eternal perspective, the new wine refreshes while the old wine is despised. It's passing away, but the new wine is eternal.

Don't be surprised if you or someone you know does not immediately desire the eternal things. Even if we don't want to go back, our flesh still desires the old ways. But as we learn to live according to the new man, the old becomes foul and the new becomes sweet. This is a maturing process.

Maturity does not come by resisting the old and force-feeding the new. Maturity comes by experiencing the goodness of God. As we grow in intimacy with God, we lose our taste for the world we are leaving behind. It's natural to pursue the things you desire. The inner man delights in the law of God, but the flesh delights in sin. This is why Paul lamented, "Who will deliver me from this body of death?" But then he answers that question. Remember Paul's answer? I thank

God through Jesus Christ our Lord! Though the flesh serves the law of sin, the mind – which is connected to the inner man – he serves (and we serve) the law of Christ.

He began by crying out, "Who shall deliver me from this body of death?" But he ended by thanking God for the answer. It was through Christ our Lord. Through Christ he found the power to serve the law of God. The mind, which is renewed in Christ, has the power to serve God and bring the body under subjection. When he served the body, sin was the result. When his mind was in Christ, the law of God naturally flowed into his life.

The same is true for you. The body is not your master. Nor is the body where you carry out the will of God. The will of God is received through the mind connected to Christ in the Spirit, and out of that mind the body is put to service for the good of the Lord's will. Only then can your body become a living sacrifice.

Deliverance is found in Christ. We rejoice that He has delivered us. In the flesh, sin dominates our lives and any who walk in the flesh will serve sin. Even the religious man serves his flesh. But in Christ, we delight in the law of God. We don't force ourselves to do God's law. We are not pursuing the law. We are not pursuing righteous works. We are pursuing Christ and discovering the relationship we have through the inner man. The natural result is the outflow of Christ. Godliness is the natural result of pursuing the desires of the heart that walks in the Spirit. That is when we experience the promise of **Galatians 5:16**

> I say then: Walk in the Spirit, and you shall not fulfill the lust of the flesh.

What work is involved in walking? It's not what you do for God. God has entered your life, invited you to join Him, and you are walking with God and growing in His grace. The Christian life is about walking where God leads. In our spirit we have fellowship, but God wants that fellowship to be part of our conscious life as He sets us apart for intimacy with Him. Now let's look at **Galatians 5:24-25**

> 24 And those *who are* Christ's have crucified the flesh with its passions and desires.
> 25 If we live in the Spirit, let us also walk in the Spirit.

Does the Bible tell us to get into the Spirit? Do we have to do something to make ourselves spiritual so we can walk with God? Or not do something so we aren't excluded from God? This was written to a church where Paul declared, "You have fallen from grace."

Do you remember the definition of grace? It is the unmerited favor of God. Mercy is God not giving us the judgment for sin. Grace takes this farther by giving us all His promises apart from any merit we may or may not have done. In fact, the Galatian church fell from grace because they were influenced by religious people who said they must fulfill the law in order to fully enter God's covenant.

The truth is, the covenant of God is between Christ on the cross and the Father. The covenant was sealed by Christ's blood, and per the terms of a blood covenant, it cannot be broken. The Father and the Son have an eternal seal based on what Jesus accomplished on the cross. Anyone who is in Christ is in the covenant. Period.

Those who fell from grace did so because they turned from grace and became self-focused. They put their trust in their efforts, man-dependent laws, and covenants that were outside of Christ. The Bible clearly addresses religion in **Colossians 2:18-23**

[18] Let no one cheat you of your reward, taking delight in *false* humility and worship of angels, intruding into those things which he has not seen, vainly puffed up by his fleshly mind,

[19] and not holding fast to the Head, from whom all the body, nourished and knit together by joints and ligaments, grows with the increase *that is* from God.

[20] Therefore, if you died with Christ from the basic principles of the world, why, as *though* living in the world, do you subject yourselves to regulations --

[21] "Do not touch, do not taste, do not handle,"

[22] which all concern things which perish with the using -- according to the commandments and doctrines of men?

[23] These things indeed have an appearance of wisdom in self-imposed religion, *false* humility, and neglect of the body, *but are* of no value against the indulgence of the flesh.

Who are those who fall from grace? It's those who let go of the head – Christ – and turn to religious practices. These have a show of

Spirit, Soul, and Body

wisdom and mimic godliness, but they have no profit. Look closely at the end of verse 23. Religious practices have no value. Period. They can't make you holy or righteous. They can't bring your flesh under control. The only thing religion can do is turn your eyes away from Christ and tempt you to let go of Him as your head.

Any practice of man's effort, regardless of how much it has an appearance of godliness, cannot improve your spiritual condition. It cannot merit salvation, blessings, or produce righteousness. The only thing religion can do is cause you to fall from grace.

Do you see the truth of scripture? Those who are holding to Christ, focused on Him, and who put their trust in Him alone, these are transformed into His perfect image, and His good works naturally flow out through their lives. The flesh loses its power, and the delight in His will emerges. It cannot work the other way around.

What happens if we have fallen from grace? The truth is that every believer repeatedly falls from grace until they understand that Christ alone is their provider and source of goodness. Once we realize we have fallen from grace, we simply look back to the cross, turn from our self-efforts, and again put our trust in Christ. Paul is warning the church for a reason. He is not saying, "You fell from grace and now you are doomed." No, he is warning them for a purpose. They have fallen from grace and are pursuing worthless things. So they are not robbed of their inheritance, he is calling them to return to the Shepherd of their souls, Jesus Christ.

The one who tries to produce his own works or righteousness has fallen from grace, but not from salvation. Let's put this into our modern terminology. The one who tries to earn God's favor in any way, has stepped outside of God's favor. God's favor is an act of grace. Grace is the expression of God's love toward us based on who He is, not who we are or what we have done.

For the purpose of expressing God's agape love, He calls us to walk in His favor. It is God's hand of invitation. When we quit trusting in God's love, we then try to earn it by our actions. Love cannot be earned, so we are pursuing the things that are contrary to love. But God calls us to abandon our hope in foolish religion that trusts in something other than Him. He calls for us to stop trying to become like Him and start trusting in His promises.

He promises that as we look to Him, He transforms us into His likeness. As we believe Him, we live in His righteousness. He has given us all things that pertain to life and godliness. None of these things are possible outside of Him. We are walking with Him and abiding in Him. God does not withdraw His favor, but we do not experience His grace when we are pursuing anything other than Christ.

We are completely sanctified once we completely believe that we are complete in Him. When we believe God's declaration that we are in the Spirit, then we'll begin learning how to walk in the Spirit.

Walking in the Spirit is summed up in this truth. We are in Him and now we ought to walk and abide in Him. We believe, therefore we look to Him alone.

Discussion questions:

Why does the word of God divide the soul from the spirit?

What is the difference between the soul and the spirit?

What is the difference between our new spirit and the Spirit of God within us?

How is our spirit connected to God's spirit?

Can our new spirit become separated from God's Spirit? Why or why not?

God said that the day Adam ate of the fruit, he would certainly die. How did Adam die?

When Adam became self-conscious, how did that affect his view of God?

How does looking to Christ change our consciousness toward our own shortcomings?

What does the Bible mean when it says, "May God of peace sanctify you completely?"

Spirit, Soul, and Body

Why does the Bible emphasize God's peace? (See Thessalonians 5:23-24)

What is the mind of Christ and how do we receive it?

Why does the immature Christian desire the old wine, but the mature believer desires the new?

When Paul sinned, what was the cause of sin?

When Paul experienced victory, how did he obtain it?

Do you have two natures?

What is the difference between the 'old man' and your flesh?

Can the flesh imitate the old nature?

Reasons for Immaturity

There are a few reasons why spiritual maturity is lacking in most churches. This is not an issue new to this generation. The Apostle Paul expressed frustration with the church two-thousand years ago. He said, "By this time you ought to be teachers, but you need someone to teach you the basic principles of God."[72] It's not an uncommon problem to have people spend their entire lives in church but never coming to an understanding of truth.

Every believer has the power of the Holy Spirit within them and is able to discern the deep truths of God, yet few actually grow beyond infancy. Though some do not want to grow and apply their hearts to truth, many desire this but don't know how to grow. There are several reasons, but this chapter will focus on two common problems that can easily be resolved.

Emotionalism

The stirring of emotions has become the most common way the church attempts to bring about lifestyle changes among Christians. Unfortunately, emotionally driven instruction does not produce lasting change. As emotions fade, old habits return.

In recent years, the Christian movie industry has produced some very moving films that address important problems. There have been movies on marriage, fatherhood, faith, teen issues, and several other topics. Some of these movies have inspired people and spawned Bible studies and Christian movements. People are touched and see their own need to change. Some of the companion books to these movies carry on with the emotions driving from the movie, and the books end with a covenant that parishioners sign and agree to cease a behavior or commit to living out a new goal.

Does this work? Maybe for a short time, but these methods never produce lasting change. The evidence for this is all around us. What movement has produced permanent change? Is the church stronger today and more holy than it was twenty years ago? Are Christians more distinguished from the world? Can the world see a

---

[72] Hebrews 5:12

difference in our life? I'm not talking about divisive issues the church has put at the forefront of their agendas, but the everyday lifestyle that make people stand back and ask, "What makes your life so much different than mine?"

Did the Promise Keepers movement reduce the divorce rate or resolve the problems in marriage that have plagued the church in recent decades? What about Love Waits or the Moral Majority movement from the 1980s? Name any movement that has produced lasting change in the Christian culture.

For a short time, emotionalism works. However, in six months we break our covenants and are back to our old behaviors and patterns of thinking. Our good intentions fall by the wayside when the emotional energy begins to run thin.

I grew up in a Baptist church. The concept of 'church revival' operates on the same principle. As members stagnate and apathy takes root, the leaders would begin calling for the church to pray for revival. They would then invite an energetic speaker to come in, preach for a week, get the members excited about the Lord, and then rejoice in the renewed energy. We called it a revived church, but what changed?

Within a few months, every person slipped back into their previous ways of living, the excitement faded, and apathy set in again. Emotionally driven change cannot have lasting impact.

Certainly we should feel the gospel. Feeling the Spirit within us is an encouragement to our hearts. Feeling bad about misbehavior discourages us from negative behaviors. But even those feelings can fade and cease having an effect on us. Not to mention that feelings are deceptive and are poor indicators of our true faith.

Don't misunderstand this to be a condemnation against touching movies, testimonies, or studies. Emotions indeed serve a purpose, but an emotionally driven method is insufficient to change the heart. Emotions can stir our hearts to receive a message, but it must be built on a solid foundation. Otherwise it will fall short. The foundation must be laid and built upon in order for true growth to occur.

A message void of emotions can appear cold. While it is rich with truth, it lacks the stirring of the heart. A message dependent upon emotions may stir the heart, but it lacks the ability to penetrate to the spirit of man. The Holy Spirit is the only person with the power to transform us into godliness, and the Spirit is not dependent upon emotions to do His work. Nor is the Spirit against emotions. But a doctrine built around emotional dependence is depending on the wrong thing. We can't trust in emotions to do the work reserved for the Holy Spirit.

There must be something stronger than emotions to drive us. Behavioral change must have a foundation greater than our human effort. Just as the Bible says, "The leopard cannot change his spots," so we cannot change the nature of the flesh.

This is why learning to walk in the Spirit is critical to the Christian life. Emotions cannot change the heart and cannot transform our lives. Emotionally driven change can only stand while emotions are running their course.

Dependence on the Milk

God never intended His people to be man-dependent. God calls for us to assemble together, teach and hear the word, and some are indeed equipped as gifted disciplers. But the call to hear and teach is not a call for dependency upon a teacher. It is a call to grow into maturity so each person becomes an edifier of the body of Christ. God's desire is to reveal Himself to each person through the word. Consider **Isaiah 28:9-10**

> [9] " Whom will he teach knowledge? And whom will he make to understand the message? Those *just* weaned from milk? Those *just* drawn from the breasts?
> [10] For precept *must be* upon precept, precept upon precept, Line upon line, line upon line, Here a little, there a little."

I use this passage often because it illustrates this truth so well. The picture being painted is that we were all once infants in Christ. It's completely natural for a baby to nurse. But as a child grows, he or she must be weaned. If a thirteen year old child was still nursing, what would our reaction be? We'd say there is something seriously wrong, for that is unnatural.

What was once good for the child becomes a problem if maturity never develops. A mother is delighted when her child nurses and begins to grow. But that same mother would be troubled if the child refused to be weaned. And those observing the relationship would be disturbed if a mother refused to allow her child to wean.

Yet this is what we see in our churches. It's also what the Apostle Paul saw in the Hebrew church. He was appalled because of the unnatural dependence upon teachers. God never intended for us to be a congregation of infants, but to grow into maturity. Let's look at the criticism of the church in **Hebrews 5:12-14**

> [12] For though by this time you ought to be teachers, you need *someone* to teach you again the first principles of the oracles of God; and you have come to need milk and not solid food.
>
> [13] For everyone who partakes *only* of milk *is* unskilled in the word of righteousness, for he is a babe.
>
> [14] But solid food belongs to those who are of full age, *that is,* those who by reason of use have their senses exercised to discern both good and evil.

Believers grow out of infancy by exercising themselves in the word, not by merely listening with apathetic ears. Every new Christian should be given the milk of the word. This is the basic principles of our faith – the things that help lay the foundation of our understanding. God never intended for you and I to be dependent upon teachers for growing into maturity. Teaching should lay the foundation of faith so you can grow into maturity. A teacher should be instructing those under them to be weaned onto the meat of the word.

If having people dependent upon me is necessary in order for me to feel valued, I am serving my ego and not the Lord. The purpose of spiritual leaders is not to be the gurus on the hill that everyone must come to, but they are those appointed by God to teach younger believers how to become true disciples of Christ. A disciple is one who follows Christ and learns how to draw close to Him, rather than becoming a follower of people. This is fully explained in **Ephesians 4:11-16**

> [11] And He Himself gave some *to be* apostles, some prophets, some evangelists, and some pastors and teachers,
>
> [12] for the equipping of the saints for the work of ministry, for the edifying of the body of Christ,
>
> [13] till we all come to the unity of the faith and of the knowledge of the Son of God, to a perfect man, to the

measure of the stature of the fullness of Christ;

[14] that we should no longer be children, tossed to and fro and carried about with every wind of doctrine, by the trickery of men, in the cunning craftiness of deceitful plotting,

[15] but, speaking the truth in love, may grow up in all things into Him who is the head -- Christ --

[16] from whom the whole body, joined and knit together by what every joint supplies, according to the effective working by which every part does its share, causes growth of the body for the edifying of itself in love.

What is the ultimate goal of those who teach? It is to bring us to a state of maturity, to make us into the perfect man. Man is used in the general sense, and this applies to all people, male and female. And how do we become the perfect person? In the Spirit, we are the perfect man, for our spirit is in Christ. The goal of discipleship is to teach people to walk according to who they are in Christ, not who they were in the flesh. The flesh is woven into every part of our pattern of thinking from birth, so growing out of this is a lifelong process.

Once someone grows into the meat of the word, they have gotten to the point where they only need to glean from the perspective of teachers rather than having dependence on being told what to think and what to do. A young believer is dependent, for they have no knowledge or understanding of truth.

Proper discipleship lays the foundation of growth, and then weans the new believer off man and onto the meat of the word. The meat is personal study, founded on our dependence upon the Holy Spirit to reveal truth and establish us in that truth. There is nothing shameful about being immature in the faith. There is shame in staying immature and remaining a spiritual dependent.

If my goal is not to equip the saints and teach them how to draw into the head – Jesus Christ, then I am not serving God. There is much to be said about discipleship that doesn't fall into the scope of this book, but failing to follow God's model for leadership and teaching is one reason why maturity is lacking.

Certainly there is a need for teachers, but the ultimate goal is to make others independent of the teacher and dependent upon Christ, as they learn how to be taught by the Holy Spirit. There will never be a

Reasons for Immaturity

time when teaching is no longer needed, for as the teacher learns, he grows deeper in his faith and then passes this on to others so they can glean from what God has shown the teacher. Eventually people will rise above our teaching and will go out and become teachers themselves. This is the greatest success a teacher can have.

Gathering dependents under your teaching is not the measure of success. The true measure is, how many have gone out and are now equipped for ministry?

We as members of Christ must realize two important things on this subject. We must learn how to wean our dependency off teachers, and we must learn how to draw close to Christ. Both go hand-in-hand. While we are infants nursing off the milk of teaching, we are not drawing near Christ. When we draw near to Christ we are also weaning off of a dependency upon teachers.

Keep in mind that this is referring to dependency. It doesn't mean that we can no longer learn from others. A spirit led teacher will constantly learn new insights we haven't discovered. If you are learning from the Spirit, you will discover insights God hasn't revealed to me, and I will learn things God hasn't revealed to you. We become unified in the faith as each of us draw into the head and we then edify each other in the love of God. Your love of God will edify me, and I will edify you. We become independently able to have an intimate relationship with God, but we don't become independent from the body. Isolationism is not God's way.

God has supplied the entire body as individual members who serve the whole. What I lack is found in others God has gifted and called into the body. What you lack is found in others God has gifted and called into the body. Anyone who truly has learned how to follow Christ will naturally be drawn to the body. God has designed the church to be supplied by each contributing member. No one is complete in themselves, and no one lacks a place in the body.

Spiritual maturity draws us into fellowship with Christ first, and by design we are naturally drawn together with others who also are drawing toward Christ. The Bible says that Jesus is the head and we are all members of the body. An amputated member has no life or service. A body that isn't connected to the head (Christ) is a corpse.

To be unified with those who are not drawing near the head is not possible – unless we abandon the head and become dead spiritually. This is why Romans 16 warns that divisions are caused by those who don't hold to the teachings of scripture and why Ephesians 4 tells us that unity comes from drawing near to Christ.

It's important to explain all of this because it's far too easy for people to misunderstand teaching. Becoming non-dependent on teachers for spiritual maturity doesn't mean we become independent people – separated from the body. It is not possible to be in God's will and be an island. God has gifted us and called us to fulfill in the body what the other parts lack. Failure to be part of the body separates us from true fellowship with Christ. Excluding members from service is also a breakdown in the body. God has left no one out of His purpose.

We mature by first learning from those God has called to equip the saints. Learn first how to draw into Christ, our Head, and then continue to grow as you learn from Christ. He will supply your lack by those He has equipped. God will also use you to supply something the church would lack without you. You have spiritual gifts, but they may remain dormant until you learn how to draw into Christ.

Don't mistake emotions for the Spirit, but learn how to walk in the Spirit through the word of God. Learn how to put off the flesh and walk in the Spirit as you also learn how to have fellowship with Christ and other believers. Consider **1 John 4:7-13**

[7] Beloved, let us love one another, for love is of God; and everyone who loves is born of God and knows God.

[8] He who does not love does not know God, for God is love.

[9] In this the love of God was manifested toward us, that God has sent His only begotten Son into the world, that we might live through Him.

[10] In this is love, not that we loved God, but that He loved us and sent His Son *to be* the propitiation for our sins.

[11] Beloved, if God so loved us, we also ought to love one another.

[12] No one has seen God at any time. If we love one another, God abides in us, and His love has been perfected in us.

[13] By this we know that we abide in Him, and He in us, because He has given us of His Spirit.

We'll revisit this topic in detail in a later chapter. For now realize that fellowship with others who love God is as much a part of our faith as our relationship with God. God has placed His love within the heart of every believer, and walking in that love naturally creates fellowship with others. When the church has true, Christ-centered fellowship, the love of God is perfected in each one of us. "If we love one another, God abides in us, and His love has been perfected in us."

If you want to have a church that has an eternal impact on the culture, abide in God's love and express that love in fellowship with other believers. Remember Jesus' words, "By this shall all men know you are my disciples, by your love for one another." True love, given from God, reveals God in us and reveals Christ to the world.

Church programs can't fulfill this. This is the promise that God will enter the church to reveal His power to those who believe enough to obey. Obedience is not founded upon human effort. Obedience is fulfilled when I learn to walk according to the Spirit instead of according to the flesh. The flesh is contrary to God, but the Spirit is the place where we abide in God's fellowship. True church fellowship flows from this.

Many reverse God's call. We aren't called to use love in order to abide in Christ. We don't love others in order to create fellowship with other believers. We abide in Christ and the love of God (not the love of man) flows into our lives and then outward to edify the church as a whole. We draw into Christ, then obedience and love are the natural outflows of walking in the Spirit.

Let's answer this chapter's opening question, "Why do people lack spiritual maturity?" People lack maturity because they are focused on things other than Christ. When people draw near teachers, they can only produce what comes from their flesh. When they draw toward church programs, success is limited to what the program can produce. But when people learn how to draw near to Christ, spiritual maturity always occurs. In Christ, we cannot help but to mature.

Sounds simple, I know. But it is simple. Paul said, "I fear that your minds might be deceived away from the simplicity that is in Christ."[73]

Mature into Christ and refuse to allow anything to distract you from that purpose. Nothing should distract you, even if the distraction is religious or has the label of Christian attached to it.

---

[73] 2 Corinthians 11:3

Discussion questions:

Can a Christian build his/her life upon a foundation of emotions?

Can emotions make something appear good that is sinful?

Can emotions make you feel bad when you are in God's will?

How does a Christian discern between emotions and the affirmation of the Spirit?

What makes a Christian a spiritual infant?

How does the Christian grow into maturity?

What is spiritual maturity?

Can a Christian grow above the spiritual level of their teachers?

Read Psalm 119:98-100. How does that affect your answer from the previous question?

If we have more knowledge than our teachers, can we still benefit from their teaching?

Does a Christian ever mature to the point where they no longer need teaching?

Read Ephesians 4:11-16. What is the evidence of maturity in the church?

If there is warring in the church, what are people focused on?

If maturity is developing, what is the evidence of this in the church?

We have the Mind of Christ

For the first few decades of my Christian life, I struggled with inconsistency, sins of weakness, and had long periods of time when I felt no presence of God active in my life. Yet once I discovered the reality of walking in the Spirit, everything changed. Previously, I couldn't fulfill what I knew I should do, nor could I overcome the things I knew I shouldn't do. Indeed, both good works and resisting sin is impossible through the flesh.

I kept making extra efforts through the flesh because I found enough success to feel like I was doing some good and had moments of joy and peace. But these were short-lived, for the next time my flesh got the best of me, all my efforts collapsed. On the outside, my religion looked good to others. Before my blinded eyes, my own efforts looked good to me. However, when I saw the glory of God's power in the Spirit, my old efforts looked foolish and the sin of my weaknesses lost its grip on my mind.

This is the problem with man-generated religion. It makes us feel good enough to keep us grappling for more. Even Christianity can slip into a man-made religion, for if we teach, preach, feed the poor, and do all our good works by human effort, it is not of the Spirit. We feel good about what we are doing, but walking in the Spirit opens our eyes to the power of God and His call to walk close to Him. Through our fellowship with Christ, works flow, and because He is the power behind our work, it has eternal fruit. My best effort may do good for the present, but His work is eternal.

Peace is always present in the Spirit, for God promises to be the one who guards our heart and mind with His peace – a peace that goes beyond human understanding.[74] Joy is always present, for we have the perspective of Christ, who for the joy set before Him endured the cross He despised.[75] Can you have joy in the midst of circumstances you despise? You can.

Another truth is that we have unlimited understanding and power available to us. Consider these two passages:

---

[74] Philippians 4:7
[75] Hebrews 12:2

1 Corinthians 2:16

For "who has known the mind of the LORD that he may instruct Him?" But we have the mind of Christ.

Look again at **2 Peter 1:3-4**

³ His divine power has given to us all things that *pertain* to life and godliness, through the knowledge of Him who called us by glory and virtue,

⁴ by which have been given to us exceedingly great and precious promises, that through these you may be partakers of the divine nature, having escaped the corruption *that is* in the world through lust.

Don't miss the weight of these passages. First, you have the mind of Christ. I have the mind of Christ. Any who are born again by the Spirit of God has the mind of Christ. This begs the question, what is Jesus lacking? The obvious answer is, nothing. He lacks nothing; therefore, we lack nothing. This is a promise given to every person born into the Spirit – we have the mind of Christ.

This truth is affirmed in 2 Peter above. His divine power has given you and I everything in order to live and fulfill our life's mission and the call to godliness. You lack nothing. I lack nothing. Yet we struggle to live out these truths. The reason is because we don't realize we are walking in the flesh, and we don't recognize this because most of us don't know what it means to walk in the Spirit. We settle for inadequacy because we don't realize there is a better way. We try to make up for the lack of spiritual power by extra human effort.

If you finish reading the passage in 2 Peter, it ends with the promise that if these things are yours and abound, you *will not* be barren or unfruitful. You can't miss God's promises and purpose for your life if you are walking in the Spirit. Fulfilling your calling and a life of godliness is a guarantee. It is not your power, for you don't have the power to change anything regarding your flesh, but it is Christ's divine power that has been given to you. In the Spirit, victory is a guarantee. Life cannot defeat those walking in Christ.

Scripture didn't say that it will be given to you, but *it has* been given to you. You already have the mind of Christ. God has already given you everything pertaining to life and godliness. Stop praying for it and look to the Lord who has already provided it. Thank God for supplying your need and receive what God has given.

God doesn't answer your prayers to overcome and be victorious because He has *already* answered this prayer. You have the mind of Christ. You have been given all things. Ask for God to open your eyes to see it, while believing that His provision is before you.

When I was a child, my mother was searching through the house for something. Frantically she lifted up the newspaper, checked chairs, searched end tables, and every surface she could find. My sister and I watched her as the frustration grew. Finally she said, "Have either of you seen my glasses?" We burst out laughing. "Okay, where did you put them?" We declared our innocence. She put her hands on her hips and said, "If you don't tell me where my glasses are, I'm going to punish you."

"They are on your head!"

We had a good laugh over that one, but it also serves as a great illustration of the Christian life. While we are searching here and there for answers, we already have what we are searching for. Instead of walking in God's provision, we walk down every hall, search every room, and beat on every door. Why isn't God answering? Because He has already answered! He plainly stated these things in His word, but instead of believing and taking on the mind of Christ, we keep searching.

Let's use the illustration of dying to self. Romans 6:11 says, "Reckon yourselves dead." How do I account myself dead when my selfishness is alive and controlling my behavior?

A Bible teacher gave this as an example once. He and two friends were meeting at a diner. This subject came up and one of the men said, "I just can't grasp the concept of being dead to my flesh. I keep praying for God to crucify my flesh. I've been praying this for years, but it just doesn't happen. I'm still the same man I used to be." They shared scriptures and discussed, but he just couldn't get it. Another person overheard the conversation and pulled up a chair and placed a thermos on the table.

"Suppose this thermos was alive. It wanted to become a thermos and began praying, 'God make me into a thermos.' For years he earnestly begged God to make him into a thermos. How do you think God would answer?"

"He would say, 'That's an absurd prayer. You *are* a thermos.'"

"Exactly. That is what you are doing. You are praying for God to make you into what you already are."

Can we apply Romans 6:11 if we don't understand Romans 6:1-10? In these passages we see, "As many as were baptized into Christ Jesus were baptized into His death. Therefore, we are buried with Him through the baptism of His death. Our old man *was* crucified with Him. The body of sin *has been* done away with. We are now raised as a new creation."

In most churches, we are taught to pray for God to do what has already been done. The answer is not *to be* crucified. It is not *to die* to self. The answer is to believe in the finished work God has declared, and then we can reckon (or account) ourselves dead to sin. I believe what God has declared and walk in God's gift of grace. It is not me accomplishing anything, but me believing in what God has accomplished and walking in it. It is trusting Christ. Only when I reckon myself dead by walking in the finished work of Christ can I also walk in newness of life by abiding in Christ through the Spirit.

The Bible says that when we are born into Christ, we are not only given a new spirit, born of God, but God places His Spirit within us and we become the temple of the Holy Spirit. He abides within us and so does His power.

God has given us instructions as to how to overcome the flesh and walk in the Spirit. Certainly God could overthrow our will and force us to walk in the Spirit, but He will not do so. Satan seeks to take captives. God calls for whosoever will to come and follow Him.

Consider the message of Gideon in the Old Testament. God called Gideon to lead Israel out of bondage. The Median army was the power of that day. When Gideon took a stand, hundreds of thousands of enemy warriors descended upon them. As far as the eye could see, the soldiers gathered to fight Israel's army. God called Gideon to the battle and gave him the most foolish battle plan this world has ever seen.

God began by stripping everything of confidence away. The Lord sent away all but three hundred soldiers. He then gave an absurd plan. Don't take swords or come up with a battle strategy. Simply put a torch inside a clay pot and surround the army. When the signal was given, they were to break the pots and shout.

How foolish this must have appeared. The massive enemy's army was sleeping, and three-hundred men were going to wake them up

We Have the Mind of Christ

and stand there with a pot and a light? Yet this was God's plan – not because there was power in the clay vessels, or power in the torches. It was a call of obedience where God would do His work through Gideon's faith. What would have happened if Gideon had refused to act so foolishly? He would have never seen God's work and would have remained in bondage.

When he obeyed, God entered the work and accomplished the mission. Three-hundred men didn't have the power to defeat hundreds of thousands of warriors. But the battle wasn't theirs. Obedience by faith was all God required. After God moved, then the soldiers were sent into action, but by then, the enemy was already defeated.

This event serves as an illustration for the Christian life. Consider God's word from **2 Corinthians 4:6-7**

> ⁶ For it is God who commanded light to shine out of darkness, who has shone in our hearts to *give* the light of the knowledge of the glory of God in the face of Jesus Christ.
> ⁷ But we have this treasure in earthen vessels, that the excellence of the power may be of God and not of us.

What gift do we have in earthen vessels? We have the light of the knowledge of the glory of God. In Gideon's example, they had an earthen vessel – a clay pot. The light was hidden within, but God's plan was to break the vessel so the light could shine forth into the darkness. Once the vessel was out of the way, God began His work. The power was not in three hundred soldiers, but in God. These men only walked in God's plan.

We have the light of God in our earthen vessel – our body of flesh. Though the power of God is within us, the power itself is not in our flesh or our personal spiritual efforts. It is God's power. But when the power of our flesh is broken, the light shines forth to reveal God's glory and He enters our obedience to accomplish the work. The power is of God, but obedience belongs to us. Obedience is an act of faith – walking as God leads – wherever and however God leads.

And what is the command God has given us? The command is to break free from the flesh and walk in the Spirit. Consider these passages:

Romans 8:13

[13] For if you live according to the flesh you will die; but if by the Spirit you put to death the deeds of the body, you will live.

2 Corinthians 10:3-4

[3] For though we walk in the flesh, we do not war according to the flesh.

[4] For the weapons of our warfare *are* not carnal but mighty in God for pulling down strongholds,

Notice one important principle these passages rest upon. It is by the Spirit that we put to death the deeds of the flesh. The flesh, or our old nature, has been crucified with Christ, but his deeds remain. God has crucified the flesh, and it was not your job to do so. In the same way, it isn't your job to break the vessel and put off the flesh. We put off the deeds of the flesh, but it is God who has broken the power of the flesh. That is accomplished by the Spirit. It is in God that strongholds fall and are defeated. We put off the deeds of the flesh by walking according to our new nature and declining our flesh's desire to regain control.

We don't purify ourselves so we can be worthy to come before God. We come before God so He can purify us. We don't subdue sin so that we are right with God. God subdues sin because we have turned to Him by faith.[76] Don't work to be right before God. Rest from your labors and take on the righteousness of Christ. It is not your righteousness; therefore, your efforts and your failures mean nothing. It is God's efforts and faith in His victory that changes behavior and transforms your life. It is God's Spirit working in you.

If your background is like mine, no one ever explained the importance of walking in the Spirit. You may have never been taught that it was possible to live according to the Spirit. Or have not been taught what it means to overcome the flesh. Most of us are taught to try harder and force obedience into our lives by efforts of the flesh. Few would call it an effort of the flesh, but if it is mere human effort, it is of the flesh. It is not possible to fulfill the Christian life through human effort. Let's look again at the Apostle Paul's rebuke of the church in **Galatians 3:3** we reviewed in an earlier chapter:

---

[76] Micah 7:19

We Have the Mind of Christ

[3] Are you so foolish? Having begun in the Spirit, are you now being made perfect by the flesh?

This is a foundational scripture and I'll refer to this often. The subject here is circumcision, but it applies to any human effort to please God or to make an attempt to make us acceptable to God through the flesh. We began this faith in the Spirit, so why would we expect anything to change as to how we live out our faith?

It is foolish to trust in the power of God through Christ to pay for our sins, but then think we must help God out in other spiritual matters. Any work done through human effort is rejected by God. One of the overarching principles of scripture is this, "That no flesh should glory in His presence."

Whether it be salvation, deliverance, good works, holiness, godliness, or any other matter, if it is born through the flesh, it is in direct opposition to God.

To fully understand this, it is necessary to explain why the flesh and the Spirit are in direct opposition to each other. In the next chapter we'll explore the perishing flesh and the new life of the Spirit.

Discussion questions:

Do you have the mind of Christ?

What must you do to become holy? Righteous? Godly?

Can a Christian live contrary to their spiritual nature?

If someone doesn't know their old nature has been already put to death, where do they focus their efforts?

If someone believes that they have been given all things in Christ, what is their focus?

Does believing our sins are paid lead us deeper into sin?

Why was the Galatian church criticized?

What happens when we pray for God to do what He has already declared?

How does the Christian receive God's power?

What is our limitation?

We Have the Mind of Christ

What is the flesh?

Let us begin this chapter by reading **1 Corinthians 15:21-22**

[21] For since by man *came* death, by Man also *came* the resurrection of the dead.

[22] For as in Adam all die, even so in Christ all shall be made alive.

Let's take a little time to understand why the Spirit and the flesh cannot agree. The Bible says that the flesh longs for the things that are against the Spirit, and the Spirit desires what is against the flesh, and these two cannot agree.[77]

These two realms are at odds, each desiring what opposes the other. They cannot agree and will never agree. It doesn't matter what Christian terms we put on the flesh, how sincere our motives are, or whose name we serve in. If an act is of the flesh, it is in opposition to the Spirit. Anything of the Spirit will be contrary to the flesh.

We as Christians must realize this. So much of God's best for us remains undiscovered because we are looking through the flesh. The same is true for our good works. It is all worthless – even if it is done in Jesus' name. As we saw previously, Jesus Himself declared this truth.[78]

So why are the flesh and the Spirit so opposed? It all goes back to Adam. Look at God's warning in **Genesis 2:16-17**

[16] And the LORD God commanded the man, saying, "Of every tree of the garden you may freely eat;

[17] "but of the tree of the knowledge of good and evil you shall not eat, for in the day that you eat of it you shall surely die."

Many get sidetracked as they try to figure out what the tree was and how it changed Adam. The purpose of the tree was to give Adam a moral choice. No one can love unless they have the option to not love. No one can submit to God unless they have the option to resist God. The tree was a moral choice. Up until this time, rebellion had no part in humanity. The curse was not in the tree, but in the word of

---

[77] Galatians 5:17
[78] Matthew 7:21-23

God, just as it was when God instructed His people when preparing them to enter the Promised Land. **Deuteronomy 11:26-28**

[26] " Behold, I set before you today a blessing and a curse:

[27] "the blessing, if you obey the commandments of the LORD your God which I command you today;

[28] "and the curse, if you do not obey the commandments of the LORD your God, but turn aside from the way which I command you today, to go after other gods which you have not known.

What cursed the people? What blessed the people? Just as with Adam, God presented His word to the people and declared that rebellion brings on the curse, and obedience gives the blessing. Adam's choice was the blessing or the curse. The power was not in the fruit itself, but in the word of God.

On one side was the tree of life. It was man's acknowledgement of his complete dependency on God. The promise was that Adam would have life if he put his trust in the Lord. The tree of life represented man partaking of God's nature.

By joining the Lord through His call, man would experience the righteousness of God. God would be man's reward. God would become man's life. All things are of God and man could do nothing to make himself great. Adam would partake of the goodness and greatness of the Lord and be glorified together with Him. The only knowledge that mattered was to know the Lord and experience true fellowship with Him.

On the other side of the garden was the tree of the knowledge of good and evil. The deceiver pointed to that tree and said, "You will be like God." Man could determine what is right and wrong based on his own understanding. Man could discover hidden knowledge that God was depriving him of. Man could experience the pleasures the Lord was hiding from him. Unbelief was behind the lie. Did God really say you would die? Does God really seek your good? You will not die and you will experience what God is keeping from you. Man believed the lie and disbelieved God. Then pride was born and sin emerged.

It's the test of faith. Did Adam and Eve believe that God was good? Did they trust the Lord to do all things for their good? Was God their sufficiency? Or did they believe the call of the world? The

What is the flesh?

world called saying that God was depriving them. He only met part of their needs. He did not want them to experience all that was available to them. Man could determine his own good and have the knowledge that allowed him to become independent of God.

Both trees still exist today in our hearts. The world calls with all the promises of knowledge, pleasures, and fulfillment. Though we can look around and see corruption and greed, which testifies that the world cannot fulfill, we still are mesmerized by the glitter of the promise. It still looks good for food, pleasant to the eyes, and desirable to make one wise. It calls us to reject faith in the Lord and put our trust in ourselves or other things.

The lie exists in the church today. Is Christ truly our sufficiency? Or do we have to do something by our own efforts to fulfill what faith can't do? Has Christ accomplished all things? Or do we need to visit the tree of human effort to complete what lacks?

Christ is the tree of life, but how few Christians believe the promise and look for the sufficiency that is there for the taking? Other ways sound like truth because they promise knowledge, accomplishments, and glory. But the simplicity of Christ doesn't sound good enough to the human heart. Only those who partake of His nature discover the sufficiency of Christ. Any who don't abide in Christ will be drawn away by everything that sounds like knowledge and human wisdom.

The call of faith says, "No good thing will He withhold from those who love Him," "All things work together for the good of those who love God and are called into His purposes," "Eye has not seen nor has the heart imagined what the Lord has in store for those who love him," and finally, "I (the Lord) am your exceedingly great reward." Each person partakes of one tree or the other.

Through Adam, we are already partakers of the tree of sin. Through Christ we become partakers of the Tree of Life. Whereas Adam could not partake of the Tree of Life after he fell, we can. The sin that prevents us has been taken out of the way through the cross, and we can freely receive new life. The curse has been removed from any who will enter in by Jesus Christ. The flesh cannot partake of the Tree of Life, but our incorruptible spirit that finds its life in Christ may freely eat.

The Lord declared beforehand that rebellion would put Adam under the curse of sin. In that day you will die. And that is exactly what happened.

Death was not an instant loss of all life, but the death of the spirit. From that day forward, man's spirit was dead to God. The spirit was made dead and the flesh came alive. In Christ, we die to the flesh and the spirit is made alive. Any who live according to the flesh are under the curse, for the Bible says in **Romans 8:13:**

> For if you live according to the flesh you will die; but if by the Spirit you put to death the deeds of the body, you will live.

Why will you die if you live according to the flesh? Because the flesh is dead to God. Romans 8:10 tells us that the body is dead because of sin. In Adam, all die. In Christ, all are made alive. Any who live after the likeness of Adam are living in the flesh that is already dead because of sin, but in Christ we find life by the Spirit.

On the day that Adam sinned, death became part of the flesh. Death came by sin and sin by Adam. Any who descend from Adam are born through the flesh. In fact, the only way to escape the slavery of the flesh is by death.

From Slavery to Freedom

What is the difference between a slave and a servant? A servant is paid for his work. It is merely a job by which someone earns a living. If a servant doesn't like his employer, he is free to walk away.

A slave is someone in bondage. In the Bible, slavery was how people settled their debts. We tend to view slavery through the lens of the 1700s and 1800s. People captured slaves and sold them for profit. This is not how the Bible deals with slavery. If someone borrowed money and then could not pay it back, they were made into a slave for a certain period of time to pay back the debt through servitude. If the debt was great enough, they could spend up to fifty years of their life in slavery. The slave wasn't surprised with this catch. When borrowing money, the borrower would have agreed to this consequence ahead of time, should they not be able to pay the debt.

Because a slave was in bondage, he had no right to be free. If the slave decided he didn't like his master, that was tough. He could not quit but was stuck until the debt was paid in full.

The Bible says that we are in bondage to sin. Because we are sinners and have a debt to sin, we cannot go free. The person in the flesh cannot simply decide to be free of the flesh and walk away. They are in debt to sin and sin is their master. Jesus explained this in **John 8:34-36**

[34] Jesus answered them, "Most assuredly, I say to you, whoever commits sin is a slave of sin.

[35] "And a slave does not abide in the house forever, *but* a son abides forever.

[36] "Therefore if the Son makes you free, you shall be free indeed.

One thing we must realize is that we are all under sin, regardless of what transgressions we may have or have not committed. People think each person sins and is therefore a sinner. But the truth is that we were born as a sinner, and therefore sin. Sin comes through our flesh and entices us to act out. We are born into the flesh before we commit any sin. This is evident, for as soon as we are able, we act out in sin from childhood until death.

The Old Testament Law is given as a living example to communicate the truth of life and spiritual principles. A person who was under slavery could be allowed to marry, but any children born while his parents were under bondage must remain under slavery. They belong to the master of the slave.[79] This is a living example of our spiritual condition. All people are born through Adam, who was in bondage to sin. Therefore, any born under that slavery remain under the slavery of sin.

Even before we were conscious of sin, we were under the flesh by birth. We are bound by birth, not behavior. Yet we still sin and then put ourselves into further debt to sin.

A child does not have to be taught how to sin. By nature they have tantrums, take from others, demand their way, and rebel against parents. It is in their human nature because the flesh died in Adam,

---

[79] Exodus 21:4

and we all inherited our flesh from Adam's lineage. Also consider
Romans 5:12-14

[12] Therefore, just as through one man sin entered the world, and death through sin, and thus death spread to all men, because all sinned --

[13] (For until the law sin was in the world, but sin is not imputed when there is no law.

[14] Nevertheless death reigned from Adam to Moses, even over those who had not sinned according to the likeness of the transgression of Adam, who is a type of Him who was to come.

The law did not come until it was given to Moses, but that didn't mean that sin didn't exist until the law. It meant that death reigned to all born into the human family, but the condition of our sinful nature wasn't fully realized until the law was revealed.

Notice two things in this passage. All have sinned and share in Adam's death, *and* everyone inherited that death regardless of whether they sinned as Adam did. Many children have died through the ages before they had the ability to choose sin, but they still suffered the consequences of the curse of death. It was not because of their actions, but because of their heritage. We are all judged for our own sins, but we are under the curse of the flesh because of Adam. Because we are born into sin, we become sinners. Not one person lacks selfishness, rebellion, and sinful tendencies. No one had to teach you sin, for it is in your flesh. Sin dwells in your flesh and seeks to exert its will through your mind (see Romans 7:19-23).

Until someone is born anew, they only have one nature to deal with – the flesh. There is no source of good by which to draw from. I say good from the eternal perspective. Even the atheist can do what mankind thinks is good. From the human perspective, good is to do things that help the flesh. From God's perspective, good is found only by that which emanates from His Spirit.

The flesh is something that rebelled against God and continues to rebel against God. Human nature is not God-seeking, but flesh seeking. It's selfish, self-focused, self-serving. Even the most noble looking efforts have selfish motives behind it. People serve others because it makes them feel good, gains praise, makes them appear noble in the eyes of others, and many other ways they feel a benefit. It is not possible for the flesh to seek the things of the Spirit;

What is the flesh?

therefore, it cannot please God. Nor can anyone who walks according to the flesh please God.

The flesh is destined for the grave. Anything of the flesh remains in the curse of sin. In fact, all of creation is destined for destruction. At the conclusion of all things, the Apostle John saw this vision, "Now I saw a new heaven and a new earth, for the first heaven and the first earth had passed away."[80] The Apostle Peter testified similarly when he said, "The Lord will come as a thief in the night, in which the heavens will pass away with a great noise and the elements will melt with fervent heat, both the earth and the works that are in it will be burned up."[81]

He concludes with this question, "Since all these things will be dissolved, what manner of persons ought you to be in holy conduct and godliness?" How should you live and what should you live for? None of these things will survive. Not your possessions. Not your works. Not the world itself.

So what does this have to do with the war between the Spirit and the flesh? Do you remember when God dealt with Adam's sin? God did not want to curse Adam, so He cursed the earth. Adam's flesh was already part of the curse, for that warning was given before Adam sinned. But sin also must be judged and instead of putting mankind under eternal condemnation, God cursed all that was around man.

Everything in this life is destined to be dissolved. The flesh will be gone. The world will be gone. Even the heavens will be gone. All that pertained to the old kingdom will pass away, for all has been corrupted by the curse of sin. But notice what God revealed in Revelation above. The old passed away to make room for the new. The old earth and heavens will pass away, and then a new heaven and earth will be revealed.

In the same way, the old life in the flesh passes away so the new life in the Spirit can be revealed. God's purpose is not to patch up the old life in the flesh. His purpose is to crucify it – put it to death. Our old life was our slave master. We were in bondage to sin and because we are also guilty of our own sin, we are indebted to the curse of sin. We cannot pay the debt, for a corpse cannot raise itself to life. A

---

[80] Revelation 21:1
[81] 2 Peter 3:10-11

penniless pauper cannot pay his bills, much less his accumulated debt. We were in bondage and had no power to escape slavery.

How does a prisoner with a life sentence get out of prison? The law does not permit him to leave and the only way out is to die. Once the prisoner dies, the sentence is over and the consequences are gone. In the same way, we are imprisoned for life as a slave to sin. Jesus accomplished two things for us in His finished work on the cross. He paid the wages of our sins. This is accounted against our life in the world to come, but the Bible says that He became sin for us that we might become the righteousness of God in Him. The debt to God has been paid, but our sinful human nature remains bound to sin. Therefore, our old nature (or old man) was put to death on the cross. It was crucified with Christ. This is explained in **Romans 6:6-7**

> [6] knowing this, that our old man was crucified with *Him*, that the body of sin might be done away with, that we should no longer be slaves of sin.
> [7] For he who has died has been freed from sin.

The body of sin, our sinful nature, has been crucified. Once we died with Christ, we became free to live for Christ. A dead man is no longer a slave.

So if the body of sin has been done away with, why do we still have a tendency to sin? Our physical bodies aren't killed; the old nature that tied us to our sin has been killed. The flesh (or body of sin) is done away with because the cords of sin have been broken. They were tied to our old nature and were crucified with Christ. A new nature has been placed within us by the Spirit of God, who also remains in us. That new nature cannot sin, for it has been born of God. Let me reiterate this by showing this passage from **1 John 3:9**

> Whoever has been born of God does not sin, for His seed remains in him; and he cannot sin, because he has been born of God.

Again let's examine how the Bible can say that whoever is born of God cannot sin, yet I have sinned many times since coming to Christ.

Our new nature finds its existence in God, and the Bible says that it is incorruptible.[82] In the passage above we also see that the one born of God cannot sin. If you are born again, your new nature cannot sin. It is impossible. A spiritual nature that is grafted into us by the Holy Spirit and maintained by the Holy Spirit within us can't sin, for it is of God. God cannot sin, so our nature that is a partaker of His divine nature cannot sin either.[83]

Remember the words of the Apostle Paul we looked at earlier? He mourned over the fact that though he delights to serve God according to his inward nature, sin rises up and attempts to seize control of his mind.

The inward man, that new nature from God, serves the law of God. It is natural for our new man to serve God, for it finds its life in Him and rejoices in the things of the Spirit. That's why the Bible says that the unlearned gentiles who knew nothing about the law, by nature kept the law of God. Without knowing the scriptures, they were already doing the things found in the scriptures. They became a law unto themselves. They did not make up their own laws, but had the natural tendency to self-govern because something within them delighted in doing the things that pleased God.

We see this same truth in new Christians. When someone first comes to Christ, they are so focused on the new life they have received that they are almost immune to sin. Their entire focus is on Christ. As emotions fade, the flesh begins to war against their minds, and it isn't long before they begin to slip back into a fleshly way of thinking – unless they are discipled and learn how to handle these temptations.

Even though we have something within us that delights in God, we also live in a body that is corrupted by sin. Our old man was kept in check by external restraints and social norms, but it was still driven by selfish desires. Our minds were tied to the old nature and did what felt right to the flesh. Sin is the result of ties to the flesh. The new nature draws from the Spirit, unless we submit our minds back to the flesh.

Often we see churches protesting the corruption of the world, but should we be surprised when the world acts like the world? No. They

---

[82] 1 Peter 1:23, 1 Peter 3:4
[83] 2 Peter 1:4

are doing what seems right in their eyes. Just as those with the Spirit do by nature what pleases God, the unredeemed do by nature what pleases the flesh. They can do no other until they also receive a new nature.

We have a new nature, yet we can still be drawn into sin. We are no longer slaves of the flesh, but the flesh still craves gratification. For this reason there must be a change of nature. The flesh, by nature does the things that are of the flesh. The new nature we have been given by God also only acts according to its natural tendencies. The flesh can do nothing but what is of the flesh; the new man can only do the things of the Spirit.

The flesh sins because it is driven by its nature. When we are in the flesh, we will act within the boundaries of the flesh.

If we walk in the Spirit, the spiritual man within us can only act according to the boundaries of its nature. Since it is born of God, it cannot sin. It is impossible for the incorruptible nature born of God to sin, for it is of God and in God. Our new nature can only act according to God's righteousness and it delights in the things of the Spirit.

The flesh cannot overcome our spirit, for greater is He who is in you, than he that is in the world.[84] Since our spirit is of the Holy Spirit within us, it cannot be overcome. This is why the Bible says that we are more than conquerors through Christ.[85] Our minds can be brought into bondage to the flesh through persuasion, but not force. Temptation persuades us to step out of the Spirit and seek immediate gratification in the flesh. We are not overcome. We are persuaded to place confidence in the flesh instead of the Spirit.

These are the two worlds in which we interact – the flesh and the Spirit. Neither can change. The flesh cannot become anything other than the flesh. Circumstances, the promise of reward, the threat of punishment, and other forces can override certain desires of the flesh, but these cannot change the nature of the flesh.

An ill-tempered man may get his temper under control by overriding it with his will, but when something pushes the right button, his temper will rise up and regain control of his life. The same is true for the critical spirit, the heart of greed, and the spirit of lust.

---

[84] 1 John 4:4
[85] Romans 8:37

What is the flesh?

Behavior can change for a short time. It will change while emotions energize us, fear threatens us, or hope encourages us. But once the overriding force fades, or something stronger arises, the restraint is lost and the flesh reveals its true identity.

The Spirit also never changes. God has declared, "I change not." The God of yesterday is the God of today, and will be the same God of tomorrow. Since the Christian life is founded upon the promise, "I will place my Spirit within you," we also rejoice with the Apostle Paul, "We have this treasure in earthen vessels."

Within our vessels of human life resides the Spirit of God. Along with the treasure of God within us is the call to walk in the Spirit. God has promised us, "Walk in the Spirit and you will not fulfill the lusts of the flesh," and warned, "Those who are in the flesh cannot please God."

The flesh cannot please God. Period. If you listen to a great message, are overwhelmed with joy, and determine in your heart to live out God's truth in your life, you will fail. That is unless you take God's truth as a call to the Spirit. In the Spirit, you cannot fail. It's a guarantee by God. Jesus said, "He who abides in Me bears much fruit." It's a guarantee. 2 Peter 2 promises, "If you do these things [of the Spirit], you cannot be barren or unfruitful," and "You will never stumble." These also are guarantees. The new nature cannot fail, but success is not found in our determination, but our faith in Christ and His completed work. He is our strength. He is our sufficiency. Believe the word and receive the promise.

Discussion questions:

Why do Christians miss out on God's best for their lives?

Why were Adam and Eve tempted to take the fruit?

How does God's picture of slavery in the Old Testament paint a picture of our spiritual condition outside of Christ?

How many natures does the unredeemed man have?

How many natures does the Christian have?

Does God try to repair the sin nature or make it godly?

Should we try to make our flesh godly?

How does the Christian become godly?

Can good works from man ever please God? Why or why not?

How do we crucify the flesh?

How do we put off the deeds of the old man?

Why do Christians sin?

How are Christians forgiven?

Why Good Deeds go Bad

John 3:6
> That which is born of the flesh is flesh, and that which is born of the Spirit is spirit.

Discerning the corruption of the flesh is often a difficult principle to communicate. When we are looking at works and good deeds from the perspective of human wisdom, what is born of the flesh can often appear good, even though God clearly rejects the works of the flesh. God not only rejects the sins of the flesh, but He also rejects all the works of the flesh – even that which appears good by human standards. Consider the explanation Jesus gave in **Matthew 7:21-23**

> [21] " Not everyone who says to Me, 'Lord, Lord,' shall enter the kingdom of heaven, but he who does the will of My Father in heaven.
> [22] "Many will say to Me in that day, 'Lord, Lord, have we not prophesied in Your name, cast out demons in Your name, and done many wonders in Your name?'
> [23] "And then I will declare to them, 'I never knew you; depart from Me, you who practice lawlessness!'

Consider the weight of this passage. These people were declaring, "Jesus is Lord," but Jesus rejected them. But doesn't the Bible also say that no one can say "Jesus is Lord except by the Spirit?"[86] What is being communicated here is not the words being spoken, but the confession of the heart.

An atheist can say the words, 'Jesus is Lord', but that is not by the Spirit. Many cults have used this passage to persuade new prospects into accepting them as Spirit led. I can name an idol, Jesus, and then call it 'lord', but it does not equate to a fulfillment of the Bible's standard of confessing Jesus as Lord. It is physically possible for the fleshly mind to say the words, "Jesus is Lord," and still remain in the flesh and far from His lordship.

---

[86] 1 Corinthians 12:3

Only the Holy Spirit can reveal the Lord and through the Spirit we have the power to truly call Him Lord. Without the power of the Spirit, we are incapable of submitting to Him as Lord. Regardless of the words of our mouth, if we remain fleshly minded, flesh remains our lord. Or perhaps a clearer way of explaining would be that we remain as our own lord.

This is the type of person Jesus is condemning. Many will serve their own flesh and declare that their works are of Christ. People will do many good things in the name of Jesus. According to the description Jesus gave above, these works are indistinguishable from the true works of God by outward appearance.

Who can say that speaking God's word (or prophesying) in Christ's name is bad? Who would think that casting out demons in Christ's name was wicked? Or doing wonders in Jesus' name is an act of the flesh? The truth is, you and I can't know. Not only can we not know the motives behind our fellow church member, we cannot discern our own motives without the revelation of the Spirit of God.

According to the Bible, the heart is deceitful above all things and desperately wicked. Who can know it? Only the Lord can search the heart, try the motives, and give us according to the true motives of our heart.[87] In Christ, there is a cleansing of the heart, but since this is part of our soul, even the Christian's heart can have fleshly motives if we are not walking in the Spirit.

Outwardly, the works always appear good to the human intellect, even when it is of the flesh. This is true when we see the good works of those around us, but how much more true is that of our own motives? My flesh can mimic the move of God through emotions, reasoning, and appearance. Yet the spiritually minded has the power of the Spirit to not only discern our own hearts, but to reveal the work God has prepared for us so we can walk in them.[88]

We don't want to spend our whole lives sacrificing, doing good deeds, and performing all the religious practices that seem right only to hear our works called acts of lawlessness and iniquity. This is why the Bible warns, "There is a way that seems right to man, but the end of it is the way of death."[89]

---

[87] Jeremiah 17:9-10
[88] Ephesians 2:10
[89] Proverbs 14:12

Why Good Deeds go Bad

The flesh is in the way of death and any works done through the flesh are dead works. But the Spirit is life. Consider again the words of **Romans 8:13-14**

¹³ For if you live according to the flesh you will die; but if by the Spirit you put to death the deeds of the body, you will live.

¹⁴ For as many as are led by the Spirit of God, these are sons of God.

All deeds of the body must be put to death. Not only must we put to death the sins of the body, but all deeds of the body. Anything born of the flesh is flesh, and nothing of the flesh can be made into something of the Spirit. The flesh cannot give birth to the works of the Spirit.

This is a very difficult concept to grasp, so let's use a word picture. Consider a plant called Digitalis purpurea. You probably know it by the common name of foxglove. Foxgloves have roots and leaves that are very toxic to people and animals. Anyone who consumes the plant will become ill and if the poisoning is severe enough, they can die. If you take the plant out of the woods and put it into your garden, the nature of this plant doesn't change. It's just as poisonous in the garden as it was in the wild.

If the plant thrives, it will send up a long stalk and will bloom. The blossoms are filled with beautiful colors and turn this common looking weed into a work of art. Even with all the gorgeous flowers, the plant is still just as poisonous as when it was only a weed. In fact, the blossoms are deadly, the seeds are deadly, and even the pollen is toxic.

If someone looked at a garden full of blooming foxgloves and said, "How can all this beauty be poisonous?" what would you say? The pretty flowers don't nullify the poison. If anything, it makes them more dangerous. No one plants poison ivy in their gardens because there is nothing to gain from them. They are harmful, but lack the beauty of flowers. But people are more than willing to take the risk of having poisonous flowers around because it adds beauty to the world around them.

This is the works of the flesh. It blooms out of a nature that is harmful. Just because it adds beauty to the world doesn't change its nature. Does this mean that people shouldn't continue doing things that make the world look better? No. At funerals we dress up the dead, surround them with flowers, and put makeup on those who have passed. But they are still dead. Making the dead more attractive makes us feel better, but it does not give them life.

Those who are of the world are those who do not have the Spirit of God within them. Jesus said, "You are not of the world for I have called you out of the world." The flesh is part of the dying world. Our bodies are dying and our flesh remains married to that which is passing away. It calls us to gratify its desire in this world. That call can come as a temptation to sin, or as a temptation to do good from the power of self. But self-power is of the flesh and anything it produces is flowers around the corpse.

So does this mean the Christian withdraws from doing good? Do we become indifferent to the suffering of the world, or the needs of the hungry, or the plethora of problems in the world? Of course not; however, we must seek to first be established in the greatest commandment and then allow God to reveal what He is doing through us. The greatest commandment can be found in **Matthew 22:35-40**

> [35] Then one of them, a lawyer, asked *Him a question,* testing Him, and saying,
>
> [36] "Teacher, which *is* the great commandment in the law?"
>
> [37] Jesus said to him, " 'You shall love the LORD your God with all your heart, with all your soul, and with all your mind.'
>
> [38] "This is *the* first and great commandment.
>
> [39] "And *the* second *is* like it: 'You shall love your neighbor as yourself.'
>
> [40] "On these two commandments hang all the Law and the Prophets."

First, let's consider the source of the question. It was from a lawyer. In that culture, the lawyers studied what was then the Old Testament scriptures. They sought to dig every practice out of the law and apply it to their culture. Yet the lawyers and the other religious leaders of that day missed the call of God. The Apostle Paul came out of that religious system and declared, "While seeking to establish their own righteousness, they failed to find the righteousness of God."

This is what people want to do in religion. Religion comes in many packages. Even the secularist serves his own religion, for they are seeking to better themselves and the world around them by good deeds. The Christian often falls into this same trap, but never realize it because in it we first declare, "Lord, Lord," before proclaiming our righteous efforts before Christ. Yet God treats these works the same as He treats the works of the secular culture around us.

The true evidence is that instead of seeking to establish ourselves, we seek the Lord. We seek His Kingdom and His righteousness, not our own. We first must establish ourselves in the love of God, and then from that love all else flows.

If we seek to please God by expressing human love to others, we fall short, for we are seeking to establish our own righteousness and do not have the righteousness of God. However, if we seek the Lord and His righteousness – which are given to us by the love God has poured into our hearts by the Holy Spirit (Romans 5:5), then we are in a position to do good works – not by human effort, but by the move of the Holy Spirit within us.

Again I feel the need to stop and explain an important truth here. The command to love God with all our heart is based on what we have received, not what we give. If we try to love God by human effort, we will fail. The command to 'love God' is the Greek word 'agapao', which is the act of expressing 'agape'. Agape is the unconditional love God has poured into our hearts. Human love is based on 'Philia' love – or friendship. It is the type of love which is returned to someone we have warm affections toward.

God is the only source of agape love. We are called to love (agapao) God with all our heart because God's agape love has been poured into our hearts by His Spirit. We are loving God with the love He has given us and has empowered us to express back. In other words, we are walking in the love of God so that we can have the full experience of His love.

If you try to love God with all your might, the best you can hope for is frustration. When things are comfortable, we might feel that warm affection, but those who abide in the love God has given are not dependent upon anything but God. Those who love God with the love He has given complete the relationship of intimacy. He first loved us, poured His love into our hearts, and we abide in that love and fulfill the commandment by living within the provision of God.

We don't love to be loved. We love because we are loved.[90] We fulfill the command to love our neighbor by directing what God has given us toward others.

Some worry that if there is no merit system, people will not do good works. Rather than becoming an excuse for not doing good works, the love of God compels us to glorify Christ by doing the good works He is calling us to do. Or perhaps I should say, the good works He works through us. The heart of man may devise many deeds that appear good, but only the person in tune with the Spirit can find the goodness of God being poured into our lives for the purpose of pouring ourselves into the lives of those around us.

Not only does the Lord call us to give of ourselves, but He chooses the works, the place, and provides His Spirit to empower us to do His purpose. Anything God calls us to give has already been given to us by His Spirit. My love to others is actually God's love given to me. My works must be the work of Christ in me and through me. I am not creating my own works. I am walking in the works God has already prepared beforehand and the need He has revealed is the path He has led me to.

Anything we establish is worthless, for it is of the flesh. Isaiah 64:6 tells us that all our righteous acts are like filthy rags in God's sight. This is a direct contrast to God's provision a few chapters earlier in **Isaiah 61:10**

> I will greatly rejoice in the LORD, My soul shall be joyful in my God; For He has clothed me with the garments of salvation, He has covered me with the robe of righteousness, As a bridegroom decks *himself* with ornaments, And as a bride adorns *herself* with her jewels.

The righteous clothing of mankind is of the flesh and cannot please God. The flesh, as we have seen, is dying. It has the aroma of death and is filthy in God's sight. But those who put on God's clothing of righteousness are well pleasing to God. He rejoices in us, and we rejoice in Him. The soul covered with the righteousness of Christ rejoices like a husband waiting for his beloved bride and reflects the beauty of a radiant bride rejoicing in her coming husband.

---

[90] 1 John 4:19

Why Good Deeds go Bad

Once we discover this beauty, the flesh has nothing of value for us.

When that radiance begins to wane, it should cause us to examine ourselves to insure we are not heeding the flesh. The flesh must be put to death by reckoning ourselves dead in Christ.

Sin is of the flesh. Good deeds done by human effort is of the flesh. Though these two may appear different to our human understanding, they are no different to God. The poison of the flesh is still poison, whether it is rooted in the filth of the mire or whether it's blooming above the world around it. It is still the flesh and still produces the same thing. Behind the blossom is a toxic nature. Behind the stalk is a toxic nature. Within its roots is the same toxic nature.

Whether the flesh is committing sin or presenting its good deeds, the byproduct is the same. It is a declaration of independence from God and seeks to present the flesh as though it were on par with the righteousness of God.

Keep in mind that Christ has dethroned the nature that once reigned in our bodies. The flesh craves to be satisfied. At the heart of the flesh is the desire of self. Self-worth, self-satisfaction, self-confidence, self-righteousness, and any other selfish desire is produced by the flesh. The flesh seeks to regain its former position and will never stop looking for any opportunity. This is why **Romans 13:14** tells us:

> But put on the Lord Jesus Christ, and make no provision for the flesh, to *fulfill its* lusts.

Don't think of lusts as only sinful desires. Lust means to deeply long for something. In most instances it is related to sin, but not always. The flesh lusts for control. At its core, the flesh lusts for self-gratification, whether that be a desire to satisfy itself through sin, through apathy, or through self-righteousness. Also consider this passage from **Galatians 5:17**

> For the flesh lusts against the Spirit, and the Spirit against the flesh; and these are contrary to one another, so that you do not do the things that you wish.

Notice that lust is not only applied to the flesh, but also to the Spirit. Both have intense desires that put them at odds with each other. The things the flesh desires are an affront to the Spirit, and the things the Spirit desires are an affront to the flesh. There can be no truce in this war. One will be suppressed and the other will be enthroned. At the heart of victory is the final phrase of the warning, "So that you do not do the things that you wish."

Victory is found in depriving self. To the human mind, this is absurd. Who would want to serve a God that requires us to die to ourselves? No self-pleasure? No self-righteousness? No self-gratification? Herein is the great irony of Christianity. False Christianity calls for us to make self better. True Christianity is the crucifixion of self. But the great irony is the satisfaction found through the denial of self. Look now at **Luke 9:23-25**

> 23 Then He said to *them* all, "If anyone desires to come after Me, let him deny himself, and take up his cross daily, and follow Me.
> 24 "For whoever desires to save his life will lose it, but whoever loses his life for My sake will save it.
> 25 "For what profit is it to a man if he gains the whole world, and is himself destroyed or lost?

Do you see why the flesh and the Spirit can never agree? The Spirit calls, "Lose your life that you may find true life," but the flesh calls, "Save your life and search for satisfaction through self-gratification." One of these calls is false. It shouldn't be hard to figure out which one is the lie. Look around. Do those who consume themselves with selfishness find satisfaction? Does gaining the whole world satisfy the soul? Or are the words of scripture clearly evident, "The eyes of man are never satisfied?"

Each day you and I stand where Adam and Eve once stood. On the one hand, the tree of self promises knowledge, satisfaction, self-sufficiency, self-righteousness, and all that the world has to offer. Through that indulgence we have the lust of the flesh, the lust of the eyes, and the pride of life.[91]

Throughout human history this choice has never satisfied, but the promise is so alluring that people spend their lives consuming its fruit. Rather than quenching hunger, this only starves the soul and

---

[91] 1 John 2:16

creates a deeper hunger, which then draws men into the never-ending quest for gratification.

On the other hand is the tree of life. Its fruit doesn't glisten. It doesn't appeal to the eyes, nor does it tempt us with the promises of self-gain. Instead, this fruit promises to put self to death. Its promise is to die in order to find life. It removes our sufficiency so that we are forced to look solely to God as our source of life, righteousness, and satisfaction.

Through this call, we take it by faith, not in what we can see, but in what God has promised. The promise is, once you have died, then the Spirit of God will raise up a new life that is completely dependent upon God. Yet this is the greatest joy, for what self could not do, God has already done for us. Those who die not only find life, but discover the true source of abundant satisfaction. Look at this wonderful promise from **Psalm 36:7-9**

[7] How precious *is* Your lovingkindness, O God! Therefore the children of men put their trust under the shadow of Your wings.

[8] They are abundantly satisfied with the fullness of Your house, And You give them drink from the river of Your pleasures.

[9] For with You *is* the fountain of life; In Your light we see light.

On one side, things, experiences, and temporal pleasures are the focus of life. On the other hand, God is our exceedingly great reward, and He is more than enough. Those who love self cannot take the fruit of life. Those who love God cannot take the fruit of self. Each decision we make is a choice between the flesh or the Spirit. There is not a third option.

To clarify, turning to the tree of life is to look to God as our complete source of life and satisfaction. It is to trust in His righteousness and receive His goodness. It is to become a partaker of God's divine nature.[92]

Good works come from God as we yield to Him. Satisfaction comes from God as we yield to Him. Both are acts of faith as we learn to trust in Christ alone. Religion says that we must do

---

[92] 2 Peter 1:3-4

something for God in order to please Him or earn a blessing. Faith says, "I have been given all things that pertain to life and godliness." I am already blessed because I am a partaker of His goodness. I am already righteous because I am in Christ. I am already favored because I am in the love of God. Works flow from a life abiding in Christ[93]. Anything else is a work of flesh.

Discussion questions:

Is it possible for the Christian to do good deeds and have those works rejected by God?

Read Romans 8:13-14. How are the deeds of the body/flesh put to death?

What is the deeds of the body? Can any of the body's deeds appear good? Are they good?

Can works of the flesh make the world a more beautiful place?

Do these works have eternal significance?

Is the love of God (agape) something we give or something we receive? Explain.

Why does God command us to love? Check your answer against Matthew 10:8.

Does God view righteous acts of the flesh as more valuable than sins of the flesh?

Is God less forgiving of the sins of the flesh than the self-righteous acts of the flesh?

How can dying to ourselves cause us to find life?

How is denying self an act of faith?

---

[93] John 15

Why Good Deeds go Bad

Read Psalm 36:7-9. According to verse 7, Who is this promise for?

Works Prepared Beforehand

In the previous chapter, we looked at how the flesh cannot produce good. In this chapter, we'll look at how God uses us to express His love and purposes to the world around us, and how He does this through our bodies of flesh. While we are in this life, we present our bodies as instruments of righteousness to the Lord.[94]

False works attempts to use the body to produce righteousness. True works begins with a life submitted to the Spirit, and the righteousness of God shines through, making our bodies subject to a godly purpose. Good works begins with God communicating to our spirit, our spirit communicating through our minds, and our actions make our bodies as an instrument of righteousness.

The Spirit abides in us, for we are the temple of the Holy Spirit. The Holy Spirit communes with our spirit, our minds are subject to the Spirit and rule our soul, and our bodies are brought under subjection to God by our Spirit led soul.

If we are led through the flesh, nothing spiritual can happen. If we are led by the Spirit, even our bodies are subject to righteousness, and we are able to accomplish the good works God has prepared for us to do. Good works must begin from the Spirit.

There are several important principles that emerge from this truth. One is that the flesh must be brought under subjection to Christ, rather than looking to it as a source for doing God's will. Look at the words of Jesus in **John 3:6**

> [6] "That which is born of the flesh is flesh, and that which is born of the Spirit is spirit.

Certainly we live and move through a physical body, but this does not mean that we attempt to live out godliness through human effort. By the flesh, I am referring to our efforts to become godly rather than looking to the power of Christ as the source of godliness. The same is true for any work or spiritual aspiration.

Anything that is born of the flesh is flesh. That includes many things we think are noble and spiritual. Worship born from the flesh is of the flesh and not acceptable to God. Jesus said, "God is Spirit,

---

[94] Romans 6:13

and those who worship God must worship in spirit and truth."[95] Spirited worship is not the same as worshipping in the Spirit. To be in the spirit it has to come through the Spirit of God. Just because worship makes us happy does not mean it pleases God. However, those who are walking and abiding in the Spirit will also be worshipping God through the Spirit.

As we saw in the previous chapter, works may appear good, but if works are born of the flesh, they are of the flesh and destined for rejection. Death cannot produce life, nor can works born of the flesh rise to the life of the Spirit. This is why getting busy for God is an act of the flesh. It's also why following our own plans and presenting them to God as good works doesn't please Him.

The Bible says God finished the works from the foundation of the world. He has woven His purposes into time and creation. Me coming to God with my well intentioned plans is rarely acceptable. God does not bless the works of man; God calls each of us into *His* works. This is why the Bible says, "You were created for good works, which God prepared beforehand that you should walk in them."

Most people look at prayer as if we are trying to petition God to act according to our will. We often think we are changing the mind of God, but in reality, Spirit led prayer is changing our hearts so we are moved into the will of God. This is why the Bible says, "This is the confidence we have in Him. If we ask anything according to His will, He hears and grants our petitions."[96]

The Bible also warns that many times we pray and don't receive because we ask with the wrong motives – our own selfish desires. Often God calls us to prayer because it's His desire to reveal His power through the heart that is completely His.[97]

The glorious truth of praying in the Spirit is that it becomes God's hand to move us into His purposes, stir our hearts to pray according to God's will, and then we become a part of God's works. Then we share in the rewards, not because we have done anything great, but because we have united with Christ so that He can work through us.

---

[95] John 4:23
[96] 1 John 5:14-15
[97] 2 Chronicles 16:9

Don't forget one important principle of scripture. "It is the Father's good pleasure to give you the kingdom." If you are born by the Spirit, you are a child of God. And God's desire is for you to be a joint heir with Christ. It is not that God needs you and I in order to accomplish His will. God desires to raise up godly men and women to share in His work so that they can share in the rewards of the kingdom.

It is not for God's benefit that we pray and do His works. It is for our benefit. God can fulfill His purposes without us, but then who would share in the joys of the kingdom? God didn't need man in order to create the universe. He didn't need our help to fashion the earth. He didn't ask for man's counsel when He built His purposes into the timeline of creation or prepared the works beforehand.

So why does God require mankind's involvement now? It is for no other purpose than for you and I to share in His glory. Your call into good works is an act of God's grace. He calls you to good works because He favors you and wants you to be a part of what He is doing. Good works are not intended for you to earn anything, but for you to join God as a child works alongside their father.

I'm a gardener. My young children want to help Daddy plant in the garden. I don't need them in order to accomplish my work. I invite them to be a part of the work because I want to build that relationship. My younger children do a poor job. When we planted strawberries, they left the roots exposed. They were haphazard in their methods, but they had such joy in being a part of growing what would soon benefit us.

I went behind them and buried the roots, or rescued the plants that were buried too deep. Sometimes I prepared the rows and said, "Put a seed here, here, and here." Sometimes they succeeded, but most of the time they did not. But I made up for what they lacked.

When the fruit and vegetables produced, they helped me pick. They missed most of the beans and picked a few under-ripened tomatoes. I finished what they missed, but they were pleased to be part of what I was doing.

When they sat at the table, they looked at the fruit of their labors and were happy to enjoy what their work had produced. They got the benefit far beyond the value of their labor, but I didn't invite them because I wanted their labor. I invited them because I wanted them to enjoy growing. I knew they would feel special to be part of

Works Prepared Beforehand

my garden. I knew they would put the strawberry on their plate and say, "I helped grow this." The food on the table had more value because they were part of its preparation.

This is what good works are all about. God doesn't need your labors. In fact, when you look to yourself as the source of labor, you are missing the heart of good works. It isn't intended to be labor, but fellowship. You have the amazing privilege of being a part of what God is doing. He is preparing His kingdom, and God has invited you to be a part of it.

When you fall short in your abilities, God doesn't look down and scold you. He embraces you as a child and approves of your desire to be a part of what He is doing. Your abilities are not needed. Your lack of ability is not a barrier, for it is God who works in you both to will and to do for *His* good pleasure (**Philippians 2:13**).

Looking to yourself misses the entire point. Good works are the pleasure of joining God as He builds His kingdom so you can enjoy both the experience, and have joy in the finished work.

Don't pollute God's works with human effort. Enjoy the fellowship! Good works are an act of God's grace to your benefit. He could fulfill the kingdom without you, but because He favors you, He invites you into His works.

God wants you to inherit the kingdom. He isn't standing afar off, watching men form their own ideas and rewarding those who figure out something that pleases Him. No, God is intimately involved in His church, that was purchased by His blood, and born through His Spirit. And His intention is to call you into His kingdom so you can have intimate fellowship with Him and be rewarded as if it were your work. Yet it must be His work through us or it is not of God and cannot be accepted as part of His kingdom.

Consider the words of **Psalm 37:23**

The steps of a good man are ordered by the Lord, and He delights in his way.

God delights in your way. He delights in directing your steps and leading you toward the promise. Certainly we can be stubborn and plop down, and refuse to go where He is leading, but why would we want to pursue worthless works over God's kingdom?

Many Christians have this attitude and don't even realize it. They claim to be followers of Christ and will do so until God is leading where they don't want to go. They can't see the promise at the end and are only interested when they can see the benefit ahead of time. They miss the joy because they are focused on something other than Christ.

How sad it is that many who name the name of Christ miss the goodness God intends for them. This is not because God isn't providing, but because they aren't receiving. Where there is no faith, the Christian is not receiving God's gifts and the love He is extending. God will lead you into the promise, but He will not drag you into it.

If we will not go where God is going, the Lord will raise up someone who will. God *will* have heirs to the kingdom. If not you, then someone else will take your place. Consider the words of **Hebrews 4:1-3**

> ¹ Therefore, since a promise remains of entering His rest, let us fear lest any of you seem to have come short of it.
> ² For indeed the gospel was preached to us as well as to them; but the word which they heard did not profit them, not being mixed with faith in those who heard *it.*
> ³ For we who have believed do enter that rest, as He has said: "So I swore in My wrath, 'They shall not enter My rest,' " although the works were finished from the foundation of the world.

This passage is comparing our promise to the Children of Israel, who didn't believe God and refused to pass through the difficulties of life and go where God was leading. They had the promise, but they missed it. And God raised up a people who would receive it.

The next generation did inherit the promise, and they had to accomplish many things in the process of taking the land. They had to do many works, yet who was really doing the work? How could they have been in God's rest, but still have to work?

They entered into God's works by ceasing from their own works. They rested in Christ while both receiving the promise and walking in the works God was leading them through. When they were walking where God led, they could not fail. It was God who went before them. It was God who fought their battles. It was God who drove out their enemies. What was their work?

This is the work of God, to believe on Him God has sent.[98] They believed God and walked in faith. The only thing dependent on man was to take what God revealed by faith, and believe it. Then they walked in God's works by faith.

God did not call them to be passive and apathetic, but to be followers of the Lord and walk in the works He had already prepared beforehand. The works were already finished in Christ, but in order to experience the finished work, they had to walk in Him by faith.

Notice the last comment in the above passage, "Although the works were finished from the foundation of the world." The work was already completed – before the world was even founded. How can this be? This fits into the words of **Ephesians 2:10**,

"We were created for good works, which God prepared beforehand that we should walk in them."

God is not calling you to accomplish His works. This has already been done. God has already made the way, accomplished the work, and fulfilled His purpose. The only thing lacking is your inheritance. And this is why you were called to faith in Christ. This is why you are called into your personal ministry. Each person has a personal ministry, for each person has the call of God on their life. And the first step in answering that call is to look to Him and trust Him alone.

God will allow you to be tested. He will allow your own flesh to rise up and tempt you. He will allow temptation from the outside to draw you. He will allow hardships to threaten you. All of these serve one main purpose. Do you look to temptation for fulfillment, or do you look to Christ? Do you desire the world, or do you desire Christ? Do you believe that the hardships threatening you have more power than Christ? Or do you trust in Christ?

When the apostles were in a ship and crossing the Sea of Galilee, a fierce storm arose. Jesus was in the boat sleeping on a pillow. He had already called them into His work, shown them His power, and promised them a place in His kingdom. Yet as the storm grew more violent, the ship began to sink. In desperation, they woke Jesus up and said, "Do you not care that we are perishing?"

---

[98] John 6:29

What was Jesus' answer? He first calmed the sea, and then said, "Why are you so fearful? How is it that you have no faith?"

Where was the lack of faith? Faith had already been revealed, yet instead of trusting in God, they abandoned faith and believed the threatening storm. The problem wasn't that they awoke Jesus. It was that they lashed out at Him because He wasn't acting as they thought He should. Faith should have assured them that they could not perish, for Jesus was with them. And He had called them to a work. Did He not have the power to preserve them? Can the storms of life overpower God's will and thwart His purposes?

No. Nothing can stand against God's hand and everything He has purposed will be fulfilled. Waking Jesus wasn't their failure. Allowing fear to rule their lives was the failure. They believed the threat had power over the word of Christ.

Let me be clear in this. Fear is not a sin. Doubt is not a sin. Temptation is not a sin. It is when we believe these things over the word of God that we fall into sin. In fact, fear can be an asset, for fear reveals our complete dependency on God. Until we are threatened with defeat, we often have confidence in ourselves. However, when we realize we have no power, that is when faith reveals the power of God. Temptations such as lust, fear, and doubt simply reveal where our confidence lies.

There is nothing wrong with getting on your knees and saying to God, "The storms make me afraid, but I put myself into your hands. Either calm the storm or carry me through it." But like the disciples, when we feel threatened, all we can see is the threat, and we forget about the hand of the Lord upon us. Or even more true, the Spirit of God within us.

How does this apply to overcoming sin in our life? Do you pray, "Why can't I defeat this weakness," or "Why aren't you fixing this?"

Faith calls for us to pray, "Lord, your promise is that Your Spirit within me is greater than the world. I have no power to defeat temptation, but you have already done this for me. Teach me how to walk in Your victory."

Sin has already been defeated. It's time to start believing in the power of God instead of the power of the storms – both those threatening from the outside, and those brewing in our flesh.

Does the God within us not see? Do we think we can abide in Christ, and yet He has no knowledge of our circumstances? Or do we

Works Prepared Beforehand

think that the God who holds the universe together with the word of His power cannot handle our troubles?[99]

The truth is that God will allow our lives to be threatened, but nothing can slip through His fingers to harm us. This is also why we are warned, "Do not fear him who can harm the body, but fear Him who has the power to both harm the body and destroy the soul."[100] In other words, fear nothing but God. And for a child of the King, that fear is cast out by God's perfect love.[101]

Persecution, troubles, and threats can do nothing but threaten the flesh. None of these have power over our true life. The eternal must remain in focus, and that means to focus on Christ as the source of life, success, and power. The enemy will try to use fear to turn us away from God's works, but those who walk by faith are bold as a lion.[102] We are bold because we serve a God whose purposes cannot be stopped. Anything that seems to cause harm is the blessing of God and leads to His rewards.

If we are of the new creation, why does sin in our lives threaten us? The things we just discussed directly apply to this question. Why do we sin? We put our eyes on the flesh. We trust in the promises of the flesh. We submit to the flesh.

Why do we turn back in fear? We put our eyes on the flesh. We trust in the threats of the flesh. We submit to the flesh. And sometimes we try to serve God through our flesh because it gives us either immediate gratification or promises faster results. But nothing done through human effort has any substance or lasting value.

We can have the biggest church in the world, but it means nothing if it is not the work of the Spirit. We can give all our possessions to feed the poor, but if it's not of the Spirit, it means nothing.[103] We can attempt to serve God with all our time, talents, and abilities, but it means nothing. God doesn't want your money, talents, or efforts. He wants one thing. Complete surrender. Trust in His love and surrender all.

---

[99] Hebrews 1:3
[100] Matthew 10:28
[101] 1 John 4:18
[102] Proverbs 28:1
[103] 1 Corinthians 13:3

God wants you to take up the cross and allow Christ to live and work through you. He offers the cross; the world offers gratification. One benefits for a moment, the other has the promise of eternal inheritance.

This is the hardest biblical principle to grasp. This is partly because in order to die to myself, I have to see my need to die. As long as I trust in my own abilities, I keep trying to do God's will through my own strength. If I have success by human standards, I am encouraged to keep my efforts going. Then I will fall into the crowd who came to Jesus saying, "I did many wonderful things in Your name. I even did miracles in Your name," but Jesus rejected these works.

God doesn't even care if you serve in His own name. If it is not born of the Spirit, it is the flesh. Any deed by human effort, even done in Jesus name, is a work of the flesh. God will reject it. Though the world and the church may praise you, if God rejects the work, it is worthless. Consider **1 Corinthians 3:11-15**

[11] For no other foundation can anyone lay than that which is laid, which is Jesus Christ.

[12] Now if anyone builds on this foundation *with* gold, silver, precious stones, wood, hay, straw,

[13] each one's work will become clear; for the Day will declare it, because it will be revealed by fire; and the fire will test each one's work, of what sort it is.

[14] If anyone's work which he has built on *it* endures, he will receive a reward.

[15] If anyone's work is burned, he will suffer loss; but he himself will be saved, yet so as through fire.

Any who are in Christ will successfully pass through the testing of Christ. Yet many will suffer the loss of all they worked for. The precious things that will endure are the things born of God. God's work is eternal and all He gives is eternal. The wood, hay, and stubble are our own works we bring before God. What we do for God will be destroyed, for the works of the flesh cannot survive God's testing. That which God produces in us will not only survive, but He will reward us for receiving what He is doing. We are rewarded for walking in the works God has prepared beforehand.

Since God has finished the work before the foundation of the world, nothing you do can alter God's preordained works. They are already finished. And God doesn't need our advice on how to improve that plan.

From the scriptures we know that God has promised our deliverance from sin and the flesh, the works were finished before the world was made, we have been predestined to conform to the image of Christ, and we have the Holy Spirit working in us to reveal all things. The scripture also states that through the word, God reveals everything to make us complete and thoroughly equipped for every good work.

Since these things are so, what reason can there be for not fulfilling the Christian life? Only one thing stands between you and being a partaker of God's purpose – your willingness to trust His word. Certainly God predestined you to conform perfectly to the image of Christ. He certainly prepared the works before the foundation of creation. Yet we are warned to be diligent lest we fall short of the promise.

If God foreordained our path, predestined us to conform to Christ, and completed the works before the world was made, how can we possibly resist anything or fall short of the promise?

This is the great misconception of many. Those who believe in predestination claim that God can't be resisted and explain away the passages where God calls for surrender and obedience. Many who hold to this system of thought deny the will of man. On the other side, those who believe in man's choice often try to explain away passages that speak on God's sovereignty, and oppose the concept of predestination. However, both concepts are clearly taught in scripture.

Does God have the right to override the will of man? Certainly. He is God and can do as He pleases. Some can point to examples, such as God's declaration that He hated Esau and loved Jacob before they were born. They had no works, yet God chose one and rejected the other before they were born.

However, none of these examples nullify the scriptures that teach that man must choose and that he has a will. Nor do the passages that say, "Choose this day," indicate that God has no power to usurp authority over the will of man. While the Bible doesn't explain why He chose to set aside certain people before birth, the Bible does call men everywhere to repent and believe the gospel.

In the next chapter, we'll discuss this and see how God's preordained plan gives us confidence in the promise that we have been given all things that pertain to life and godliness.

Discussion questions:

What makes a deed good and what makes it fleshly?

If good deeds or worship makes you feel good, does that mean it is of God?

Is every need you see a call of God?

Is it possible to work in the church and not please God?

Why does God call us into His works? Can God accomplish His purposes without us?

When we do good works, does God owe us a reward?

Why does God reward the faithful Christian?

Did God save you because He needed workers, or because He desires to share His glory with you?

When you goof up God's work, is He angry?

Does God desire more effort or more communion from your life?

Can we walk by faith if we have fear? Or doubt?

Why does the Bible say that some will lose all their works by the Lord's fire, yet they will still be saved?

What does that tell us about earning salvation or God's approval?

Predestined for Good Works

At the end of the previous chapter, I made the statement that God has the right to usurp authority over the will of man. While this is true, another truth should be considered as well. Never do we see God's promise received without faith.

Let's take the example of Esau and Jacob. God said, "Esau have I hated and Jacob have I loved."[104] Yet how did Jacob receive the promise? After a twenty-year journey where he fled from his brother's wrath, God told him to return home with the promise, "I will bless you and make you a great nation."

When Esau heard Jacob was returning, he pursued him with a band of four-hundred men. Jacob prayed, "I fear my brother and am afraid he will strike down my children and their mother, but you said, 'Return and I will bless you.'" He then claimed the promise of God by faith. He confessed his fear, and that fear drove him to trust completely in the Lord. By faith, he stood upon the promise and received the promise.

The will of man does not nullify the sovereignty of God. Nor does the sovereignty of God wipe away the clearly taught principle of man's will.

The works were finished before the world was founded, but God does not force us into that work. In the letters to the churches found in Revelation chapters 2 and 3, Jesus warned the churches to repent, from false beliefs and false works. Eight times Jesus gave the churches a command to repent or face consequences. And what is the primary consequence?

"Repent...or I will remove your lampstand from its place." Consider the words of Christ in **Luke 19:41-42**

[41] Now as He drew near, He saw the city and wept over it,
[42] saying, "If you had known, even you, especially in this your day, the things *that make* for your peace! But now they are hidden from your eyes.

This was spoken to Jerusalem just before they crucified Christ. Jesus added further to this when he cried, "O Jerusalem, Jerusalem,

---

[104] Romans 9:13

the one who kills the prophets and stones those who are sent to her! How often I wanted to gather your children together, as a hen *gathers* her brood under *her* wings, but you were not willing!"[105]

When Jesus wept over the city, what was God's hope for the people? This day was meant for their peace. But they couldn't accept God's plan and now it was hidden from their eyes. In Jesus' cry He expressed the longing of the heart of God – to gather them under His wings. God wanted them to be part of the glory of His kingdom, but they refused to let go of their ways in the flesh and could not trust in the life-giving word that was meant for their peace.

In spite of this, Jesus had spent years foretelling of God's plan. Also, hundreds of years before Christ God foretold of the sufferings He would have to endure. God foreknew, yet He also desired to bless. He knew of the coming rejection and even built the sufferings of Christ into the plan of God. He used man's rejection of Him for man's deliverance from sin. Yet this does not change the fact that God desired their peace and meant the day of visitation to be part of their glory. This is not an assumption that we can deny. This is the testimony of Jesus Christ.

What happened when God's people rejected Christ? The works were finished from the beginning of creation. God's purposes will be fulfilled. So God raised up a new people and completed His plan through the Gentiles.

What God does is always consistent with how He works. Though He works uniquely in our lives, the principles of God never change. God meant the events of your life to be for your peace. He longs to gather you under His wings and bring you into His inheritance to share in His glory. But God will not cast your will aside in order to force you into His promises. Instead He calls you to die to your will and say, "Not my will, but yours, Lord."

The words mean nothing until our eyes are on Christ and our love is upon God. He has indeed predestined you to conform to His image. He has indeed finished the works beforehand and calls you to walk in it. He indeed desires for you to inherit the kingdom. But if you reject His perfect plan, and pull away your shoulder like a rebellious son or daughter, God will allow you to fall short of that

---

[105] Luke 13:34

glory. And He will raise up someone who will join Him as God accomplishes His purpose.

The works are complete. The only thing incomplete is our place in that work. Not one of His foreordained purposes will fail. If you walk according to the flesh, you will fall short of God fulfilling this in your life, but God's purpose will be completed. Or perhaps I should say, have been completed.

It is an amazing thing that God has chosen to make us part of that glorious plan. God could just make it happen. One word and it is finished. Yet God takes joy in your inheritance. It is a delight for Him to direct your steps so you don't miss any part of God's plan for you. But He will not force you into obedience. Obedience must be an act of faith and a response to His love.

This is where the power of the resurrection comes into our life. I do not have the power to do God's will. Just as I can't crucify my own flesh or forgive my own sins, I also cannot produce good works or create spiritual things from my own life. I overcome the flesh by looking to the cross. I find power by looking to the resurrection. I conform to His death by receiving the power of Christ in order to get the flesh under subjection to God, and then I also receive the power of His resurrection by which I live according to the Spirit and not according to my own abilities. Everything has been given through Christ.

God cares nothing about your abilities. He can raise up a talentless, uneducated person lacking any confidence to do His work. In fact, the less personal ability we have, the more we trust in God instead of in our flesh. Consider **2 Corinthians 4:7**

But we have this treasure in earthen vessels, that the excellence of the power may be of God and not of us.

Though we live in a body of flesh, we do not act according to the flesh.[106] We dare not trust in ourselves, for then we will fall short. Instead, we look to Christ. He crucifies our sins, confidence, and hopes born of the flesh. From this position we can look at His resurrection and find the power to walk in the Spirit and understand that the power is not of us, but of Christ.

---

[106] 2 Corinthians 10:3

By putting our trust in the power of His resurrection, we walk by faith. Faith is not believing in our abilities, but in the power of Christ.

Now the flesh has no dominion over you, so the character flaws that once drove you to failure have been taken out of the way, and the power of His resurrection enables you to respond in obedience and confidence. Now you have the power to act in a gentle spirit, turn from lusts, abandon greed, shun pride, and do good as the Spirit gives opportunity.

The battle to overcome is not an attempt to complete the work of God, but the struggle to learn to walk by faith instead of walking in the flesh. We fail when we are drawing from the flesh. We overcome when we are walking in the Spirit. It's a life-long learning process to shun the flesh and receive from the Spirit.

Why do people war with one another? The flesh rises up to defend its rights. That could be the right to be respected, claiming credit for deeds done, getting rewarded for work, or any other self-focused demand. But if we are crucified with Christ, how can these things control our life? If you insult a dead man, what will he do? Can a corpse demand his rights, insist on being recognized, or manipulate others to get his way? No, he's dead. Nothing in this life matters to the dead man.

We are dead to this world and if we are in the spirit, one thing matters. Christ is glorified. Did I get credit? Who cares? My only hope is that Christ is glorified. What is the meaning behind works? That Christ is glorified. What if my spouse offends me? Let Christ be glorified.

Living in this truth is only difficult because we heed the flesh. We get offended because sin in our flesh is presenting to our minds comments like, "I'm not going to take that. That person is frustrating me." Sin always presents the temptation of the flesh in first person, as though 'I' were speaking. Yet each of us has the power to say, "Not my will, but Christ's." The flesh has no power and the Spirit points us to the will of God. Our only concern is abiding in Christ and glorifying God. The 'I' speaking only becomes your action if you accept the will of the flesh over the will of God.

Once this dawns in your heart, it will change everything about your life. The flesh will always try to rise up, but as we learn to turn

Predestined for Good Works

from it, the flesh starts becoming a distant distraction. It will always beckon for our attention, but has no power unless we yield again.

When you first begin living in the Spirit, pride will seek to turn you away. God will call you to return a curse with a blessing, but the pride of sin will say, "I won't let that person get away with wronging me." God will call you to turn away wrath with a soft answer, but pride will say, "I must defend myself."

You are dead to the flesh. You must not defend your reputation. The Bible says that men will speak evil of you, but our only concern is that they will one day glorify God when He visits them with the promise of salvation.[107] Just as God did for us while we were offending Him with our sin, He will call those who have offended us to His grace.

You will want to be recognized when your works go unnoticed, but the Lord says that those who seek the praise of men already have their reward,[108] but those who do good works cannot be hidden, for God will either exalt them, or reward them in the life to come.[109]

One thing I can tell you from personal experience is that selfish pride will try to cause you to mourn over what is being lost to the flesh. When I began to answer the call to stop defending myself, God impressed Proverbs 15:1 on me, "A soft answer turns away wrath." There were situations where people used contentious words, and this often led to disagreements and arguments. I did not want to give a soft answer when the other person offended me. I wanted to confront the behavior, yet the end result was always more bitterness.

With great wrestling, I surrendered my right to defend myself (and still wrestle against this pride). It was especially difficult the first few times I put this into practice. But two things happened. God gave me a peace that amazed me, and in time, the other person began to respond in a positive way. At first I hid my feelings and gave a gentle answer. In a short time, I discovered that my feelings were no longer ill and I felt at peace – even when the other person was confrontational. It wasn't long before the words of others began to lose their impact.

---

[107] 1 Peter 2:12
[108] Matthew 6:1-2
[109] 1 Timothy 5:25

Then something strange happened. As the relationship became better, I found myself wanting to point out the reason for the change. I felt sorry that the other person would never recognize any wrong. And then I felt it would appear as if I was affirming that they were right. Because I had surrendered, it would appear as if I was the only one in the wrong. Certainly I shared some of the blame, but now I was looking like the only one to blame.

Then the Lord reminded me that this was part of dying to the flesh. It doesn't matter who gets credit or who shares in blame. A lifetime of living for the flesh had no fruit or positive results. Am I now willing to abandon God's ways simply because others would not feel ashamed at their behavior when I felt they should?

Oh how subtle the flesh can be! When it couldn't defeat me with anger, it became the kisses of an enemy, empathizing with me as a victim. Is my reward in being right? Or do I trust in God who sees my obedience and rewards me according to His own goodness? Did I count the pride of my flesh as more valuable than the call of God? Again I must look to the cross and declare my faith in the work of Christ. The deeds of the old nature are dead, along with my pride. When pride rises up, I again remind myself that the old man is dead and his deeds have no power. I then look to the resurrection as I trust in Christ to empower me to live according to the Spirit.

If you follow this truth, you will see victory. You will also have times where the flesh gets the best of you because you allowed your mind to adopt sin's temptation as your own. Don't grovel in defeat, but step out of the flesh and into the Spirit. At times you will have to pray, "Lord, I have no strength to overcome this. I am trusting in you to live through me. You must respond through me, because I can only respond selfishly. I am dying to myself and my rights. Love this person through me."

Let me stop for a moment to clarify an important truth. God does not reward me because I obeyed. I didn't earn a few blessings because I agreed with God and decided to act according to my new nature. I didn't earn God's favor because I answered His call to turn from the flesh and trust Him.

Even obedience can be turned into an act of legalism. If I am obeying in order to merit, then my obedience becomes an act of the flesh. I realize this can seem confusing until you understand the call of grace. I must obey because I trust the Lord. His word promises that

He will lead me to what is good when I walk in obedience. When the Lord says, a soft answer turns away wrath, I obey because I believe this is true, not because I think God will love me more.

I am blessed. You are blessed. We have been given all things that pertain to life and godliness – blessings, power to overcome, righteousness, and all good things have already been given to us. My obedience is an act of trust in God's perfect way. I am not earning anything. Through obedience I am refusing to be drawn outside of God's perfect will knowing that the flesh has nothing to offer. All God's blessings have already been given and any who abide in Christ are also abiding in everything God has already provided.

In me, that is in my flesh, no good thing dwells (Romans 7:18). I cannot rise above these things. Nor can I attain to the righteousness of God. I can't fulfill the call of obedience or walk in His works while my flesh is my strength or the source of my efforts. It must die and Christ must live. Only then can I live counter culture to the world and in agreement with God. **Galatians 2:20** says

> I have been crucified with Christ; it is no longer I who live, but Christ lives in me; and the *life* which I now live in the flesh I live by faith in the Son of God, who loved me and gave Himself for me.

It is not me working to please God. It is Christ living in me. When I abide in Christ, I am living by faith and making no provision for the flesh.[110] When I act through the flesh, I'm seizing the reins from His hand and driving myself to react according to the flesh instead of by my nature in Christ.

Surrender your life, look to Christ, and allow His life to be live through you. Though it may seem like a great sacrifice in the beginning, you will discover what it truly means to live in the joy of the Lord.

Discussion questions:

Why did Jesus say, "This day was meant for your peace," yet they found destruction? Was God's purpose thwarted?

Is it God's will for you to inherit His kingdom?

---

[110] Romans 13:14

Is it possible to fall short of God's intended inheritance?

Read Hebrews 12:15-17 and Colossian 2:8. What are we being warned about?

How can we be predestined by God and still miss out?

Can God's work be stopped or His purposes thwarted?

Can God's will for our life fall short? Why or why not?

How does sin work through our flesh to deceive us?

If God's works were completed before the world began, and God works through us to perform His good will, how does this give us confidence?

Does this make us robotic and without a will?

Does God's predestined plan contradict God's call to surrender our will?

Does obedience earn a reward? Why or why not?

Walk by Faith

2 Corinthians 5:7

For we walk by faith, not by sight.

These eight words speak volumes. Think about the message of faith throughout the scripture. "The just shall live by faith."[111] This one phrase is mentioned four times in the Bible, once in the Old Testament and three times in the New.

How many times did Jesus say, "Be it unto you according to your faith?" Once He looked at four friends and when He saw *their* faith, Jesus healed their paralyzed companion. Twice Jesus told His disciples that if they had faith merely the size of a mustard seed, they could move mountains and uproot immovable trees. The message Christ was conveying is that nothing can stand in the way of true faith. The opposite is also true. Consider the words of **Hebrews 11:6**

But without faith *it is* impossible to please *Him,* for he who comes to God must believe that He is, and *that* He is a rewarder of those who diligently seek Him.

Faith means to believe God. But it is much deeper than mere human belief. Many people make themselves believe, and declare God's healing or provision, but their prayers and hopes fall short. Yet when Jesus asked a man if he believed enough for his son to be healed, he cried out, "I believe. Help my unbelief!"[112] Jesus did not require the man to be free from unbelief. He still acted in the midst of a grieving father's declaration of weakness.

Without any declaration at all, the Apostle Paul perceived a man's faith during his preaching, stopped in the midst of his sermon and said, "Stand on your feet." A man born as a cripple leaped and walked – two things he had never done in his life.

Why do some people see the miracles of God through faith, while others believe with all their might and never see God act? Why do some people try to live out their faith and do all the right things but never experience the fullness of God's power in their lives, while

---

[111] Habakkuk 2:4, Romans 1:17, Galatians 3:11, Hebrews 10:38
[112] Mark 9:24

others crawl out of the gutters of sin, and after having done nothing right, experience God's transforming power?

Simply put, it isn't about you at all. In fact, religious people have a harder time than those raised outside of church because their vision is obscured by traditions, their own righteousness, apathy, or faith in people or organizations. The unlearned only know, "I was blind, but now I see." Then they are able to fully trust in the God who offers deliverance to them.

Faith is believing, but not believing through human effort. All man-made faith is worthless in the realm of the Spirit. Contrary to common teaching, faith does not make God act, and doubt does not make the devil act. Satan uses doubt to blind us to the revelation of God's purposes so we don't trust, or so that we think we must help God along by creating a little more faith to satisfy a perceived lack.

The truth is, faith is of the Spirit; doubt and unbelief are of the flesh. The flesh will never cease creating doubt, unbelief, or masquerading itself as spiritual through superstition – or manmade faith. Mark Twain once said, "Faith is making yourself believe something you know isn't true."

This is an accurate definition of human-created faith, but it is not true of the faith of the Spirit. Manmade faith is forcing yourself to believe out of superstition, but true faith is the assurance of what is hoped for and the confidence in what is not seen. True faith is confidence in what God has revealed to our spirit and is not bound by what the human eye can see. To understand this, let's dig a little deeper.

I mentioned the man who cried out, "Lord I believe. Help me with my unbelief." This is a perfect example of the war between the Spirit and the flesh. The flesh pounded the man with unbelief, but Jesus stood before him with the offer of grace. God revealed His purpose, to heal the man's son, and then called for the man to believe God's power to accomplish that purpose. The flesh warred against his mind by pointing to the impossibility of overcoming the plague his son had been enduring.

The man did not deny his doubts. He declared his trust in God's purpose while casting the burden of the flesh on Christ, where it belongs. Jesus did not hold the man accountable for his doubts, but instead acted according to the fact that the man put his trust in the faith of Christ over the doubts of his flesh.

Walk by Faith

Faith comes by the revelation of God's purposes to us in our spirit, and we act by faith by trusting in His purpose. Belief without revelation is superstition. Disbelief after revelation is an act of unbelief. The Bible says that whatever is not of faith is sin,[113] because to reject faith is to cast God's revelation aside, because we trust more in the flesh. Unbelief is to trust in the flesh. Faith is to trust in what God has revealed.

Let me give another example. In Genesis 15, God took Abraham and revealed to him the purposes He intended. Abraham received the revelation, and believed God. He trusted that the Lord was able to accomplish what He had revealed and promised to Abraham. He believed even though his body was already dead in the flesh and what God promised was humanly impossible.[114]

Two things happened at that point. Abraham's faith was accounted to him for righteousness, and God set Abraham on the path to receive those promises. It took more than twenty years before the promise came to fruition, but during that time, God blessed Abraham even beyond what had been promised.

We see many examples in the history of the kings of Israel where men disbelieved God and missed the promises. Even earlier, we see that none of those who came out of bondage to Egypt received the promise, except Caleb and Joshua. God revealed His purpose, but the people trusted in fear, and that caused them to disbelieve God. When they rejected God's purpose, the Lord led them away from the promise and they spent their lives in the desert of unbelief.

This is a good time to stop and consider the message of the desert. The Bible says that the message of the desert wasn't just for the faithless children of Israel, but for our example to learn from.[115] The Bible also says that Abraham's response to faith was also for our example.[116]

Both the faithlessness of those wandering in the desert and the faithfulness of Abraham reveal God's purposes in your life. What caused Abraham to trust in the Lord? His flesh was already accounted as dead – **Romans 4:19-22**

---

[113] Romans 14:23
[114] Romans 4:19-25
[115] Hebrews 4:1-11, 1 Corinthians 10:11
[116] Romans 4:23-24

[19] And not being weak in faith, he did not consider his own body, already dead (since he was about a hundred years old), and the deadness of Sarah's womb.

[20] He did not waver at the promise of God through unbelief, but was strengthened in faith, giving glory to God,

[21] and being fully convinced that what He had promised He was also able to perform.

[22] And therefore "it was accounted to him for righteousness."

Abraham accounted his flesh as dead and put his trust in God's promise. What happened in the desert? Those who could not believe had to wander in the desert until they died. The only two who did not die were Joshua and Caleb. They were already God-dependent and there was no need to die. The flesh had to die so a people of faith could emerge. Abraham accounted himself as dead and God gave life. A faithless nation lost their lives because they tried to save it.

In the same way, when you cannot believe God, the Lord sends you into the desert, not to punish you, but to strip away the confidence in the flesh. Most people spend their lives in the desert because they will not allow the flesh to die. The flesh cannot inherit the promise. Because it is God's desire for you to inherit His promises, He will keep you in the desert until the flesh is put to death, and you learn to trust in the Spirit.

Let me be clear on this. God is not punishing you for unbelief. It is God's good pleasure to give you His kingdom. But that promise can only be received by the Spirit. Those who try to enter by the flesh will always be driven back to the desert. The desert is designed to put to death the stronghold of the flesh, not to punish the believer.

The flesh cannot inherit the kingdom of God. It needs to be buried in the desert. Once we allow God to apply the work of Christ so we abandon the flesh, then we can freely enter the promise of God's rest. Account yourself dead to the flesh but alive to God in the Spirit.[117]

Unlike the Children of Israel, everyone born anew has the Holy Spirit within them. God's Holy Spirit reveals His purpose to our spirit, and then calls us to believe. Jesus made an interesting statement in **John 6:44-45**

---

[117] Romans 6:11

Walk by Faith

[44] "No one can come to Me unless the Father who sent Me draws him; and I will raise him up at the last day.

[45] "It is written in the prophets, 'And they shall all be taught by God.' Therefore everyone who has heard and learned from the Father comes to Me.

No one can believe in Christ or in anything of the Spirit unless it is first revealed. Sincerity does not make human faith any less dead. Religious reasoning does not transform human effort into spiritual life. God draws us to Christ and then calls for faith. Christ is first revealed and then the call is heard.

After salvation, nothing changes. To try to believe in our purposes does not make God act. Consider the words of **1 John 5:14-15**

[14] Now this is the confidence that we have in Him, that if we ask anything according to His will, He hears us.

[15] And if we know that He hears us, whatever we ask, we know that we have the petitions that we have asked of Him.

The prayer of faith is to pray in agreement with God's revelation of His intended purposes. God reveals His will to us, and we believe by faith or disbelieve according to the flesh. Faith is never by the will of man. Period.

According to the Bible, it is God who deals each person a measure of faith.[118] Faith is a gift given by the Holy Spirit for the purpose of edifying the church.[119] In the individual life of a believer, faith is the fruit of the Spirit.[120] Do you see a pattern? Faith comes from God in order to empower us to act according to God's spiritual standard. God reveals His purpose to us through His Spirit within us. He communicates the perfect will of God to our spirit, and then calls for us to believe in Him and His purpose. Carefully read this passage from **Ephesians 1:11-12**

[11] In Him also we have obtained an inheritance, being predestined according to the purpose of Him who works all things according to the counsel of His will,

---

[118] Romans 12:3
[119] 1 Corinthians 12:7-11
[120] Galatians 5:22

^{12} that we who first trusted in Christ should be to the praise of His glory.

How does God determine His purposes? According to our prayer? According to our faith? No. God predestined His purposes according to the counsel of His own will. Before you and I were born, God's purposes had already been determined. He is calling us to be a part of what He is doing. He is not asking us to determine what He will do. We touched on this when we discuss works by the Spirit. Now it's important to realize that our prayers are either according to our will or according to His will.

Only one will can be fulfilled. God is not seeking your counsel, but your partnership in what He is doing.

God reveals His purpose to you, and then asks you to believe. Not merely to believe with a nod of the head, but to believe to the point where you place your trust in Him and His purposes. God reveals the call of salvation by speaking to us through the Spirit and then calls for us to put our trust in Christ.

This is true for discovering the will of God in our own lives. It is also true when it comes to receiving Christ before salvation. Until Christ is revealed, saying a sinner's prayer means nothing. This is clearly stated in **John 1:12-13**

^{12} But as many as received Him, to them He gave the right to become children of God, to those who believe in His name:

^{13} who were born, not of blood, nor of the will of the flesh, nor of the will of man, but of God.

No one is saved by willing themselves to believe the gospel. God calls, God draws, and God reveals Himself. Then the call of faith is issued and the person either surrenders to the will of God by faith, or rejects the call and trusts in the flesh. Believing the gospel must come by God first revealing Himself to the lost soul.

God's ways don't suddenly change after salvation. We don't begin by revelation in the Spirit and then have to walk according to human understanding. God reveals His purposes in our lives the same way He revealed His will to save us. In the Christian's life, God reveals His purpose, and then calls for faith.

Faith comes by hearing the word of God, because through our understanding of the word, we see the revelation of God's call in the

Spirit. The Spirit of God is always communing with our new spirit that was born from God. However, that understanding in our spirit cannot make it into our minds until the revelation of God occurs. The primary avenue of revelation is the scriptures.

Remember the passage we looked at earlier? We are all taught by God. Not one Christian lacks this promise. Any who are in Christ have been given the power to understand and believe. The only thing preventing spiritual maturity and understanding is our ignorance to the fact that we should look to the Spirit for revelation, or our unwillingness to do so.

This revelation comes either through the word, or through a life founded upon the word. When I hear (or read) the word, my mind understands and the Spirit reveals. What the Holy Spirit has been revealing to my spirit comes alive in my understanding once the word is received. That's why certain passages come alive at certain times. As God works in our spirit, our understanding is excited by the word of God, and the purposes of God are revealed to our minds as we listen by faith.

Don't allow commentaries to be your only focus. Look to the Spirit for understanding. A listening heart receives the revelation of the word. There has to be a time where we are listening for the Spirit's revelation with an uncrowded mind.

It's no coincidence that the message being preached on Sunday is often what God has been working in you throughout the week. Or why the Sunday school teacher hits on the same topic the preacher addresses on the same day. God often works within the church in unison, and because He has preordained all things, He brings the right word into our life at the right time – the time when He is working within us to reveal His purpose. Faith then becomes the call to believe what God has revealed and to walk according to His purposes.

People spend their lives trying to please God and attempting to produce spiritual fruit, but this is not our calling. God is pleased by our faith. Without faith it is impossible to please God.[121] So what is the call of faith? Jesus said, "Abide in Me." He went on to explain

---

[121] Hebrews 11:6

that outside of that abiding relationship, we can do nothing, but within that abiding relationship, a fruitful life is the natural result.[122]

Stop working and start abiding. Rest in His grace and let the Spirit flow through you. God is expressing His love to you, and to love God with all our heart is to believe in His love, receive it by faith, and abide in it. Let's bring in this passage from **Philippians 2:12-13**

[12] Therefore, my beloved, as you have always obeyed, not as in my presence only, but now much more in my absence, work out your own salvation with fear and trembling;
[13] for it is God who works in you both to will and to do for *His* good pleasure.

Work *out*, not *for* salvation. And what is the work of God? When the people ask Jesus how to do the works of God He said, "This is the work of God, that you believe on Him whom God has sent." That 'whom' is Christ. The work is faith in Him. Notice the above passage, right after we are told to work out, we are told that it is God who does the work. Our work is to believe.

In truth, the only act on our part is to reject the call of the flesh with its doubts and fears, and to believe in what God has revealed. Our fear is that we don't fall short of God's promises, and it should cause us to shiver with fear to think of missing out on God's call. How sorrowful it would be to abide in the flesh in the desert when the promise was within our grasp the whole time.

What gives God pleasure? He is pleased to work His will in you. Our work is to believe and surrender, then walk where He is leading. You are not working for God. You are allowing God to work through you. You are walking where He has made the way.

Don't mistake good works as being human effort. Abiding is the key to serving God and experiencing His pleasure. God's pleasure is to give His promises to you. In fact, the promise is already yours. All you must do is let go of the flesh and take hold of what God has provided. Look to the cross. In the cross your sins are paid, the flesh has been crucified, and you have been raised to life. Here is another passage that clarifies what is meant by fear. Look at **Hebrews 4:1-2**

---

[122] John 15

¹ Therefore, since a promise remains of entering His rest, let us fear lest any of you seem to have come short of it.

² For indeed the gospel was preached to us as well as to them; but the word which they heard did not profit them, not being mixed with faith in those who heard *it*.

There is a promise, and many will fall short of it. Yet it is available to all. And what is our work? To enter His rest. Your goal is not to do anything for God, but to enter His rest. You enter the rest by believing on Christ.

He is our rest. Before Christ, we worked to become good people. Religion is filled with those who are laboring to please God. The church is filled with people who are working their lives away on useless labors. The work is not to apply your efforts to build His Kingdom, but to enter the rest. This is explained further in **Hebrews 4:10-11**

¹⁰ For he who has entered His rest has himself also ceased from his works as God *did* from His.

¹¹ Let us therefore be diligent to enter that rest, lest anyone fall according to the same example of disobedience.

What are you to be diligent to accomplish? Be diligent to enter His rest. Not to work the works of religion. Not to feed the poor, visit the sick, clothe the homeless, do chores for the elderly, write books, teach and preach, or any number of works people do. Indeed these things will emerge from the Christian life, but unless they are the outflow of the love of God within us, works mean nothing.

If you are working to please God, your works mean nothing. The work of God is to believe on Christ and enter His rest. Cease from your labors, rest in His Spirit, and then allow God to work in you and through you.

Works come from God. Works cannot lead to God. Rest is to stop working to earn grace and to believe in God's invitation to enter his Kingdom without cost. He paid the cost. You must be diligent to keep your eyes upon Christ and not allow the cares of this life to draw you out of that rest. Yes, the church can be part of the cares of the world. If works are not the path God has created beforehand and called you to walk in[123], your works are worthless efforts of the flesh.

So to work out our salvation is to work the works of God by believing on Christ, and to fear lest we fall short of the promise of entering His rest by faith. Many hear the word preached, but fall short because they cannot trust in the work of Christ.

A person who turns over a new leaf is depending upon human effort and will only have the limited strength of the flesh. There is no contentment in the flesh; therefore, religion based on man's effort can only lead to legalism, self-righteousness, self-deception, and frustration. But those who discover life in the Spirit will understand the words of the Apostle Paul, "Whether hungry or full, imprisoned or free, whatever state I am in I have learned to be content."[124]

Are you content in every situation? Do you have perfect peace? A consistent gentle spirit? What about Jesus' words, "You must be perfect, even as your heavenly Father is perfect." Are you perfect?

We've all heard the statement, "I am not perfect, just forgiven." But God's will doesn't stop with your forgiveness. Consider these passages:

Ephesians 4:13
Till we all come to the unity of the faith and of the knowledge of the Son of God, to a perfect man, to the measure of the stature of the fullness of Christ;

Colossians 1:28
Him we preach, warning every man and teaching every man in all wisdom, that we may present every man perfect in Christ Jesus.

Romans 8:29a
For whom He foreknew, He also predestined *to be* conformed to the image of His Son...

Is Christ the image of perfection? Certainly. And we have been predestined to conform perfectly to that perfect image. So why do so few people attain to that image of perfection? The answer is

---

[123] Ephesians 2:10
[124] Philippians 4:11-12

profoundly simple. In the flesh, no one is perfect, but in the Spirit, everyone is perfect. The Bible says that our inner man is incorruptible,[125] and we've already discussed the Bible's declaration that whoever is born of God cannot sin because His seed remains in him.

I realize I'm being a little redundant here, but since this issue comes up often, it is necessary to reiterate this point. Whoever has been born of God does not sin, and he *cannot* sin. That which is born of the flesh is flesh and can be nothing but the flesh, but that which is born of the Spirit is of the Spirit.[126] The flesh can do nothing but draw from the flesh and produce that which is of the flesh. It might gloss things up a bit so it appears noble, but it is still of the flesh. This is why Isaiah 64:6 warns that all our righteous acts are filthy in God's sight. The reason?

Everything in life has its origins in either the Spirit or the flesh. Those who are in the flesh cannot please God.[127] Even if something appears good to our human eyes, if it does not come from the Spirit, it is still the flesh.

So in the flesh, we aren't perfect. We were sinners who have been saved by grace. But the grace that God has shown us through forgiveness also calls us to have perfect communion with God in the Spirit. God's desire is to not leave you in the flesh, but draw you into the Spirit where His power to live out the Christian life is found. You cannot successfully live out the Christian life. It is humanly impossible. Until you realize you can't do it, legalism will appear to have value. But once this truth is realized, you will also understand that grace is the only way.

One important truth to note is that this book cannot do the work of God in your heart. To walk in the Spirit by faith three things are required.

1. Knowledge. If you are unaware of God's higher calling, you cannot seek to attain it. This book is a tool that hopefully will give you this knowledge and stir in you a desire to reach for these things.

---

[125] 1 Peter 1:23
[126] John 3:6
[127] Romans 8:8

2. God's revelation. The Lord has to draw you by the Spirit and open your eyes to see both your need, and the provision of His Spirit. Just as a blind man cannot open his own eyes, we cannot open our own spiritual eyes. The Lord opens our eyes and calls us to come.

3. A heart willing to act according to God's faith. God will not only open your eyes to what He intends to do, but He will call you to step out of the flesh and into the Spirit to be part of it. This requires abandoning the flesh. And the flesh will call with fear, the promise of pleasure, apathy, and all its tools. Unless someone is willing to step into God's call, they cannot experience what it means to walk in the Spirit.

Just as Abraham was called to step out in faith to journey to the promise not yet revealed, you also will be called out to step into the Spirit and receive what God has not yet revealed.

The Bible says that the natural man cannot receive the things of God and that they are foolishness to him. In your flesh and through the carnal mind (which we all have until we take on the mind of Christ that has been given to us) the way of the Spirit doesn't make sense. Being called to abandon self seems foolish, for we are dying to everything we once valued. How does dying give life? How does sacrifice give satisfaction? How does leaving our security equal peace? And abandoning the pursuit of happiness bring contentment?

By faith, we abandon our place in this world to find the sufficiency of Christ in the Spirit. The promise cannot be seen with human eyes, but when you discover the deep richness of walking in the Spirit, nothing in this life can satisfy.

History has sprinkled examples of a few men and women who found this way and abandoned all. Go and find their testimonies. Is there one person who truly tasted of the goodness of Christ and wanted to go back? Is there one example of a miserable Christian who truly abandoned all to follow Him? No. In fact, it is quite the opposite. While those few rejoice in supernatural joy, those who are unwilling to abandon this life continue grappling for joy, peace, and satisfaction, but cannot find it.

History is also filled with those who regretted living for themselves, but not one person who laid down their life for the sake of the gospel lost it. It is impossible to see the richness of God until we first empty ourselves.

Having said all these things, let's go back to a question asked in a previous chapter. If God has guaranteed a fruitful life, perfect position of godliness, and that we are complete in Him, lacking nothing, why don't people experience this?

The answer to this basic question is the purpose of this study. All goodness, all power, a fruitful life, and a perfect personhood is found by walking and abiding in the Spirit. The flesh rises up and attempts to gain control, but we have the power in Christ to overcome the flesh and live in perfection.

Though we fall short, all we must do to experience the victorious Christian life is turn from the flesh and draw near to God in the Spirit. We look to the cross for the payment of sin, but the Christian life doesn't stop there.

Jesus shed His blood to pay for our sins, but that is not all Jesus accomplished on the cross. Jesus also was put to death in the flesh so our body of flesh could be put to death in Him. Not only were our sins paid, but we were also freed from the body of sinful flesh. These two truths were accomplished on the cross, but this isn't where the work was finished.

Jesus also rose from the dead so we could have life. Consider **1 Peter 1:3-5**

> [3] Blessed *be* the God and Father of our Lord Jesus Christ, who according to His abundant mercy has begotten us again to a living hope through the resurrection of Jesus Christ from the dead,
> [4] to an inheritance incorruptible and undefiled and that does not fade away, reserved in heaven for you,
> [5] who are kept by the power of God through faith for salvation ready to be revealed in the last time.

This is the completed work of Christ. He did not just die for your sins. Jesus also put your flesh to death, and rose to give you life, hope, and power. The promise that we are kept by the power of God through faith is what is lacking in the life of most Christians.

I say the promise is lacking, but in reality, the promise is there for any who will receive it by faith. It is the realization that we have already been given all things that people are lacking. I am complete in Christ. You are complete in Him. We live outside of God's power because we don't understand that we have been crucified with Christ *and* we have received life and power through His resurrection. The hope is for the future, but the power is for your life today.

This power is only found in the Spirit and only experienced by those who trust in Jesus' crucifixion power against their flesh and the resurrection power of His life. The promise is received by faith.

His power is for your life. This is how you overcome. Your purpose is not to conform your flesh to the image of Christ. Nor is your purpose to take the reins of your flesh to control your lusts, anger, unruly tongue, or any of the countless weaknesses of the flesh. It is not for you to control your flesh. It is for you to look to the cross and believe in the power of Christ to crucify your flesh – which has already been accomplished. It is for you to look at His resurrection for the power of life by walking in the Spirit – which has already been accomplished for you. You *were* crucified with Christ. You *were* raised with Christ as a new creation.

Do you believe this? Pray for God to open your eyes to reveal the truth of these things to you. Once you find the power of the Spirit, the flesh will not have dominion over you. Even when you recognize you are stumbling, it is also a realization that you are stepping into the flesh. The solution is to simply turn from the flesh and trust in the power of Christ given to you. Looking unto Jesus, the Author and Finisher of your faith is the secret to living as a perfect man or woman.

Though we may fall, the power of the Spirit is just a heartbeat away. My hope is that the struggle between the flesh and the Spirit will become clear to you, and that you will believe God's promises so you can walk in His life-changing power. My life is a testimony to the truth of scripture. Each day comes a deeper realization as to how much God has yet to reveal, but continues to reveal as I submit to His word. The same is true for you.

Any who are in Christ have the Spirit of Christ – and we are complete in Him.[128] The reason the flesh dominates our lives is because we lack the faith to receive the promise. The reason we don't see the power of the Spirit in our lives is because we lack the faith to receive it. All of God's promises are received by faith.

---

[128] Colossians 2:10

Walk by Faith

Don't lose sight of this truth: you cannot produce faith, for making yourself believe is a human effort and profits nothing. God has dealt you the measure of faith.[129] The power of faith is revealed through the word of God – for faith comes by hearing and hearing by the words of Christ.[130] Faith is lacking because we trust in the flesh. Through the flesh, unbelief is produced. Having faith is to see the word of God and respond in belief to what God has revealed to you. Faith is a gift of God. It is Him revealing His will and calling us to believe and receive, or disbelieve and choose another way.

When the Bible speaks of faith coming by hearing, the subject is the good news of Christ. Romans 10 presents the message of our acceptance with Christ, so the message of faith is that Jesus has made us acceptable to God, and through Him we have the invitation of joining God in fellowship.

Some translations say, "Faith comes by hearing the word of Christ," which is an accurate explanation of what is being summarized in Romans 10. How good are the feet who bring the good news, is immediately followed up with the words, faith comes by hearing the word of God/Christ. Faith comes by seeing our position of righteousness in Christ, and from this firm assurance, everything in our walk of faith flows. Having a good conscience toward God is essential for living by faith.

We need to walk in these truths by faith so we can experience them in our spiritual walk. This is the beginning of what it means to walk in the Spirit. Look to Christ, for He is the embodiment of grace and our complete sufficiency. He is the Author of your faith and the Finisher of your perfection in Him.

Discussion questions:

Can a person walk by faith while struggling with fear or doubt? Why or why not?

Why did God force His people into the desert?

---

[129] Romans 12:3
[130] Romans 10:17

Did Abraham have to beg God for blessings? Did he have to name it or claim it?

What does it mean, faith comes by hearing the word of God/Christ?

What does it mean to work out your salvation with fear and trembling?

What three things did Jesus accomplish for us through the cross and resurrection?

If we stop at the promise that Jesus paid it all, are we acknowledging the complete work of Christ?

How does the word of God reveal to our minds what is already being revealed in our spirit?

Can a person choose to believe without the Spirit of God revealing truth to them?

What does the Bible mean when it says, "The word didn't profit them, not being mixed with faith?"

Sonship – The Spirit of Adoption

Living in victory begins with you understanding your relationship with God. God's Spirit communicates with your spirit – the new creation given to you when you were born again – and through this communication, you discover the truths of God. It is important to understand the relationship with your Heavenly Father. Look at **Romans 8:14-17**

> [14] For as many as are led by the Spirit of God, these are sons of God.
>
> [15] For you did not receive the spirit of bondage again to fear, but you received the Spirit of adoption by whom we cry out, "Abba, Father."
>
> [16] The Spirit Himself bears witness with our spirit that we are children of God,
>
> [17] and if children, then heirs -- heirs of God and joint heirs with Christ, if indeed we suffer with *Him,* that we may also be glorified together.

This is an amazing revelation, but it's a small piece of the picture, as we shall soon see. I want you to take to heart a few important truths in this passage.

God's Spirit affirms our adoption as a child of God. Consider the legal implication of adoption. When a child is adopted, what is the legal difference between an adopted child and a natural born child? There is none. An adoptive parent doesn't say, "Here is my real children and this one is my adopted child." Any parent who did this wouldn't be worthy of adoption. They would say, "Here are my children," making no distinction between adopted and natural born children. If anything, an adopted child should understand the love of their parents more, for they were chosen out of the world to become an heir.

This is why the Bible speaks of Christ being the only begotten and we are given the right to become the children of God,[131] yet when

---

[131] John 1:12

scripture speaks of God's children, it puts no distinction between us and Christ, the Son. As stated above, if we are children, then we are also joint heirs with Christ.

None of this changes who Christ is. But it does change who we are in Christ. Though Jesus existed in the form of God, He willingly veiled His glory to become a bondservant in the likeness of the flesh.[132] Is Jesus any less God because He humbled Himself in order to lift us up? No. This is the greatness of God's mercies and love.

Instead of condemning man because he fell short of God's glory, God made Himself of no reputation and came in the likeness of sinful flesh that He might redeem us out of the bondage of flesh.[133] It is through God's power to overcome sin in the flesh that He gave us the power to overcome the flesh through Him, so we also could be joined to Christ and inherit the kingdom through adoption.

Adoption doesn't change us into gods. Instead, adoption changes our inheritance from being the wages of sin to becoming inheritors of the kingdom of God.

Christ is the only begotten because He came forth from God.[134] He was with God in the beginning.[135] From the beginning He was the Word of God, was God, and yet became flesh. The world was made through Christ, but did not recognize Him.[136] Becoming a man did not change who Christ was. He was fully God, but veiled His glory for the purpose of rescuing us from the condemnation of the Law.

In the same way, becoming a child of God does not make us the creator of the universe, but rather we become adopted children with the same right of inheritance as Christ.

God did not do this because He had to, but because it is God's good pleasure to give you His kingdom[137]. And that kingdom is only inherited through Christ as we unite with the Spirit of God. Uniting does not transform the created person into the Creator, but instead makes us children of God by adoption. The Spirit transforms us into the likeness of His character, but not into the divinity of His being.

---

[132] Philippians 4:6-8
[133] Romans 8:3-4
[134] John 16:27-28
[135] John 17:5
[136] John 1:1-12
[137] Luke 12:32

Sonship – The Spirit of Adoption

I say all of this to dispel a misconception in some teachings that attempt to exalt man above what scripture allows. We are exalted through glorifying Christ. The Bible says that we are glorified together with Him. This doesn't mean that we glorify ourselves to God's level, but that we glorify God and He lifts us up to share in His glory. It is still His glory and not our own.

Take special note of the word 'Abba'. This word is what Jesus used when in His darkest time of life. Just before His crucifixion, Jesus cried out, "Abba, Father," and then poured Himself out in prayer as He prepared to face the cross.

The word 'Abba' means 'Daddy'. Our heart should call out to God as a Daddy. His Lordship does not put him out of the arms of those calling Abba, Daddy. Nor does calling God 'Daddy' diminish God from being Lord of all. Jesus called the Father, Daddy, and through that intimate relationship, He learned how to submit in obedience.[138] Don't become so formerly reverent focused that you forget to look to God as your Abba.

What happens when a child is afraid? The child calls out for a parent. When my youngest daughter is fearful over something, she reaches up and says, "Hold me, Daddy."

Never forget that intimacy does not justify disobedience. My children may want to sit in Daddy's lap, but they also understand that what Daddy says has to be obeyed. They respond to my voice when I give instructions, and I respond to their voice when they call out. They may want to experience a father's love, may want to feel safe from the fear, or they may want something from me.

I receive them as a child regardless of their performance. If they disobey, I will correct their behavior, but I don't reject them as my child. In my limited human ability, I guide them to the right way so they don't experience unnecessary consequences in life.

This is our relationship with God as we call Abba, Father. The Spirit of God reveals our relationship with God and affirms that He indeed cares for us. No longer do we merely view God as the instruction giver, but God has now been revealed as a loving Father. Through the Spirit, we can confidently come before our God as though He's a Daddy who loves His children, and not a God far away.

---

[138] Hebrews 5:8

Once we experience the Spirit, we find joy in the understanding that we are indeed sons. Not just sons waiting for the day we get to heaven, but sons now. God wants us to experience this intimate fellowship each day on this side of life as well.

There is another important truth to understand about the passage that introduced this chapter. The word 'sons' is very significant. We need to bring in **Galatians 3:28**

> There is neither Jew nor Greek, there is neither slave nor free, there is neither male nor female; for you are all one in Christ Jesus.

Why didn't God say the Spirit affirms that we are sons and daughters of God? Let's go back and look at the legal declaration being given. Adoption is a term that communicates the rights of a child to be treated as a natural born child. The adopted child shares in the same rights as any existing biological children. Legally, there is no distinction between an adopted child and one born from the womb of the adopting mother.

In the same way, we are legally sons so that we have the right to share in the inheritance of God. The passage from Romans above declares that God confirms we are children, but as heirs, we are sons.

In that culture, a son inherited the possessions of the father. A daughter did not inherit the estate of her father. Through marriage, she entered into what her husband possessed, but legally, the possessions are handed down from fathers to sons. Yet God has declared that in Christ, we are not measured based on gender, for there is neither male nor female. There are different roles in the family and church for males and females, but that has nothing to do with our relationship with God or the inheritance of God's kingdom.

Unlike the culture of that day, God legally declared that each believer has the inheritance as a son of God. His Spirit declares we are children of God, and legally, both male and female have the inheritance of sons.

Regardless of how human culture treats the genders, in God's kingdom, whether you are male or female, you are a joint heir with Christ.

Discussion questions:

Read Romans 8:29, Galatians 3:26, Hebrews 2:9-11. What portion do we have in the kingdom of God?

Why does Christ call us brethren?

Read Revelation 17:14. Does Jesus calling us brethren of the adoption devalue who He is?

Read Philippians 2:9-11. Does the adoption make us equal to Christ?

How can we be a joint heir of the kingdom and still be lower than Christ?

Does making us heirs of His kingdom mean that God is dethroned or man is exalted to the level of godhood?

What does Abba mean?

Why does God declare we have the adoption as sons instead of saying as children?

In God's kingdom, what is the difference between male in female?

Is this different than our roles on this side of life?

The Strength of Weakness

Once we understand our sonship – God's adoption which has created our relationship – we then will have the foundation to dig deeper. In fact, this is where the Christian walk begins to transform our way of thinking. Until this understanding has dawned, we have been dependent on the flesh to aid us in discerning the spiritual life we are now part of. But this is not possible, for the natural man cannot understand anything but superficial spiritual matters, and even basic things are misunderstood. Consider the words of **1 Corinthians 2:14**

> But the natural man does not receive the things of the Spirit
> of God, for they are foolishness to him; nor can he know
> *them,* because they are spiritually discerned.

The ways of the Spirit cannot be understood by the natural man – those discerning good and bad through the flesh. We often apply this passage to how the world views the Bible, but it equally applies to us as Christians. The Christian who discerns God's will through natural means will always reject the deeper things of faith, for God's ways always appear foolish to the natural mind.

This is why we talk the talk, but when God brings us to the point of total surrender, we can't do it. The natural (or carnal) mind begins to question the wisdom of obedience. What about my job? What about my family? What about my future? What about the things that have always seemed important to me? My dreams, hopes, and affections will always draw me away from God's will if I am drawing my understanding from a mind grounded in the flesh.

Let's face it. God asks us to do many foolish things. To trust God when there is no certain outcome is not a comfortable place. Men and women have walked away from lucrative careers to the dismay of their families because they knew the will of God and sought an inheritance greater than this life. If your own natural mind cannot understand God's call, don't expect friends and family to praise you for sacrificing the seventy-year life for the eternal.

Unfortunately, for every person who discovers the greatness of God's call, there are countless people throughout history who have turned from the call because it appeared more foolish than their own reasoning. In truth, we all have fallen into this trap to varying degrees. Have you ever said, "If that man came to Christ it would do so much good for the church?" The wealthy could provide resources. The great speakers could use their talents for the kingdom. The athlete or the famous actor can use their platform for God.

That is the reasoning of the natural mind. God doesn't need the wealthy, for He owns everything in this earth. God doesn't need the great speaker, nor the famous celebrity. Quite the opposite. God said, "I use the weak and feeble things to bring to nothing the strong, and the foolish things to bring to nothing the wise."[139]

We look at outward appearances and think how much God could use these gifts and talents. But God looks at the heart and often chooses those who are the least qualified, the least talented, and the least desirable. The reason? "That no flesh should glory in His presence."[140]

Throughout history, God has raised up leaders from people we would have never chosen. And God has bypassed those we think could do so much for the kingdom. That's why the Bible says, "Not many mighty or noble are called."

God didn't say He wouldn't call any great men, but that it would be rare. The mighty tend to trust in their own abilities, and the rich tend to trust in riches. It's hard for those among the everyday crowd to learn to depend on the Lord and not themselves. How much more difficult is it for the gifted speaker, famous celebrity, and billionaire?

Think about all the religious leaders around the time of Christ. They were gifted men, educated men, and men who dedicated their entire lives to knowing the scriptural law. It was a valued profession that required a life dedicated to learning and working.

Out of the thousands of Pharisees, scribes, and lawyers throughout Israel and the Jewish people scattered throughout the Roman Empire, how many were called? Knowing the scriptures was something essential to understanding the work of Christ. Yet the only Pharisee we have record of being called into the ministry of Christ was the Apostle Paul. Even Paul had to first be broken before he could be used.

---

[139] 1 Corinthians 1:19, 27
[140] 1 Corinthians 1:29

As discussed previously, God gave Paul a weakness in the flesh in order to make him God-dependent and humble. Paul's thorn in the flesh kept him in a state of brokenness so he didn't trust in his own abilities. It's hard for the mighty, noble, and wise in this world to abandon themselves and count what they have always depended upon as worthless. Because people praise their abilities, they learn to glory in who they are in the flesh.

In order to receive God's power, the gifted must learn to count all things as worthless except what is given and empowered by the Spirit of God. This is what must happen in our lives as well. We looked at brokenness at the beginning of this book, and examined how it's easier to depend upon God when we know we are in need, rather than when we feel adequate in ourselves.

If you talk to those who truly understand what it means to walk in the Spirit, one thing is common among them. They have reached the point in their lives where they came to the end of themselves and realized their complete dependence upon Christ.

When we are broken, we cease looking to our flesh and personal abilities, and we begin looking to the Lord. Once you learn to trust in the Spirit instead of your flesh, you will discover the true richness of the Christian life. This is where walking by faith begins. This is also where we learn to commune with the Spirit of God. Let's review this passage again, for it is a foundational passage. **1 Corinthians 2:11-16**

> [11] For what man knows the things of a man except the spirit of the man which is in him? Even so no one knows the things of God except the Spirit of God.
>
> [12] Now we have received, not the spirit of the world, but the Spirit who is from God, that we might know the things that have been freely given to us by God.
>
> [13] These things we also speak, not in words which man's wisdom teaches but which the Holy Spirit teaches, comparing spiritual things with spiritual.
>
> [14] But the natural man does not receive the things of the Spirit of God, for they are foolishness to him; nor can he know *them*, because they are spiritually discerned.
>
> [15] But he who is spiritual judges all things, yet he himself is *rightly* judged by no one.

¹⁶ For "who has known the mind of the LORD that he may instruct Him?" But we have the mind of Christ.

Understanding this scripture is one of the greatest gifts you will receive. This passage teaches you how to discern the Lord's will instead of depending on your own intellect. I'll give you both a warning and a promise. When you learn what it means to be taught through the Spirit, you'll discover that God is calling you to act contrary to many things you would have once thought was right. That's the warning. The promise is that you'll experience God on a deeper level and understand the scriptures more than you ever thought possible. And you'll never again be satisfied with living status-quo Christianity.

Let's break down this passage for a closer look.

This passage begins with a comparison. Just as the human spirit understands the perspective of man, even so, we must understand that the Spirit of God is what provides understanding of the things of God. Your human spirit cannot understand God in itself. If you are looking to your own intellect in order to understand the things of God, you've already stepped into error. In your natural mind, you have zero ability to understand God or His ways.

Certainly you can understand some things about God. The unbeliever recognizes the things that are easy to understand about the Bible and about God from the natural perspective. But they cannot understand fellowship with God or the things of the Spirit. Have you ever wondered how the atheist can spend so much time combing through the Bible and looking for perceived mistakes, but they can't see the truth all around them? Or how cults can know enough about the Bible to create a religion of deception, but they can't discern Christ through the scriptures?

Some truths are plainly seen – even by the fleshly mind, but only the Spirit of God can reveal the things of the Spirit.

The majority of Christians are using the same methods as the world. They are using the human spirit as the interpreter and discerner of the things of God. Then the truths of scripture are applied through the flesh.

That is when the focus of Christianity shifts from Christ to personal ideals. Christianity becomes about what I can get – happiness, material possessions, and gratification. Then if the music doesn't appeal to me, I can't worship. If I'm not sitting in perfect comfort, I'm unable to praise and worship the Lord. Or praise and worship is centered around how good it makes me feel instead of a heart of gratitude for who God is and what He has done.

Most church resources are more focused on making people happy rather than fulfilling the call of God to reach the world and make disciples. Wars and fightings within the church and between denominations stems from this very thing.

Organizational Christianity is often reduced to satisfying the human spirit instead of learning to abide in Christ, where we can commune with God's Spirit. The human spirit cannot be satisfied outside of perfect fellowship with Christ; therefore, perceived needs are never fully met. Then the church member is more focused on what they want than expressing God's love back to Him and outward to each other.

The first principle to understand is that the human spirit cannot discern anything but the perceived needs of the flesh and not the truth of the Spirit. Until you learn to look beyond human understanding you cannot discern the truth of God.

Thankfully, the Bible doesn't stop there. The next principle is that you have God's Spirit within you. If you are born into the Spirit, you are the temple of the Holy Spirit and you already have everything you need in order to understand truth. You don't have the same spirit you see in the world and around you in daily life. You have something greater. You have the immeasurable greatness of God within you, and a new spirit, one born for fellowship with God and receives revelation from God.

God is within you in the form of the Holy Spirit. And God is not your spirit. The Spirit of God has been placed inside you at your new birth and communes with the new spirit He has given you. The old nature of sin has been done away with, a new spirit has been born of God within you, and that new spirit is not left alone. Along with your new creation you also receive the indwelling of the Holy Spirit. He is the Helper and comforter who never leaves you. Look at this promise Jesus gave in **John 16:13-15**

> [13] "However, when He, the Spirit of truth, has come, He will guide you into all truth; for He will not speak on His own *authority,* but whatever He hears He will speak; and He will tell you things to come.

The Strength of Weakness

¹⁴ "He will glorify Me, for He will take of what is Mine and declare *it* to you.
¹⁵ "All things that the Father has are Mine. Therefore I said that He will take of Mine and declare *it* to you.

The Holy Spirit (who is the Spirit of truth) speaks to you, reveals the things to come – God's will for your life – reveals Christ and His glory to you, and teaches you all things. Is this not the greatest promise ever given?

When Jesus spoke to the Samaritan woman at the well, He used her thirst for water as a picture of the satisfaction of the Holy Spirit within us.[141] He promised that the person who drinks of this water will never thirst. Instead, there will be a fountain of living water within us that will spring up and quench us with everlasting life.

This begs the question: if the Christian has the promise that life will be always springing up like a fountain, and we'll never thirst again, how can we ever feel dry? I once had a pastor tell me, "I feel dry as a bone. I haven't felt God's presence in months."

So why is this fountain missing from the lives of so many Christians? This is the wrong question. Maybe the real question is, why can't most Christians see that fountain? If you are a new creation, born of God, you have the Spirit within you and you always have this fountain springing up. The problem is that you don't have eyes to see it. Or there is something keeping it from flowing into your soul. If you have new life, you have this fountain. Look at **John 7:38-39**

³⁸ "He who believes in Me, as the Scripture has said, out of his heart will flow rivers of living water."
³⁹ But this He spoke concerning the Spirit, whom those believing in Him would receive; for the Holy Spirit was not yet *given,* because Jesus was not yet glorified.

This is the end of Jesus' conversation with the woman at the well. She was trying to understand spiritual truth through human eyes, and couldn't understand the value of this gift. The Holy Spirit within you water's your soul, gives life, and quenches every need. But those who are looking to the flesh or live in a fleshly mindset

---

[141] John 4:7-13

can't see the fountain, even though it is already flowing in the believer's spirit.

Let's use a couple of word pictures from the Old Testament. First, we'll look at Hagar, the mother of Ismael, who journeyed through the wilderness with her son. Soon she ran out of water and began to thirst. Lost with no source of water for days, she became desperate. Still unable to find water, she placed her crying child under a tree and abandoned him. She knew they could not survive any longer and she said, "I can't watch the death of my son."

Hagar began weeping as she gave up all hope. Then an angel of the Lord came to her. Because the child was a descendent of Abraham, God promised Abraham that the child would become a nation. As the angel spoke, a miraculous thing happened. God opened her eyes and she saw a spring of water.[142]

The Bible does not say that God created a spring, or opened a spring. He opened Hagar's eyes to see the spring that had been there all the time.

In the same way, the wellspring of life is already within you if you have the Spirit of God. The Lord must open your eyes to see it and that can only happen when you look to Him to reveal these things to you. You cannot open your own eyes and you can't muster up your own faith to stir God into action. It is God who draws and we who surrender. In this scenario, we are letting go of our trust in the human spirit and placing our faith in Christ alone. As we look to Him, we discover that Jesus is all we need.

Until we are looking to Him, we can never see His sufficiency. Look to Christ and believe His word, "He who believes in Me, as the Scripture has said, out of his heart will flow rivers of living water." This is a guaranteed promise. Are you receiving? If not, look expectantly to Christ and pray for your eyes to be opened.

The second word picture also comes from the Old Testament. It's the story of Abraham and his son Isaac. Abraham received many promises from the Lord, was blessed, and became great in wealth and stature. We are referred to as children of Abraham by promise, but what does that mean? Let's look at Isaac and see.

Isaac inherited everything he possessed and worked for nothing. It was given to him from his father. By birthright, he had God's

---

[142] Genesis 21:19

The Strength of Weakness

covenant that through him the promise would flow, and without any work on his part, he inherited the Promised Land and everything his father possessed.

The Bible calls us joint heirs with Christ and we also inherit the kingdom of our Heavenly Father. We did nothing to merit it. We didn't build the kingdom. We didn't earn the promise. Jesus said, "It's your Heavenly Father's good pleasure to give you the Kingdom." It is ours by birthright when we are adopted as children of God.

To see how this applies to the living waters of our promise, let's examine the word-picture of **Genesis 26:18**

> And Isaac dug again the wells of water which they had dug in the days of Abraham his father, for the Philistines had stopped them up after the death of Abraham. He called them by the names which his father had called them.

Who dug the wells of water? Not Isaac. The water was already there, and just below the surface the water flowed. But the water was stopped up because the mouth of the well was filled with the earth.

In the same way, the living waters of God are already present in your life. The things of this earth clog the Christian's life and prevent us from experiencing the watering things of the Spirit. What can you do to produce this living water? Nothing. Your Heavenly Father has already placed this life within you. The only role you and I play is removing the things from our life which stops the Spirit from flowing. I appreciate the way this is explained in

James 4:6-8

> 6 But He gives more grace. Therefore He says: "God resists the proud, But gives grace to the humble."
> 7 Therefore submit to God. Resist the devil and he will flee from you.
> 8 Draw near to God and He will draw near to you. Cleanse *your* hands, *you* sinners; and purify *your* hearts, *you* double-minded.

How do we cleanse ourselves? How do we purify our hearts? By submitting ourselves to God. The devil is the enemy. Just as the Philistines came into the land to clog the wells of water, Satan seeks to clog your life with the cares of this life.

Resisting the devil is not the message of this passage. Submitting to God is the message. Through submission, the devil flees. We then resist his call to be drawn again into temptation. Through submission to God, the things that clog our soul are removed, we are cleansed, and the water of the Spirit flows. Through temptations Satan attempts to clog the wells, but he has no power over the life submitted to the Spirit.

You cannot produce the living water, but you can dig the earth out of your life. You cannot produce anything of the Spirit. The promise of God is, "His divine power has given us all things that pertain to life and godliness."[143] If you have the Spirit of Christ, you lack nothing. Any lack is the result of the world clogging your life with things that are contrary to the Spirit. So then the only role we have is to remove that which quenches the Spirit[144] and submit ourselves to God. Our inner being flows with life, but the well of life is clogged by the world and prevents the flow from the Spirit to our outward life. Consider **Romans 6:13**

> And do not present your members *as* instruments of
> unrighteousness to sin, but present yourselves to God as
> being alive from the dead, and your members *as* instruments
> of righteousness to God.

Notice, we don't make ourselves righteous. We don't present our plans to God. We don't do things to make God accept us or earn His favor. We simply present ourselves to God. When we do so, God receives us and He uses our physical bodies to interact with the world around us and to reveal Himself to others.

Sometimes we present ourselves to Him and the Lord helps us by digging out the things of the earth that stops the wells. Sometimes He refreshes us with green pastures and quiet waters. Sometimes He tells us to follow Him through the valley of trials. Sometimes He calls us to be still while He prunes away the dead growth from our life which prevents us from producing the fruit of spiritual maturity.

Once I present myself to God, I am trusting fully in the work of Christ for my life. It is a declaration that my old life is dead through the cross, and He has the right to remove anything carried over from

---

[143] 2 Peter 1:3
[144] 1 Thessalonians 5:19

that dead life. It is also a declaration that I am trusting in the resurrection of Christ so that I am now living as one alive from the dead.

We must have both. There must be death on the cross *and* resurrection into the Spirit. To present myself to God I am counting my life in this world dead and surrendering to the life of the Spirit and the purposes of God. It is to live for God's will and not my own. If I cling to the dead works of the old life, I cannot cling to the Spirit. I am then clogging the wells with dirt instead of receiving life from the Spirit.

You can trust God. Because we know that we are highly favored through Christ and are submitted to the Spirit, we also can have confidence that all things are of God. The flesh may suffer, but in the Spirit we rejoice in the goodness of the Lord. In difficult circumstances, we will understand that God is not angry, but is delighting in our steps. The eternal perspective puts the flesh into the right perspective as well.

God has given us all things that pertain to life and godliness. If these things are lacking, it isn't because God hasn't provided them, but that we are stopping the flow of God's life with other things coming in that have no eternal value.

Discussion questions:

Why do God's ways appear foolish to the mind rooted in the flesh?

If we live by faith, will we appear foolish to the world? What about other Christians?

Will God lead you into a situation where you struggle between acting foolishly and trusting in safety?

Why did God say that He chooses the weak things of this life for His purposes?

What does this tell us about our own lives? How do we enter God's purpose?

Why can't the natural mind discern the things of the Spirit?

What happens to Christianity when it is understood and lived out through human understanding and not by the revelation of the Spirit?

How do we understand the deep things of the Spirit?

Name three functions of the Holy Spirit in John 16:13-15.

Read John 15:26. What is the role of the Spirit in this passage?

Jesus said that the Spirit will be a spring of life in the believer. Does the spring of living waters apply to every Christian?

Read 1 John 4:1. If a spirit claims to be of God, but does not glorify Christ, is it the Holy Spirit?

Can false spirits turn our focus to things that sound good but are not of God?

Can the things of the world prevent us from experiencing the living waters?

If a Christian isn't watered, what could be clogging the living waters from flowing into his/her life?

The Anointing of Christ

Proverbs 20:5

> Counsel in the heart of man *is like* deep water, But a man of understanding will draw it out.

This is the call of every Christian. When you receive Christ, you receive all that Christ has accomplished for you and provided for you. As we read earlier, we – the believer – have the mind of Christ. You do not need anyone to teach you the things of the Spirit, for the Spirit abides in you and teaches you all things. Certainly God has appointed teachers, preachers, and those who equip the saints, but this is not to rule over us, but to teach us how to grow into our head – Jesus Christ.

The Bible teaches that each person is under the anointing of Christ, and as we shall see, this empowers us to fulfill our calling and walk victoriously in the Christian life. Before digging into this, let's examine the Bible's explanation of the body of Christ.

The role of leaders in the church are to equip the saints so that they also learn to abide in fellowship with Christ and are equipped for the ministries He has gifted them to do[145]. Let me clarify one important truth here. You aren't dependent on teachers in order to grow spiritually, but you do need the body in order to be part of Christ. We are called the body of Christ. He is the head, the church is the body of Christ, and each of us are members of that body.

Each member has a role in the body, but no member is above the others. In God's eyes, the pastor is not greater than the one with the gift of helps. Authority and gifts in the church are not intended to create a spiritual elite class. God has appointed each person in the body as He wills so each member can edify the whole. The purpose of each person's role in the body is to unify the entire body in the purpose of glorifying Christ. Anytime my gift is used for personal glory, I have detached from the body and am serving myself and not God.

We are not independent, but interdependent as we draw into the head – Christ. In a moment we'll review the New Testament role of leadership we looked at in a previous chapter. We'll reexamine this

---

[145] Ephesians 4:11-19

from the perspective of God's anointing to gain a clearer picture of how roles in the church fulfill the call of unity and put us under that anointing. Once again we'll see how certain passages must be examined from different perspectives in order to gain a firm understanding of God's plan of walking by faith.

Leadership does not equal anointing. In our modern era, people mistake our calling to ministry as an anointing. They are adopting the Old Testament anointing as if it applies today. In the Old Testament, Christ had not yet paid for sin, and man was limited in his fellowship with God. The average person could not approach the Lord and only the High Priest could enter the holiest place of the temple. And he could only do this once a year after going through many tedious cleansing rituals. Even then, his life was in danger, for if he sinned or made any mistake in the ritual, he would become an offender before God and would die in the Holiest of Holies – the inner part of the temple.

The other priests would tie a rope to the High Priest when he entered in, for should he die, this would be the only way to get him out. God used these things to reveal the vast barrier of sin between man and God. Yet when Christ paid for our sin on the cross, God shook the temple to its foundation and the canvas that veiled the holy of holies was torn from top to bottom.[146] The barrier of sin that kept us from God had been removed through Christ.

The temple was no longer the holiest place and man was no longer forbidden to approach God. Christ became our covering so our sin no longer prevented us from fellowship with God. What was once limited to a few who were set apart for God, now is freely available to all who are in Christ.

This was why some were anointed in the Old Testament. A prophet, king, or priest was anointed with oil and set apart for God.[147] This is also why the Bible warned the people, "Touch not My anointed." It wasn't as it is misused today. Today people use this passage to avoid having their teachings compared to scripture, but the warning was that God has set this person apart as king or priest and no one but God had the right to remove them. Anyone trying to remove God's anointed was challenging God.

---

[146] Matthew 27:51
[147] Leviticus 4:5, 1 Samuel 10:1, 1 Samuel 16:13,

The Anointing of Christ

Another important note is that God's Spirit came upon his prophets and kings. Never do we see the Spirit of God indwelling men in the Old Testament. You see things like, "The Spirit of the Lord came upon him and he spoke..." Even when King Saul became an enemy of God and tried to kill Samuel the prophet and David, the newly anointed king, the Spirit came upon him and he was powerless to do anything but prophesy the word of the Lord.[148]

How can a man that the Prophet Samuel said has become the Lord's enemy[149] also have the Holy Spirit prophesy through him? The Lord's Spirit came upon people but did not indwell people. In the Old Testament, the temple was where God resided with man, but once Christ paid the price and was glorified, man became the temple of God.

Man is no longer anointed as an individual, for God does not need to set a single person aside to be a representative to the people. Now we are anointed through Christ. He is the head and anyone who is part of His body is under that anointing. In the Old Testament, the oil represented the person being covered by the Holy Spirit. The Spirit would come upon the person in the form of anointing, but today Christ is anointed and the Spirit is within us – not merely upon us. The picture of our anointing can be seen through a few passages of scripture. Look first at **Psalm 133:1-2**

> [1] Behold, how good and how pleasant *it is* For brethren to dwell together in unity!
> [2] *It is* like the precious oil upon the head, Running down on the beard, The beard of Aaron, Running down on the edge of his garments.

Where is the anointing oil applied? When someone is anointed, it is always poured on the head. Jesus Christ is the head and we are the body. He was anointed and we have His anointing upon us. We are not anointed; we draw near the head where the oil of the Spirit runs down and reaches us.

The only examples of anointing that we see in the New Testament is the anointing of Christ, and that His anointing abides on

---

[148] 1 Samuel 19:11-24
[149] 1 Samuel 28:16

those in His body. Christ is anointed, and the church is anointed. Never is the anointing directed at a special class of Christian.

Jesus is called the anointed one. In fact, the word 'Christ' means 'anointed'. We are called believers and children, but only He is called 'the anointed.' The church and all who are in the church have His anointing in them through the body of Christ, but are not anointed individually.

We are not 'anointed to preach'. We are not 'anointed for ministry'. We are not anointed individually at all. We all have an anointing because we have the anointing of Christ. The Bible explains that we all are anointed. Look at **1 John 2:20-29**

> [20] But you have an anointing from the Holy One, and you know all things.
> [21] I have not written to you because you do not know the truth, but because you know it, and that no lie is of the truth.
>
> ...
> [26] These things I have written to you concerning those who *try to* deceive you.
> [27] But the anointing which you have received from Him abides in you, and you do not need that anyone teach you; but as the same anointing teaches you concerning all things, and is true, and is not a lie, and just as it has taught you, you will abide in Him.
> [28] And now, little children, abide in Him, that when He appears, we may have confidence and not be ashamed before Him at His coming.
> [29] If you know that He is righteous, you know that everyone who practices righteousness is born of Him.

Where is the anointing? On those God has picked out with a special calling? No. It is given to those John called, 'little children'. It is the believer, the church, and includes the most immature among us. It is not upon a special group, but within all who are in Christ. The anointing is not upon the elite, but within all of God's children.

Jesus Christ is the anointed of God, and because we are in Him and under His anointing, we have the anointing of the Holy Spirit.

Many will come in to claim authority over the church. These claim to be your covering, but we have only one covering – Christ.

The Anointing of Christ

Deceivers will declare themselves to be the head, but we have one head, Christ. Some even teach that they are the source of our spiritual strength and that no individual can grow beyond their covering – which they claim as themselves or through an organization.

Nothing could be farther from the truth. The only limitation to your growth is your willingness to abandon all and draw closer to Christ. You are the only limitation to spiritual maturity. Not once do we see any man called to be the covering of another man. Not one time do we see anyone other than Christ called to be our head.

Some misuse passages in the Old Testament where the husband or father was called the covering of their wives and daughters. These passages have nothing to do with spiritual maturity or our relationship with Christ. In the home, God has appointed the man to be the head of the family, but not the intermediary between Christ and the woman. Nor is any person our intermediary. There is one mediator between God and man – Jesus Christ (See 1 Timothy 2:5).

Let me reiterate this again. The anointing has been given to the entire body – all believers. This is not to selected individuals, but it is written to the children of God. It's not merely for the leaders or for a special class of Christian, as some now teach, but the anointing is over everyone in the church. And John is addressing the church who others are trying to deceive into thinking that only a select few have the anointing. If you have the Spirit, you have the anointing. We are not dependent upon an anointed class, but the same Spirit that anointed Christ also anoints and teaches you. John is not the only apostle to teach this. Look at **2 Corinthians 1:21-22**

> [21] Now He who establishes us with you in Christ and has anointed us *is* God,
> [22] who also has sealed us and given us the Spirit in our hearts as a guarantee.

Who is anointed? Us who are in Christ. Paul is writing to a church struggling in the faith, yet he still identifies them as the anointed along with himself. The apostles of Christ identified all believers as having the anointing, not just the apostles or specific leaders. Jesus Christ is the one anointed and we receive the anointing by drawing into that head. Let's look at how this functions in the body through the passage mentioned earlier – **Ephesians 4:11-16**

¹¹ And He Himself gave some *to be* apostles, some prophets, some evangelists, and some pastors and teachers,

¹² for the equipping of the saints for the work of ministry, for the edifying of the body of Christ,

¹³ till we all come to the unity of the faith and of the knowledge of the Son of God, to a perfect man, to the measure of the stature of the fullness of Christ;

¹⁴ that we should no longer be children, tossed to and fro and carried about with every wind of doctrine, by the trickery of men, in the cunning craftiness of deceitful plotting,

¹⁵ but, speaking the truth in love, may grow up in all things into Him who is the head -- Christ --

¹⁶ from whom the whole body, joined and knit together by what every joint supplies, according to the effective working by which every part does its share, causes growth of the body for the edifying of itself in love.

I realize I'm throwing a lot of passages into this discussion, but these paint a beautiful picture of how the Christian life is designed by God. Once again, we see the warning of deception, but this time by the Apostle Paul. Men will craft many convincing arguments, but do not be taken by those who usurp authority for themselves. Those claiming a special anointing attempt to put people under their bondage, but the truth sets us free. This passage explains the true role of leaders in the church.

What is the goal of those appointed into leadership by God? It's three-fold. To equip the saints for ministry. To teach each person and the body as a whole how to draw near to Christ – the head. Finally, it's to teach the body how to edify itself in love. And where does that love come from? It is poured into our hearts by the Holy Spirit.[150]

Now we need to be taught or reminded how to take what God has given us and to minister to others – both in the church and to those who we are calling into the church. When I say church, it isn't only your local assembly, but the entire church. The universal church is the body of Christ.

Many people call themselves 'the church', but fulfilling God's call is how we identify the true church. Is your local organization

---

[150] Romans 5:5

The Anointing of Christ

teaching others how to draw into the head? Is it teaching others how to be equipped for ministry? By ministry we are talking about fulfilling God's calling and building His kingdom by giving of ourselves for the eternal benefit of others. Finally, does the church focus solely on glorifying Christ?

The true church is comprised of the members of Christ. This crosses church walls, denominational lines, race, and geographical locations. But it does not abandon the truth of scripture or join to another head. We are the body of Christ. The church is not a corpse and is not a two-headed monster. We take what is given through the head and submit ourselves as members of His righteousness.

The body of Christ is formed by the unity of individual members who have joined into that head and are dependent upon all that is supplied by Christ. We are not supplied from any other source. Nor do we serve any other head. We are unified with one body, but that requires each member to understand their role. We are not serving God as individuals – as though we individually are a body. You are not the body. You are a member of the body.

God has equipped you to supply a need for the body. This is why we are told not to forsake assembling together. Church is not just where you get spiritual input from others, but where you unify with other believers to supply what they lack and be supplied in what you lack – all with one purpose – to be united in Christ.

Having said that, it is important to understand how each member contributes to the edifying of the body. Your fellowship with God directly affects the body. Or as the Bible says, when one member suffers, the body suffers with them. When one member rejoices, the body rejoices with them.[151] We are not losing our individual identity, but are drawing near to Christ so our individual relationship with God edifies the entire body.

You make a difference. Your walk with God affects everyone around you – for good or bad. God corporately joins us together, but He rewards us for our individual faithfulness and communes with us as a son or daughter. Your fellowship with God is essential for the church as a whole, and for your individual spiritual health.

This fellowship with God is the greatest reward in the Christian life.

---

[151] 1 Corinthians 12:26

The Church in the Spirit

Understanding how the Spirit of God communes and communicates with our spirit is one of the great essentials of truth in the Christian life. We spend so much time wandering in the desert, having no direction, and unable to discern our place in God's plan simply because we are trying to communicate with God through the flesh.

You may be struggling as I was. Almost my entire Christian walk was inconsistent and without clear direction because I tried to hear God through my ears of flesh, read the scriptures through my eyes of flesh, pray through my flesh, and understand spiritual things through the mind of the flesh. It is impossible to understand spiritual things without understanding how God's Spirit communes with our spirit.

God's Spirit does not change. The same power you receive is the same power I receive, for the power is not of us, nor is it imparted to us. The power is in God and if His Spirit is within us, the power of God is also within us. And the purpose of God's Spirit is not to impart some mystical power, but to reveal Himself to us, reveal His plan to us, and to purge out of our lives the things that oppose the Spirit so we can conform to the likeness of Christ.

The Spirit of God is not limited by our perception of anointing. We all have different callings, but the same Spirit. We all have different gifts, but the same Spirit.[152]

In Acts 8, we see that Philip was sent by the Spirit to Samaria to preach Christ. Many believed the gospel, including a man named Simon, who came out of witchcraft. When the work of God in that city became known to the rest of the church, they sent the apostles down and they performed miracles and great works by the Spirit. Simon saw this power and offered them money to give him that power.

They rebuked this man for the sinful thoughts of his heart. He thought the gift of God could be bought, but there is also another truth that isn't as apparent. Philip was greatly used by the Spirit. He was sent to meet a man of great authority in Ethiopia as he rode in a

---

[152] 1 Corinthians 12:4-11, Ephesians 4:11-16

The Anointing of Christ

chariot heading home. This man received Christ and when the apostles later visited that region, the church had already begun.

Philip was caught up in the Spirit and sent to Samaria, where a great revival broke out. Yet Philip could not do what the apostles Peter and John were doing. This is why the Bible says that each believer is part of the body of Christ, and that the body works according to what each member supplies. Peter and John could not overtake the role God had given Philip, nor could Philip produce the power of the Spirit given through Peter and John.

God has chosen to divide our gifts, abilities, and callings this way so that no one is lifted up in pride, and so that no member appears to be unneeded.

Many members fail to fulfill their calling in the body of Christ because few people understand their calling and become ineffective in the role God has given them. In fact, most Christians are unaware of the role or gifts God has given them. This is why we have a few people working themselves to the breaking point while the majority of the church sits back and resists getting involved.

A crippled body tries to find crutches and other methods to limp along without the missing members. One such crutch is guilt. Through guilt or empty promises, the church attempts to persuade members to take on work in the church. This creates a new problem. Now members who respond through pleas for help are taking on roles God has not gifted them to do, nor called them to do. So then the church loses focus.

Instead of having a passion to follow the Spirit's call, we often operate in the flesh and try to discern the call of God without ears to hear it, eyes to see it, or the mind of Christ to understand it. Then the mission of the church becomes to serve the church instead of to serve God. And because the Spirit isn't being understood, the church is unaware that they are going their own way and not doing anything of eternal significance.

Decades pass, then generations pass, and tradition takes the place of discernment, and it is treated as if denominational traditions are on par with scripture. All the while, people are serving traditions in the flesh, thinking they are pleasing God, yet the Lord says that nothing of the flesh can please God.

Look at how God rebukes His own people throughout biblical history? God gave the people the Law of the Old Testament and God established the feast days and all the ordinances they practiced. Yet as the people lost focus on Him, they served the traditions and God said:

> "I hate, I despise your feast days, And I do not savor your sacred assemblies. Though you offer Me burnt offerings and your grain offerings, I will not accept them, Nor will I regard your fattened peace offerings. Take away from Me the noise of your songs, For I will not hear the melody of your stringed instruments." Amos 5:21-23

How can God despise what He commanded be done? They are singing praises and playing music, yet God stops His ears and declares that He will not listen. Sacrifices meant nothing to God, nor the feasts that were supposed to honor Him, nor the best offerings the people could present. The people offered their talents, assembled in His name, sang songs to the Lord, and offered the best of their possessions, but God said, "I hate these offerings."

How can this be? The answer is found in **Romans 8:8**

So then, those who are in the flesh cannot please God.

Jesus affirmed this when He said, "Those who worship God must do so in Spirit and in truth."[153] How must we approach God? In the Spirit. How must people learn how to serve God? They must be in the Spirit.

It begins with you, the individual Christian, discovering your life in Christ. When you came to Christ and were redeemed, a new spirit was given to you, and this is how God communes with you and reveals His will and all the things of the Spirit. This is how we experience the promise we saw earlier, "You have the anointing and know all things." His anointing abides in you and teaches you all things.

The only thing between you and experiencing the fullness of Christ is your flesh. And God has provided a way to overcome the flesh. We'll explore how to walk in this truth in the next chapter.

Discussion questions:

---

[153] John 4:24

How were the Old Testament prophets and kings anointed?

Why did God require oil to be poured onto their head?

Why couldn't God indwell man in the Old Testament?

What does 'Christ' mean?

Can you find any person other than Christ anointed in the New Testament?

Read 1 John 2:20-29. Per verse 27, who is anointed?

Who is the head of the body of Christ?

Read Mark 10:42-45. What is the difference between church leadership and world leadership?

Why did Jesus forbid creating leadership that puts one person over another?

According to 1 John, why do people claim to be anointed over others?

If someone claiming a special anointing threatens to curse those who refuse to submit, can they curse members of Christ?

Does God permit authority in the church?

How can we have authority, roles, and spiritual gifts without exalting one person over another?

Can God's model work effectively without a church walking in the Spirit?

We are in the Spirit

Romans 8:8
So then, those who are in the flesh cannot please God.

Galatians 5:16-17
[16] I say then: Walk in the Spirit, and you shall not fulfill the lust of the flesh.
[17] For the flesh lusts against the Spirit, and the Spirit against the flesh; and these are contrary to one another, so that you do not do the things that you wish.

Few people realize how foundational the above passages are to living the abundant life Jesus promised. Until we learn how to walk in the Spirit, we cannot consistently live out the Christian life, and this doesn't happen until the flesh is in its proper place.

God said, "My ways are not your ways," and the apostles of Christ stated that the message of the cross is foolishness to the world. Not only is it foolishness to the world, but it is foolishness to any who walk according to the flesh. This includes Christians and people within the church. There are two ideologies that are diametrically opposed. The wisdom of this world is foolishness to God, and the wisdom of God is foolishness to the world. Keep in mind that the flesh is part of the world.

You and I must choose who we are going to follow, and who will count us as a fool. We must choose whether we desire to invest our lives into a world that is passing, or into a kingdom we have not yet seen. You cannot have both. Any who teach otherwise either does not know the scriptures, or does not believe God.

Does God bless us in this life? Certainly He does. But there are two things we must consider. First, how do we define blessing? Second, what role does the 'thing' we count as a blessing play in our lives?

The true blessing is that which is eternal. Cars are not eternal. Houses are not eternal. Yet even these things can be used for purposes which have eternal significance. Do I love my car? Or do I view my car as something I have been loaned by God for the purpose of fulfilling my walk of faith? If my car caught fire and was

We are in the Spirit

destroyed, would I mourn for my car? Or mourn for my house? Or do I believe these belong to God and He has the right to do what He deems good – even if that falls outside of my perspective of what is good?

Consider the life of Job. Satan accused Job of loving God only because of the temporal blessings he received from God. If you read the book of Job, you'll notice that God initiates the challenge. God knew Job's heart and his limitations. "Have you considered my servant Job?" The Lord asked Satan. "There is none like him. He is blameless and upright. He shuns evil and fears God."[154]

Satan then accused Job of loving God only because of his possessions. Yet when God allowed Satan to put Job to the test, He allowed Job to be stripped of everything but his life. When Job lost everything, what was his reaction? He lamented at the string of bad news that kept coming in, but he said, "The Lord gives and the Lord takes away. Blessed be the name of the Lord."[155]

When his wife questioned God's faithfulness, Job said, "Shall we indeed accept good from God and not adversity?"[156] He understood God's right to bring adversity into our lives, plus he had the assurance, that regardless of all adversity, good would be the end result. Consider the amazing words of Job's faith in **Job 19:25-27**

[25] For I know *that* my Redeemer lives, And He shall stand at last on the earth;

[26] And after my skin is destroyed, this *I know,* That in my flesh I shall see God,

[27] Whom I shall see for myself, And my eyes shall behold, and not another. *How* my heart yearns within me!

What was the true desire of his heart? He lost everything this world calls good, but his hope rested fully upon the day when he would see Christ in person. His heart did not yearn for the things of this world, but rather for the day that faith would become sight.

Job understood what God told Abraham, "I am your exceedingly great reward." The items in God's hand are not our rewards. God is our reward. The riches of heaven may be a part of

---

[154] Job 1:8
[155] Job 1:21
[156] Job 2:10

our reward, but God is our exceedingly great reward. Do we love our friends because of what they can give us? Do we love our kids because of what they can do for us? Or do we love them for who they are? Hopefully the latter.

The average Christian views God as someone looking down from heaven, who sprinkles blessings on us when we do enough things right, and tosses adversity in our lives as punishment for wrong. The accurate view of God is someone who is intimately involved in every part of our life – a God who draws us into deep fellowship with Him and works in our lives to lead us through this life as we journey toward eternity. He's leading us to the time when faith will be sight and God's presence will not only be within us, but face to face.

Let me state this as plainly as possible. If you are born into God's kingdom as a child of God through faith in Christ, adversity is always an act of God's love. Because all our transgressions have already been punished through Christ, we are promised that we cannot be under God's wrath.[157] The wrath of God against sin has already been satisfied in Christ. God didn't require you to receive wrath while you were His enemy. He certainly isn't going to require it now that you are His child.

Is Christ sufficient to pay for the sins of the world, but His sacrifice is not sufficient to pay for the sins of God's children? Christ *is* sufficient. So take the word wrath and strike it from your vocabulary as you think of your relationship with God. Wrath has no role to play.

The truth is that everything fleshly in our lives is accounted as the flesh. This is true whether we think of it as sin, or we think of it as good. Worship expressed through the flesh is of the flesh. Lust expressed through the flesh is flesh. God doesn't look at our flesh and say, "That act of the flesh is better than that act of the flesh, so I'll accept it." No. God looks at our actions and is only concerned about one thing. Is it of the flesh, or is it of His Spirit?

Nothing of the flesh is acceptable to God. Period. All of your righteous acts are just as harmful as all of your acts of lusts and corruption. There may be different consequences here on earth, but everything that is not of the Spirit will be destroyed by the fire of

---

[157] 1 Thessalonians 5:9

We are in the Spirit

Christ's judgment – whether it is what we consider righteous or what we consider to be sin. Consider **1 Corinthians 3:11-15**

¹¹ For no other foundation can anyone lay than that which is laid, which is Jesus Christ.

¹² Now if anyone builds on this foundation *with* gold, silver, precious stones, wood, hay, straw,

¹³ each one's work will become clear; for the Day will declare it, because it will be revealed by fire; and the fire will test each one's work, of what sort it is.

¹⁴ If anyone's work which he has built on *it* endures, he will receive a reward.

¹⁵ If anyone's work is burned, he will suffer loss; but he himself will be saved, yet so as through fire.

What happens to our works of the flesh? What happens to our acts of blatant sin? They burn up and will not be allowed to pass over to the next life. What happens to our service toward God, worship, acts of kindness, and all good deeds done through human effort? They will be destroyed by the fire of Christ and will not be allowed to pass over. There is no difference. If you belong to Christ, you pass over without your human deeds. Good or bad in your sight, they cannot go where you are going.

The truth of the Christian life and God's testing in this life is that He is shaking loose that which is non-eternal, so we can clearly see what is eternal and put our focus on Christ. He is the only thing that is eternal. All good works come through Christ. No other foundation can be laid, or built upon. You can't build upon Christ with things of the flesh. You cannot lay a foundation upon your own moral excellence and expect God to accept it. No flesh will glory in His presence.[158]

All adversity serves one of two purposes. It is to either shake loose that which is not of God, or it is to break our dependency on the flesh. The tighter we cling to our flesh, the more difficult adversity will be. If we cling to our own righteousness, we are hindering the work of God and increasing our need for adversity to break the flesh. If we cling to our lusts, we are hindering the work of God and

---

[158] 1 Corinthians 1:29

increasing our need for adversity to break the flesh. There is no difference in God's eyes.

That which is of the flesh is flesh.[159] Righteousness born of the flesh is flesh and cannot inherit life. Sin born of the flesh is flesh and cannot inherit life. Overtly sinning is a declaration of being independent from God and placing our need in the world for gratification. Placing our need into works of righteousness of the flesh is to declare ourselves to be righteous by human effort and not by Christ.

Human good works is a declaration that we can make ourselves righteous, independently of God. Whether sin or religion, there is no difference. Flesh is flesh.

The greater threat comes from righteous acts of the flesh. It's much easier to persuade a murderer, thief, or adulterer that their actions are sinful than it is to persuade a religious person of this fact. The greatest tool in Satan's hand is religion. And he has no problem using the name of Jesus to persuade you to look to yourself instead of to Christ. We have already seen Jesus' explanation that many will come to Him declaring how many good works they have done in Jesus name, but He calls them workers of iniquity.

This is you and I, not just the world. Putting the label of 'Jesus' on our religious efforts does not make them works of God. Calling my works, Jesus' does not transform a work of the flesh into a work of the Spirit. That which God performs is the work of God. That which man performs is a work of the flesh. Period.

Legalism, or religious acts done through man's effort to legalize himself, is the most powerful weapon in the enemy's hand.

Oh, how much joy we miss because we are investing our lives through the flesh instead of through the Spirit. Intimacy with God transforms everything into joy, and only then can we testify along with the Apostle Paul, "I have learned that whatever state I am in, therewith to be content."[160] Only the Christian can have a joyful heart regardless of circumstances.

An important step toward victorious living is to understand the difference between walking in the Spirit and living according to the flesh. The flesh craves sin and the only way it can be gratified is to

---

[159] John 3:6
[160] Philippians 4:11

We are in the Spirit

war against our mind and seek to bring us back into captivity. Until we learn to both recognize the attack of the flesh *and* learn what it means to walk in the Spirit, the flesh will have success in its desire to satiate its cravings. The flesh's gratification comes when we are persuaded to step out of the Spirit.

We begin by understanding our choice. We have the promise, "Walk in the Spirit and you will not fulfill the lusts of the flesh."[161] Not only will you squelch the cravings of the flesh, but you will be abundantly satisfied with the river of God's pleasure.[162]

Let's digress for a moment so we don't slip into a misunderstanding of what it means to walk in the Spirit. Walk in, not merit – that is the message. We are not achieving something in the Spirit in order to overcome the flesh. We are walking in what God has done instead of walking in the call of the world. To understand this, let's bring in a few passages of scripture. First look at **Romans 8:9-10**

> [9] But you are not in the flesh but in the Spirit, if indeed the Spirit of God dwells in you. Now if anyone does not have the Spirit of Christ, he is not His.
> [10] And if Christ *is* in you, the body *is* dead because of sin, but the Spirit *is* life because of righteousness.

Who is in the Spirit? You. If you belong to Christ, you *are* in the Spirit. I missed this truth for many years. I wrestled against my flesh, trying to overcome it so I could walk in the Spirit. I looked at life as though that once I quit walking by the flesh, I would obtain the opportunity to walk in the Spirit. I viewed the Spirit as the goal line and the flesh as a strong defender standing between me and the goal. In truth, I am already in the goal and the flesh is trying to call me out of what God has placed me into.

Another false way of looking at this is that we must enter the Spirit in order to overcome the flesh. The idea is that if we can become spiritual, we can use that against the flesh. Again, this misses the point being made. Walk in the Spirit – not *do* to receive the Spirit.

Read the above passage again. If you are in Christ – born after the Spirit and as a new creation, you ARE in the Spirit. You ARE

---

[161] Galatians 5:16
[162] Psalm 36:7-8

NOT in the flesh. The Apostle Paul is trying to help the church understand who they are, so they can stop living by a standard that contradicts their new nature.

I grew up with a friend whose parents constantly said, "You are sorry. You'll never amount to anything. You are bad." Do you know what happened? He believed who they told him he was, and began to live out that life. It still haunts his life today. Yet I met someone a few years back who was bullied his entire life. He was called weak, worthless, and a nobody. His confidence took a beating, but one day he discovered technology and realized he loved it. He learned quickly and got a job in IT. Suddenly people were praising him for his skills. One day he said, "You know, I realized that the peers of my childhood were jerks. I wasn't the person they said I was. When I quit believing the lies, I quit acting like that worthless child."

If this is true in the world, how much more true is that for us who are children of God? The apostles were telling the church to live according to who they are, and then the person they used to be will have no power over them. They weren't trying to change who they were; they were being called to live according to who they are.

"You are in the Spirit if you are in Christ." That is the message. If you walk in that truth, the flesh has no power. The flesh has power over the old man, but he is dead. We are called to walk according to the new man. This is explained beautifully in **Galatians 5:24-25**

²⁴ And those *who are* Christ's have crucified the flesh with its passions and desires.

²⁵ If we live in the Spirit, let us also walk in the Spirit.

Let's look at the first phrase of verse 25. The word 'if' comes from the Greek word 'ie', which means: if indeed, if after all, or since. Knowing this makes it clear that this isn't a 'maybe' statement. The apostle speaking is not saying "If you are in the Spirit," as if it were a question. He's not asking if they are in the Spirit. He's saying, "Since you are in the Spirit." It's a declaration of who they are, not what they hope to be.

This may seem like splitting hairs, but it's actually a critical distinction. The Bible is not saying, "If you can get into the Spirit, you can have victory." The Bible is saying that you *are* in the Spirit and since this is true, you should be walking in victory.

We are in the Spirit

You are not in the Spirit because you have accomplished something worthy of being there. It is not because you have broken through a barrier and have obtained the Spirit. You are in the Spirit because you are in Christ. Any who are in Christ are in the Spirit. It cannot be otherwise. You are in the Spirit because of what Christ has done for you, and because you are born again, by the Spirit. You are now of God in Christ and He is always in you. You are always in Christ. The call of the flesh is to war against your mind, persuade you to act according to who you were, and then convince you that because sin is present with you that you are still of the flesh.

Take some time to read the epistles (or letters to the churches) in the New Testament. The apostles of Christ are writing to help keep the churches from drifting away from the truth. Frequently you will see them reminding the Christian of who they are in order to correct behavior. In fact, you will notice that when addressing poor or sinful behavior, the Bible almost always points to who they are. The message isn't, "Act like this so you can become godly." The message is, "Christ has set you free and made you into a new creation. Walk in what He has done for you and be what He has made you. Walk according to your new nature. Act like who you are."

Certainly we wrestle with the flesh, but it isn't an effort to defeat the flesh, but to resist its call to follow the desires of the old nature that is now dead and buried. And we overcome, not by looking at the flesh and trying to resist, but by looking at the Spirit. Since we live in the Spirit, let us also walk in the Spirit. We are called to walk according to who we are, and not according to what we have been delivered from. We simply need to learn how to identify what is of the flesh and what is by the Spirit.

Until you recognize these two opposing ways of focusing on life, sin will gain ground and spiritual things will seem just out of reach. Learning these truths was life-changing for me. The weights that easily ensnared me lost their grip when the focus of my life changed. Instead of trying to survive, I began to see deeper things of God that were once hidden in plain sight.

If we could sum up the whole matter, we should say something like this: You are in the Spirit. Believe in what God has done and walk with that focus. Stop trying to get in the Spirit, and start believing you are in the Spirit as God has declared. Then walk according to who you are in Christ.

Looking back I realized that faith was lacking because the word was lacking. It's not a coincidence that the Bible says, "Faith comes by hearing and hearing by the word of God." When we don't know the principles of faith, we miss out on many things. The topic at hand is one of those things. How many people struggle with sinful habits and personal weaknesses because they don't understand the promise that our flesh has been crucified and we have the power to walk in the Spirit – the place where sin cannot go?

Faith Without Works is Dead?

Since we've touched on faith by hearing a few times, it is necessary to clarify some misunderstandings about faith and how it applies to works. Why does faith come by hearing the word of God? Does hearing the word create faith? No. In Hebrews 4:2 we see that people can hear the same word of God we hear, but it cannot profit them if it is not mixed with faith. The word of God plus our faith equals fulfillment of God's purposes in us.

Faith is a gift of the Spirit and each person has been dealt a measure of faith. In the Spirit, we have faith. Unfortunately our minds are often ignorant to the reality of the Spirit. When we hear the word of Christ, the Holy Spirit affirms in our spirit what God is revealing to us and calling us to do. Our minds are illuminated with His truth and faith comes alive in our soul. To get an understanding of this, let's look at **James 2:20-26**

20 But do you want to know, O foolish man, that faith without works is dead?

21 Was not Abraham our father justified by works when he offered Isaac his son on the altar?

22 Do you see that faith was working together with his works, and by works faith was made perfect?

23 And the Scripture was fulfilled which says, "Abraham believed God, and it was accounted to him for righteousness." And he was called the friend of God.

24 You see then that a man is justified by works, and not by faith only.

25 Likewise, was not Rahab the harlot also justified by works when she received the messengers and sent *them* out

another way?

^{26} For as the body without the spirit is dead, so faith without works is dead also.

James' discussion is confusing if you don't understand the perspective of what He is saying. In Ephesians 2:8-9, the Apostle Paul explains that we are saved by faith through grace and not of works. Salvation is by faith apart from works. There is nothing you can do to merit salvation. Yet now James is pointing to faith without works and saying that it is dead. We are justified by faith through our works. Is this a contradiction? Of course not.

Paul is addressing the topic of salvation, but James is addressing the apathy of Christians. Paul is talking about God's work of salvation, which Christ accomplished for us. James is talking to those who are children of God who think that the message of grace is passivity. An apathetic Christian is not the evidence of grace – nor is apathy the evidence that a person has a life grounded in faith.

We who have the Spirit can become so fleshly minded that the word of God does not move us. Church is filled with those types of people. Some are religious but do not have the Spirit, but some do have the Spirit and have become apathetic. These hear the word, never mix it (or apply it) by faith, and the word profits them nothing.

In their soul, their faith is dead and lifeless. There is no activity, no revelation of God, and no true work of righteousness.

But those who hear the word, feel the stirring of the Spirit, believe the word, and walk in it, faith springs to life in their soul and the evidence comes out in their lives and works. It is still the work of God, but they have responded to that call, believed God, and the joy of the Lord blossoms into action. It isn't their decision to create good works. It is their submission to what God is revealing through their spirit.

The word of God shines a light into our soul to reveal the purposes that God's Spirit is already revealing to our spirit. Then when we hear the word, we see God's revelation in it, believe in what God is doing, and the word is mixed with faith so it comes alive within us to accomplish what God desires for us. God's word will always accomplish what He desires. The question is, will we be partakers in what God is doing?

Those who hear the word and resist God's revelation will not profit from the word because faith has been pushed aside by the fleshly mind. When God's revelation interferes with our fleshly desires, the carnally minded Christian suppresses it. Suppressing revelation can become so common-place that we don't even perceive we are doing this. Our response springs through the flesh so we no longer recognize the intuition of our spirit. Then all our actions come through the flesh and even good works are merely human effort.

One of the dangers of living under the law as a legalistic Christian is that law requires human effort. When our focus is on the law – rules we must keep – then our focus is on the flesh and revelation is suppressed. Legalistic thinking turns man into the focus, and we are blinded to God's revelation. Just as Jesus said to the Pharisees, "If you were blind, your sins would be forgiven (for God would open their eyes to grace). But because you say, 'I see', your sin remains."[163] They were blind because their trust was in the law and not Christ. What Jesus revealed was received by those who focused on Christ. Revelation was hidden from the eyes of religion and human effort.

In truth, human effort only comes into play when it comes to resisting God. I don't make spiritual things happen. I don't decide to choose God's will. I don't decide to do good works. I don't decide to become spiritually mature. These are natural outcomes of the life in the Spirit and are all according to the works of Christ within us. I can only decide not to do these things. The Spirit reveals God's will and draws us into God's work, and we either follow or resist. The flesh calls us to follow its ways of thinking, and when the flesh rises, the outflow of the Spirit is suppressed.

Self-deception is a subtle form of disobedience. I can justify my own ways while convincing myself that it is of God. When God calls to abandon all, I can resist that call by pointing to all the good I can do with what God has given me. When I am called to wait, I can convince myself to act. When I am called to act, I can convince myself to wait. I can give all that I have because of human will and not realize that God has other purposes. Or I can save all I have when God's purpose is to release all and trust Him.

---

[163] John 9:41

How then do I know when self is the motivation and when the Spirit is calling? The truth is that a specific circumstance is not how I learn to discern between God's call and selfish trust. Spiritual discernment comes through intimacy with Christ. As I learn to hear His voice, I also learn to recognize that anything that isn't His voice is a deception.

Antique dealers don't learn how to identify the counterfeit by studying thousands of counterfeits. They learn to study and intimately know the characteristics of the pieces they value. Then when a counterfeit appears, they identify it by the fact that it falls short of the real thing. A counterfeit has many, many good qualities and closely resembles the original craftsmanship. But it is worthless because it is only an imposter of the original.

We don't learn to discern the Spirit's prompting by looking at what calls to us. We learn to discern the Spirit by knowing God. Through intimacy with Christ, the Spirit reveals Himself first, and then His purposes are made plain through that ongoing relationship.

Don't try to discover the will of God if you are not learning how to walk with Him. God's purposes and His will for your life are not independent of a relationship with Him. Out of the relationship everything flows. Without intimacy with God, works slip into human effort and our own ideas often are mistaken as the prompting of the Spirit.

Once we understand the truth of faith, we have the foundation of overcoming.

Discussion questions:

When Job was stripped of everything, what did he declare as his hope? See Job 19:25-27.

Does God view good works in the flesh as better than sins of the flesh?

When the Christian sins, do we place ourselves under God's wrath?

Are there consequences to sin?

According to 1 Corinthians 2:13, what is the purpose of the fire of God's testing at the throne of Christ?

If we commit sin in order to fulfill ourselves independently of God, or do good deeds independent of God, is there a difference in God's eyes? Why or why not?

Why did Jesus call those who did good works in His name workers of lawless acts?

Is it harder to convince a good person of their need for Christ than it is to convince a criminal?

Review Romans 8:9-10. How does the Christian get in the Spirit?

Review Galatians 5:24-25. How do we crucify our old fleshly nature?

Why is faith without works dead?

Who is James focusing on in his discussion? Is he contradicting Ephesians 2:8-10?

How do we learn to hear God's voice and know His will?

Christ's Threefold Work

Now that we've addressed the foundation of faith, let's consider the finished work of Christ. This book has alluded to some of this information, but it's important to be intentional and specific. Understanding Christ's finished work and how it affects our daily walk is of the utmost importance. And it is one of the most untaught or under-taught truths in the church.

There are three parts to the crucifixion event. Christ has provided three things that are foundational to living victoriously in the Christian walk. The first we already know and hear frequently in the church. Jesus shed His blood to pay for our sins. But that is not all Jesus accomplished.

Through Christ, we have been given all things that pertain to life and godliness. His death, burial and resurrection did more than pay for sin. We also died in Christ that our body of sin, the fleshly nature, might be done away with.[164] He died, was buried, and rose again.

Each of these facts directly affects your life. Let's first look at the crucifixion. This is where we have been set free from this body of sin. Take a look at **Colossians 2:13-14**

[13] And you, being dead in your trespasses and the uncircumcision of your flesh, He has made alive together with Him, having forgiven you all trespasses,
[14] having wiped out the handwriting of requirements that was against us, which was contrary to us. And He has taken it out of the way, having nailed it to the cross.

All the debt we have to sin was paid by Christ. Just before His death, Jesus cried with a loud voice, "It is finished!" The Greek word is 'Tetelesti' which means, paid in full. Tetelesti was what was written on a bill in the Greek culture when a loan was repaid or a debt was paid off. Jesus died for the sins of the whole world. Consider **1 John 2:2**

And He Himself is the propitiation for our sins, and not for ours only but also for the whole world.

---

[164] Romans 6:6

All sin has been paid, but it is applied to the cross by faith, and we receive Christ's righteousness by faith. All your sin has been paid. In fact, all sin has been paid. It is like God's grace in our lives. Though grace is offered and all things have been given to us that pertain to life and godliness, this profits nothing until it is received by faith. We can walk as ignorant Christians, not knowing the greatness of what we have been given.

In the same way, the world can walk in sin, not knowing that Jesus has already delivered them from it. Or as the Bible says, "He who does not believed is condemned *already*, because he does not believe in the name of the only begotten Son of God."[165] No one is condemned for not believing in Jesus. The world is already under condemnation. Jesus is the escape from that condemnation.

We have all heard that Jesus died for our sins, but what does that mean? There is a deeper meaning in Christ's death that most people don't realize. Jesus made the statement, "If anyone desires to come after Me, let him deny himself, take up his cross, and follow me."[166] As we have already seen, Jesus then goes on to explain that the one who loses his life will find it, and the one who saves his life will lose it.

The cross has been misunderstood as a call of suffering. We've heard people say about a problem, "It's just my cross to bear," but this misses the entire point of the cross. Certainly Jesus suffered, but the cross is the place of death. It is where the flesh died, but the Spirit was made alive. Let's see the Bible's explanation in **1 Peter 3:18**

> For Christ also died for sins once for all, *the* just for *the* unjust, so that He might bring us to God, having been put to death in the flesh, but made alive in the spirit; NASB

Jesus did not die spiritually. This is often misunderstood. Spiritual death is the state we are in before receiving the Spirit of God and our new spirit. Jesus did not have to suffer in hell because any who die without Christ have done so because they refuse God's mercy. The suffering of spiritual death does not occur until what the

---

[165] John 3:18
[166] Luke 9:23-24

Christ's Threefold Work

Bible calls the second death.[167] Sin is in the flesh; therefore, every mention of Christ's death and suffering points solely to the flesh. He suffered in the flesh. He died in the flesh. But He was made alive in the Spirit.

Some translations use the phrase 'by the Spirit', but the word 'by' is not in the text. The original Greek states 'is alive' (zoopoieo) spirit (pneuma). Literally this can be translated as: alive spiritually, quickened by/in the spirit, or to give increase of life in the spirit.

There is no need for Jesus to suffer in hell because man was not intended for hell. Hell was created for the devil and his angels.[168] Man only joins the damned if he refuses life. Some have a hard time accepting that Jesus didn't go to hell. Who knows why people cling to this erroneous thinking, but look at every scripture that speaks of Christ's suffering and death. Not one goes beyond the flesh. Part of the confusion is because older translations use the word 'hell' for both Greek words, 'Hades' and 'Gehenna'.

Hades is the place of the dead, while Gehenna is described as the place of torment. Yet some translations make no distinction between these two words, so when the Bible says that Jesus went to Hades, because it is also translated as hell, some teach that Jesus was condemned to hell. The truth is that according to scripture, Jesus went to Hades to preach to the spirits in prison.[169] He had the keys to the grave,[170] and the saints of old were freed[171], appeared with Christ after His resurrection,[172] and then disappeared after His ascension. Once their sin was paid, they received the same opportunity to be present with the Lord after death that we are promised in the New Testament.[173]

Don't forget that Jesus' final words were, "Father, into your hands I commit My spirit." This is not the declaration of one destined for hell, but for life.

---

[167] Revelation 2:11, Rev 20:6, Rev 20:14, Rev 20:8
[168] Matthew 25:41
[169] 1 Peter 3:19
[170] Revelation 1:18
[171] John 8:56
[172] Matthew 27:52-53
[173] 2 Corinthians 5:8

All sin is paid through Christ. According to scripture, it is impossible for the blood of animal sacrifices to take away sin.[174] The Old Covenant sacrifices were merely a yearly reminder that pointed to Christ. The Old Testament saints kept the law by faith, but their sins were not paid until Christ's atonement for sin. Until that time, they had no right to come before God, but after the debt was paid, the veil that prevented them was taken out of the way.[175]

Man was once kept out of the Holy of Holies because death was eminent for any who approached God bearing their own sin. Now we come freely before His throne because the payment for sin was made by Christ, and His blood was sprinkled on the altar in heaven.[176]

That is the atonement for sin. The word 'atonement' means to make reconciliation for sin by covering it. Once atonement was made, the wages of sin were satisfied. And this is where most Christians lose sight of the cross. They look at the atoning blood of Christ as the end of Jesus' work. But atoning for sin, though necessary, is not all we need. Something had to be done with the sin-maker. Our flesh.

So why does the Bible say we were put to death? Through Adam, our spirit was dead to God because of sin, but our flesh was very much alive through a fallen sinful nature. Through human nature, the flesh controls the mind, will, and heart of fallen man. Until the old man is crucified, that nature is in control.

Just as Christ was put to death in the flesh but made alive in the Spirit, we also must be put to death in the flesh and made alive in the Spirit through faith in Christ. Let's look at this explanation from **Romans 6:8-11**

> [8] Now if we died with Christ, we believe that we shall also live with Him,
>
> [9] knowing that Christ, having been raised from the dead, dies no more. Death no longer has dominion over Him.
>
> [10] For *the death* that He died, He died to sin once for all; but *the life* that He lives, He lives to God.
>
> [11] Likewise you also, reckon yourselves to be dead indeed to sin, but alive to God in Christ Jesus our Lord.

---

[174] Hebrews 10:3-4
[175] Luke 23:45
[176] Hebrews 9:12, 23-24

Christ's Threefold Work

If you died with Christ, you also live with Him. This is not only speaking of the resurrection of our bodies, but also the promise that we shall experience Christ's life now. Your flesh was crucified with Christ and you were raised as a new creation. Both the future resurrection of our bodies and our current life in Christ are promised through Jesus's completed work. Let's look at this by bringing **2 Corinthians 5:17** into view:

> Therefore, if anyone *is* in Christ, *he is* a new creation; old things have passed away; behold, all things have become new.

Before Christ you were dead spiritually, but alive in the flesh. Of course the flesh is destined for the wages of sin – which is more death, but it's alive in our physical existence. As we'll examine shortly, life doesn't come through the cross, but through the resurrection of Jesus. Before there can be resurrection, there must be death. In our lives, we experience resurrection power now through the death of the flesh. The flesh dies to remove the old. It is taken out of the way, having been nailed to the cross. With the flesh dead and out of the way, we then receive the resurrection life of Christ in the form of a new spirit, born of God.

Jesus said a seed must first fall into the ground and die, then it raises up into new life and becomes fruitful.[177] A dry dead seed remains dry and dead. But the seed gives up itself in order to become a new creation. The old is taken out of the way and the new emerges.

Your flesh must die before you can be made alive. That old nature, born from the flesh, was crucified with Christ. Past tense. This is one of the mysteries of God that we have a hard time grasping. Let's focus in on verse 8 above: **Romans 6:8**

> Now if we died with Christ, we believe that we shall also live with Him,

Did you know that you died with Christ? If you are born into God's kingdom, you were put to death. Not will die, but did die. This will be an important truth to understand. When Jesus died, He died once for all. Yet the Bible says that while we were dead in our sins,

---

[177] John 12:24

we were crucified with Christ that the body of sin (the flesh) might be done away with.

One Nature or Two?

In the early years of my teaching, I subscribed to the view commonly taught in many churches – that we have two natures. One is the old sin nature of Adam, and the other is a new nature from Christ. In my youth a pastor explained it to me this way, "Inside your heart is a black and white dog and they are fighting. The black dog is your sin nature, and the white dog is your godly nature. The one that wins is the one you say, 'Sick him' to the most."

I think most Christians view spiritual life this way. Whichever beast you feed the most, encourage the most, or help the most is going to win. If you fall down, try harder. If that doesn't work, try harderer.

There is a problem with this view. Actually, there are several problems with this view. First, it is man dependent. Under this belief system, God is dependent upon you to accomplish righteousness on His behalf. He gave us a new nature, but now we must raise it like a puppy and teach it how to fight. If we do well, our nature will do well. If we blow it, then our Christian life will flop.

Unfortunately, no one has yet to succeed in this endeavor. Since we approach both natures as man-dependent, we are empowering the flesh either way. We are either using the flesh to produce righteousness, or we are using the flesh for sin. As we saw in a previous chapter, whether we are using the flesh for good deeds or bad, they are still acts of the flesh. And flesh and blood cannot inherit the kingdom of God.[178]

The second major problem is that the concept of two natures simply isn't true. The Bible says that we are the temple of the Holy Spirit.[179] The Bible also says that a house divided cannot stand.[180] Scripture teaches that darkness and light cannot abide together and we cannot be joined to both.[181]

---

[178] 1 Corinthians 15:50
[179] 1 Corinthians 3:16, 1 Corinthians 6:19
[180] Matthew 12:25
[181] 2 Corinthians 6:14

Christ's Threefold Work

Since God is not the author of confusion,[182] why would He bring us into confusion by giving us two contradicting natures and then leave it up to us to figure out which one to listen to and which one to feed? According to the Bible, the old has passed away. Review this passage from **2 Corinthians 5:17**

> Therefore, if anyone *is* in Christ, *he is* a new creation; old things have passed away; behold, all things have become new.

What happened to the old creation? It passed away to make room for the new. The old things have passed away – past tense. You were buried with Christ – past tense. You have died with Christ – past tense. Now all things are new.

If you live in the mindset of wrestling against the flesh, you've already lost the battle. The flesh can't overcome the flesh. It is the Spirit that gives life, the flesh profits nothing.[183] God did not create a house divided. God did not create a temple divided. The light of God does not abide in a house of darkness. You are new. The old is dead. The old is gone.

Unredeemed man has one nature – a sinful nature born from Adam. Those who are born of God have one nature – a godly nature born of the Spirit.

The natural question everyone asks when this truth is presented is, "If I only have one nature, and it's from God, why do I sin? Why is it so hard to live a godly life?"

Let's review this struggle again from the perspective of the Apostle Paul. I realize that I've used this passage a few times already, but now we are going to view it from yet another perspective and glean more truth and encouragement from it. Look again at **Romans 7:19-23**

> [19] For the good that I will *to do,* I do not do; but the evil I will not *to do,* that I practice.
> [20] Now if I do what I will not *to do,* it is no longer I who do it, but sin that dwells in me.
> [21] I find then a law, that evil is present with me, the one who wills to do good.

---

[182] 1 Corinthians 14:33
[183] John 6:63

^{22} For I delight in the law of God according to the inward man.
^{23} But I see another law in my members, warring against the law of my mind, and bringing me into captivity to the law of sin which is in my members.

There was a time when I misused this passage. I thought Paul was saying that a sinful nature warred against his spiritual nature, but that is not what he said. Sin did not dwell in his nature, but in his flesh. Sin in the members of his body presented evil to him, and persuaded him to follow a different law than the law of God.

The inward man, that eternal nature that has been born of God, delights in God's law. Notice what is said – he desires what is good. He delights in the law of God. He's not trying to keep rules in order to please God or become godly. His new nature is godly. That nature desires good. The inward man delights in the law of God because that nature is born of God. Its life is in Christ and it naturally desires what is good. The inward man does not have to be forced to conform to a godly standard – it is born into a godly standard. It is godly by birth and it is incorruptible because it is of God.

When the new nature is the focus, the mind naturally delights in what is of God. It can do no other. Satan knows this, so what is the primary place of attack? To war against the mind and drag it into a different law – the law of sin. The flesh is corrupt and bound under the law of sin. Paul explains this as Romans rolls into the next chapter. Look at **Romans 8:2**

> For the law of the Spirit of life in Christ Jesus has made me free from the law of sin and death.

In Christ, we are freed from the law of sin. This is plainly stated in **Galatians 5:18**

> But if you are led by the Spirit, you are not under the law.

Those who are in the Spirit need no law, for our life is in Christ. In Him, the law has already been fulfilled, and because we are partakers of God's divine nature, keeping the law of righteousness is part of our nature. We cannot sin, because we have been born of

Christ's Threefold Work

God.[184] Though the flesh is subject to the law of sin, righteousness is now part of our eternal nature.

Our old nature was spiritual, but dead. It was subject to the flesh because it had no life or power to live for God. Our new nature is spiritual, but it is in Christ. The flesh wars against our minds because sin in our flesh desires the same control it had under the old nature.

Sin will use any tools available to deceive our minds. This includes using the commandments of God in order to deceive us. Sound strange? Look at **Romans 7:11**

For sin, taking occasion by the commandment, deceived me, and by it killed *me.*

Look at legalism, self-righteousness, guilt, and other things in the church and in the lives of Christians that pretend to be godly, but produce bondage. Does the legalist have freedom? No. He is bound to keeping the law in the flesh. While it promises liberty, sin is using the law of God to bind the Christian. How many Christians hear the word, and instead of finding freedom, they feel shameful and guilty? Sometimes it is their misinterpretation of the word. Sometimes the word is taught as legalistic from the pulpit. Yet Jesus said the truth sets us free.

As far back as Genesis, God warned, "Sin crouches at the door, and its desire is to rule over you. But you should rule over it."[185] So how do we rule over sin? By setting our minds on things above, where Christ reigns.[186] Sin not only uses temptations of lusts, but temptations of legalism. Don't forget that when Satan tempted Christ, he used scripture to do so. Satan attempted to use scripture for serving the flesh, but Jesus turned the focus to God's glory.

Our inner man – that new nature – is free from the law of sin, but sin in our flesh is still bound by that law. It is sin in our flesh that wars against the mind, trying to take our focus off of Christ and into the flesh.

Temptation is revived through the law. This is true whether we are trying to resist through the law, or trying to create righteousness through the law. The power of sin is the law. But we are dead to the

---

[184] 1 John 3:9
[185] Genesis 4:7
[186] Colossians 3:2

law and it has no power over us. Yet if sin in our flesh can persuade us to put our trust in the law, sin wins. The mind is brought under subjection and the sins we have been freed from are revived. Paul goes on to explain this further. Let's look at the passage just mentioned in a fuller context. **Romans 7:10-11**

> [10] And the commandment, which *was* to *bring* life, I found to *bring* death.
>
> [11] For sin, taking occasion by the commandment, deceived me, and by it killed *me.*

Notice that it is sin in our flesh that is using the law against us. If we step out of the Spirit by forgetting our faith in Christ, we are now in the flesh. Then sin takes advantage of the opportunity and with the law slays us.

This is why there are defeated Christians. It is not that sin has conquered them. It is that they have shifted their faith away from Christ and onto the law. The law cannot save you. The law cannot teach you how to overcome sin. The law's main function is to reveal your guilt and inability to measure up to God's perfect standard so you are driven to Christ.[187] Now we have come to Christ for salvation, but then abandoned Christ in order to serve the same law that condemned us. It isn't the law that teaches us godliness. It is grace! Look at **Titus 2:11-15**

> [11] For the grace of God that brings salvation has appeared to all men,
>
> [12] teaching us that, denying ungodliness and worldly lusts, we should live soberly, righteously, and godly in the present age,
>
> [13] looking for the blessed hope and glorious appearing of our great God and Savior Jesus Christ,
>
> [14] who gave Himself for us, that He might redeem us from every lawless deed and purify for Himself *His* own special people, zealous for good works.
>
> [15] Speak these things, exhort, and rebuke with all authority. Let no one despise you.

---

[187] Romans 3:19, Galatians 3:23-24

What does grace do? It teaches you how to deny ungodliness and worldly lusts. What does the law teach you? The law teaches that you are a sinner, are guilty, and then it slays you with guilt, shame, and defeat. Before salvation, these things revealed our need for deliverance through Christ. Now that Christ has set us free from these things, why do we desire the law over God's grace?

Will men despise you if you teach grace? Yes. For the law births legalism, and legalism views grace as a threat. Knowing this, God has commanded us to not allow men to despise us. In other words, it isn't our concern how people react against the truth. Stay focused on Christ. Walk by faith, not by sight, and not human effort.

The power of sin is the law; therefore, sin seeks to overcome anything that threatens its power. But sin cannot defeat grace. It can only war against your mind to persuade you to deny the power of Christ and submit back under the law. Then you become one of those whom Paul warned, "You have become estranged from Christ, you who attempt to be justified by law; you have fallen from grace."[188]

What does it mean to be estranged? It's the Greek word, 'apo' – to separate from or flee from something or someone. The law persuades you to flee from the grace of Christ as insufficient and to put the weight of self-righteousness upon your own back. And that is a burden you cannot bear and a task you cannot accomplish.

How then do we become reunited with Christ? We already have seen that Christ is in us, and we in Him. Yet our will can abandon Christ and pursue temptation. What causes us to break from following Christ and pursue the will of sin? We took our eyes off Christ and looked to the law. To reunite in God's purpose, we simply take our eyes off everything else and put them back onto Christ. He is our sufficiency. He is our life, our righteousness, and we are partakers of His nature.

The separation is not a loss of life, but a loss of focus. We have quit pursuing the grace of God (where God's will is) and have pursued works of the law. We place ourselves back into God's grace by believing His word and looking back to Christ. We deny ungodliness by taking our eyes off the flesh and placing our focus back to Christ. We overcome meaningless religion by placing our eyes on the grace of God in Christ.

---

[188] Galatians 5:4

Do you see a pattern? Everything points to the complete sufficiency of Christ. Anything that is man dependent is of the flesh. Everything that is Christ focused is of the Spirit.

Take special note of verse 14 above. Who purifies us from every lawless deed? Who purifies us from sin? Who creates in us the heart for good works? It is Christ. Purification is the work of Christ. The desire for good works is not born out of guilt, but out of a love for Christ. He creates in us the zeal for good works when we focus on His completed work on the cross.

Sin wars against us as an enemy, using our flesh, and trying to draw our attention away from the Spirit and onto human effort. Satan knows your weaknesses. One of the greatest weaknesses of every person is their emotions. Satan will use guilt to persuade you that you have fallen short, and that you must do something to make yourself right with God. He will use shame to condemn you in the flesh and use it to war against your mind to draw you back into the flesh. He will use good works and sinful lusts. Whichever it takes to draw you into the flesh, he will use.

Feelings are a terrible focus of our faith. When guilt condemns, Christ is greater than our hearts. When shame points to our failure, feelings have no bearing on reality. Feelings may say, "You are falling short," but God has declared, "You are complete in Christ." Get your focus off feelings and onto Christ.

Your weaknesses of the flesh are irrelevant. God has condemned sin in the flesh through the cross. Have you fallen short of God's standard? Of course you have. Will you blow it? Of course you will.

Each time you fall short, Satan uses that sin as a tool against you. Sin will take occasion of your failure, use the law of sin to condemn you, and will either lead you farther into temptation, or convince you that the burden of recovery is on you. You'll then feel like you have to do something to make right the wrong. Like the lamentation of the Apostle Paul, sin will take advantage of the law and try to slay you.

That is guilt. That is shame. But you must realize that God has already overcome that sin, and it is understanding God's grace that teaches you to overcome ungodliness. When you try to make right your sins, you are giving more power to sin and you will live the defeated Christian life. It's a guarantee. Either pride will blind you

Christ's Threefold Work

and persuade you that you can be righteous by human effort, or guilt will pound you because you can never do quite enough to measure up.

You know what? You cannot measure up. It's a sin to try to measure up. It's a sin to try to become righteous. You read that correctly. It is a sin to attempt to produce righteousness, for you are declaring independence from Christ and you are professing that His work was insufficient to accomplish what the Bible says Jesus accomplished for you.

The answer is to not focus on the sins of your failure, but the gift of God's grace. Then you will rejoice with the Apostle Paul. He began by pointing to the problem and lamenting, "Who will save me from this body of death?" but then rejoiced in the answer in **Romans 7:25**

> I thank God -- through Jesus Christ our Lord! So then, with the mind I myself serve the law of God, but with the flesh the law of sin.

If you try to serve God through the flesh, you are actually serving sin. There is only one way to serve the law of God – through Jesus Christ our Lord. Set your mind above,[189] where Christ is seated on the throne of victory.[190] Abide in Christ and the victorious Christian life is a guarantee.

Predestined for Victory

The victorious Christian life has been given to all who will receive it by faith. There is nothing for you to accomplish in order to obtain spiritual maturity, for all has been accomplished through Christ and we are in Him. You were in Christ on the cross. Your sinful nature was put to death on the cross. You also were raised as a new creation at His resurrection. All that Christ accomplished is already yours.

To some, this sounds confusing, but that is because we can only view life as a timeline. We are stuck in our 70-80 year life perspective. But God is not bound by these things. God views time as

---

[189] Colossians 3:2-3
[190] Ephesians 2:5-6

an object in His hands. He saw the end from the beginning and created all things to fulfill all His will. This is also why we can have such confidence in His promises. They are accomplished facts. We are either in the promise by faith, or trusting in the flesh.

God does not have to find a way to force His will into the world in order to intervene in our lives. God saw every moment of time and created the beginning with the end in His hands. While you are praying for God's will to be done, God has already placed your future in the center of His will, so your prayer (which He knew beforehand) will be answered. This is why we pray according to His will. And why our primary focus is to set our love upon Him rather than trying to find a way to fulfill our love of self. Consider **Ephesians 1:4-6**

> [4] just as He chose us in Him before the foundation of the world, that we should be holy and without blame before Him in love,
>
> [5] having predestined us to adoption as sons by Jesus Christ to Himself, according to the good pleasure of His will,
>
> [6] to the praise of the glory of His grace, by which He has made us accepted in the Beloved.

When were you chosen in Christ? Not during your lifetime, but before the creation of the world. Knowing beforehand that we would be in Christ, you were crucified with Him and your sins were taken out of the way. The only thing hindering your life was your unbelief. Once you recognized the gift of God that was already prepared for you, you believed, and God placed you in Christ to receive the gift of salvation He had waiting for you all along.

The same is true for your holiness. The same passage that testifies of God's love for us beforehand also promises that God has prepared the way for you to be holy and blameless before Him. This goes back to the passage we saw earlier – we have been given all things that pertain to life and godliness. Everything you need in order to live the abundant life, conform to the image of Christ, and inherit all God's promises has already been given to you. You lack nothing. Consider **Romans 8:29-31**

> [29] For whom He foreknew, He also predestined *to be* conformed to the image of His Son, that He might be the firstborn among many brethren.
>
> [30] Moreover whom He predestined, these He also called;

Christ's Threefold Work

whom He called, these He also justified; and whom He justified, these He also glorified.

[31] What then shall we say to these things? If God *is* for us, who *can be* against us?

Do you realize that there is nothing preventing you from conforming perfectly to the image of Christ? It truly is possible to be like Him in all ways of character and faith. When God established creation, He built into your life everything you need to be perfect and complete. You lack nothing.

So why do so few people fulfill this purpose? Herein is the great paradox of scripture. Does predestination equate to robotic behavior? No, it doesn't. While it is not possible to fully understand God's ways, two things are certain. One, God has foreordained your path and given you everything needed to live out the Christian life and fulfill all of God's will for you. This also includes inheriting all that God prepared for you to receive in His kingdom.

Second, faith and obedience are part of God's plan. A Christian can be faithless and disobedient. In fact, very few find the abundant life God has prepared for them. Why did Jesus say, "To Him who overcomes, I will give…" and then promise all the greatest promises to those few people? And what are we trying to overcome?

I spent many years pondering over this question. Overcome what? It wasn't until I grew in my understanding of the war between the flesh and the Spirit that I understood this question. Overcoming is to put our flesh under subjection so that the Spirit can reign. The flesh is the one way the enemy gets a stronghold in our lives, churches, and culture. The culture can be influenced by our faith, but they will always be driven by the flesh. However, the church and our individual lives should be led by the Spirit and not flesh-driven.

Consider the struggle of Paul we looked at earlier. What was Paul lamenting over? "The sin in my flesh rises up and wars against my mind, trying to bring me back into bondage." What is your battle? And what is my battle? It is our flesh, rising up, and trying to bring us back into bondage. The flesh rises up and turns our eyes to lust. It rises up in the form of jealousy. Or outbursts of wrath. Or greed. The flesh rises up in countless ways and its desire is to rule over you.

This is what we must overcome. And it is the most difficult undertaking of the Christian life. When anger burns, God says to turn wrath away with a soft answer. This sounds great until we are angry. Then the flesh rises up to take control and we want to answer wrath with wrath. Turning our eyes away from sin sounds great until our flesh craves lust. Not allowing money to become our master sounds great until wanting more drives us to greed. Everyone has weaknesses and they all fall under one word – flesh.

Overcoming the flesh is difficult because it is so engrained into our lifestyle and patterns of thinking. This is why God promises the greatest rewards to those who overcome. Overcoming is a guarantee for any who will allow God to transform their lives into His likeness, and this is preordained into your life. All you must do is allow the Holy Spirit to lead you into the path of life while answering the call to abandon the flesh. It is to believe God over your fleshly desires. This includes all desires and not just the ones we deem as sinful.

This is also why we must understand the difference between the flesh and the Spirit. If you are trying to overcome through human effort, you will fail. I know this from personal experience. Why did I try for so many years to break the strongholds of the flesh, but always failed? I had enough short-lived successes to keep me trying, but nothing ever lasted. And then I understood the Spirit's role. I soon understood the promise Jesus gave, "Those who enter into His rest have ceased from their own labors." I quit laboring in the flesh, and began resting in His Spirit. Suddenly things changed. The flesh lost its dominion and I began to see a new world of spiritual living I had never perceived, but it had always been within my reach.

Let us lay a foundation of understanding so we can learn to walk in the Spirit and experience what it means to be an overcomer. If we are more than conquerors, then we should be seeing victory in our lives as we seek to walk in Christ's rest.

The first step is believing this basic truth. You have been crucified with Christ. Have been. Not will be. Not want to be. You can't try to be. You *have been* crucified, the power of sin has been broken, and the body of sin has been done away with. This was given to you by God before the world began, but you have to believe God.

Consider again the words of **Hebrews 4:1-3**

¹ Therefore, since a promise remains of entering His rest, let us fear lest any of you seem to have come short of it.

² For indeed the gospel was preached to us as well as to them; but the word which they heard did not profit them, not

Christ's Threefold Work

being mixed with faith in those who heard *it*.

³ For we who have believed do enter that rest, as He has said: "So I swore in My wrath, 'They shall not enter My rest,' " although the works were finished from the foundation of the world.

There are a few things to draw from this passage. The subject is the Children of Israel, who were given the promise, but didn't receive it. They heard the same word being preached to us, but they did not profit from it because the word wasn't mixed with faith. Knowledge is not enough. We have to see God's promises, believe them, and then walk in them by faith.

Also note another important fact. The work was completed from the foundation of the world. In other words, God predestined them to receive the promise, but because they rejected the promise through unbelief, they did not profit from it and never received what God had prepared for them.

Look at the promises of God we have discussed so far. God has finished your work before the foundation of the world; you were in Christ; your flesh has been taken out of the way; the body of sin has been done away with; you are now free to live according to the Spirit. We are more than conquerors through Christ. You have overcome.[191]

Do you still struggle with the flesh? Have you perfectly conformed to the image of Christ? Are you more than a conqueror? Or does your flesh still rise up and seize control of areas of weakness in your life? If we're honest, we must acknowledge how we fall short of these promises. But it doesn't have to be this way.

Each day you should be seeing your spiritual nature rising up and your flesh should be losing its grip. The work is already done, but we have to learn to recognize the flesh and put our faith in God's word. Most of us pray, "Lord help me to overcome my temper. Help me to stop being selfish. Help me to not lust. Help me to..." name the weakness. The truth is that God has already helped you overcome these things. "Lord, crucify my flesh," is a prayer of unbelief, for God has already declared that He has crucified it.

The focus of our lives must be to look to the Spirit where our power resides, and stop beating the air with prayers against the flesh.

---

[191] 1 John 4:4, Hebrews 4:1-3, Colossians 2:14, Romans 6:6

The flesh is dead in Christ. Our body still has sin in its members, but we are instructed to reckon ourselves dead to sin. To reckon means to account. God has declared that the flesh is dead in Christ and I must agree with God and account myself dead in Christ. From that position, I have the freedom to live. This is explained in **Galatians 2:20**

> I have been crucified with Christ; it is no longer I who live, but Christ lives in me; and the *life* which I now live in the flesh I live by faith in the Son of God, who loved me and gave Himself for me.

We have been put to death in the flesh through Jesus on the cross so that we might live with Him in the Spirit. We have died in the flesh, but made alive by the Spirit. You must choose to live in that promise or live according to your own understanding.

Jesus' death on the cross freed us from the power of sin, and Jesus' resurrection from the dead gave us new life. We were in Christ on the cross, and the only thing lacking was our faith in His work. Once we believed, the promise was fulfilled and Christ came into us.[192] Now we are in Him, and He in us. Christ began residing in us when we became the new creation.

Just as we believed in the cross to receive forgiveness of sin, we also must believe in the cross for the power over the flesh. But don't stop there. We also must put our faith in Christ's resurrection, which gives us power to live victoriously in Him. In the next chapter, we'll examine how we not only died in Christ, but also now live according to an eternal nature.

Discussion Questions:

Why was Jesus put to death in the flesh?

Where is sin born in our lives?

What is the handwriting of requirments that were against us?

According to 1 John 2:2, whose sins did Jesus die for?

---

[192] John 14:20

Christ's Threefold Work

Does the Bible teach that Jesus' spirit had to be tortured in hell? Are there scriptures to support this?

Why does the flesh have to die before receiving life in the Spirit?

Does not believing in Jesus condemn people?

Can scripture be used for ungodly purposes?

How did Jesus take Satan's deception by twisting the scriptures, and put the word into the right perspective?

How do we rule over the sin trying to rule our minds?

Review Titus 2:11-15. How does grace teach us to deny the desires of sin?

Why does legalism despise grace?

Why does sin despise grace?

Why did Paul warn the church, "You have abandoned Christ and fallen from grace?"

How does someone restore grace to their life?

When we blow it, what must be done to make right the wrong?

According to Romans 7:25, how is the law of sin served? How is the law of God served?

If we have been predestined to live victoriously, how does this affect our faith?

Do we pray, hoping God will fulfill His word, or do we seek with confidence, knowing He has already fulfilled His word for us?

Dying to Live

Understanding the power of the resurrection is the most neglected part of Christianity, and the most limiting factor of our faith. Dying to our old nature is only the beginning of the Christian life. While our goal is to overcome sin, we aren't called to focus on our sinful behaviors. No one overcomes by dwelling on what is dying. We don't set our eyes on what is passing away, but what is emerging as new life. The new focus of the Christian life is the resurrection power of Christ and how that power is made manifest in us.

The first step toward eternal life is the understanding that we have redemption through His blood, and have the forgiveness of sins.[193] The law not only reveals the righteousness of God, but it also reveals our inability to measure up to the fullness of God. When a person comes to the realization that they can't measure up to God's perfect standard, they are now in a position to see the value of the gift of God's grace.

Do not fall into the trap of thinking that God's grace gives you the power to measure up to the law. Any who are in the Spirit are not under the law. Period. There is no law to keep. Our only focus is the grace of God that welcomes us into eternal life. That life is not merely for the future, but it is for now. Grace invites us to walk in the Spirit by our eternal life during this present time. Our main concern is to not allow the flesh to draw us back into a temporal standard or carnal way of perceiving life.

Whether something is of the flesh or Spirit is what we judge. Jesus said, "Do not judge according to appearance, but judge with a righteous judgment."[194] Righteousness is only found in the Spirit, so righteous judgment is based on what is in the Spirit and what is not.

Sin or not sin isn't the focus, for anything that is not of faith is sin.[195] Whatever is not of faith is of the flesh. Period. Whether something is religious or secular, sinful or pious, indulgent or disciplined, these are not the evaluators of good. The flesh can be expressed through acts that appear good, or acts that appear sinful.

---

[193] Ephesians 1:7, Colossians 1:14, Romans 3:25, Romans 5:9
[194] John 7:24
[195] Romans 14:23

Dying to Live

But if it is of the flesh, it is still standing on a corrupt foundation that is passing away and will not enter into eternal life.

Don't fall back into the human standard of evaluating right and wrong. Our liberty is measured this way: **1 Corinthians 10:23-24**

23 All things are lawful for me, but not all things are helpful; all things are lawful for me, but not all things edify.

24 Let no one seek his own, but each one the other's *well-being.*

If we are in faith, all things are lawful because the law has already been fulfilled in Christ and we are in Christ. Our standard of measure is two-fold. One, does it help or edify others? If the answer is 'no', then we should use restraint because of our love for the brethren. Second, does it shift our focus away from Christ? If it draws me into the flesh, then it is also drawing me out of the Spirit. **Galatians 5:18** says:

But if you are led by the Spirit, you are not under the law.

In the flesh, we only have the law, but in the Spirit, the law is not our concern. Looking to Christ is our focus – not religion, works, liberty, or restrictions. Works and godliness will flow naturally into our lives, but do not put your focus on any of these. It's a trap that will take you out of the Spirit and put you back into the flesh where you are trying to measure up to the standard of the law. If God wanted us to be under the law, He would not have placed us in Christ and declared us free from the law.

After we are born anew, nothing changes. Let me reiterate this critical point again. We have a tendency to fall back into the old way of thinking. People often try to live out the Christian life the way they tried and failed to find salvation. Just as our eyes were opened to salvation once we realized our need for Christ, we also find victory in Christ once we realize our inability to become godly by human effort.

As we have already discussed, in Adam we had a nature that is bent toward sin. Yet we were created in God's image, meant to reflect the glory of God. The law reveals God's nature and character, and because we were created to reflect that character, sin causes us to fall short, thus "all have sinned and fallen short of the glory of God."[196]

---

[196] Romans 3:23

After receiving the gift of grace, the flesh still falls short and we are still dependent upon grace. We will always be dependent upon grace. We will never be dependent on human effort.

From the beginning, God warned that the wages of sin was death and that in the day man rebelled, he would die. He would die spiritually, and he would be destined for the wages of sin – death in judgment. Yet God so loved the world that He gave Himself as the payment for sin.[197] Christ was born under the law, fulfilled the law, and condemned sin in His own flesh. Justice demands a penalty, but in Christ, we have already received the penalty of death.

In our culture, we see the same thing. If someone breaks the law, we expect there to be consequences. A judge that ignores the law is considered corrupt. Where there is no law, there can be no order. Civilization cannot survive without the rule of law. This is no different in spiritual civilization.

Because the law demands justice, the Bible says that God remained just, while being the justifier of the one who has faith in Jesus.[198] God did not break His own law in order to extend us mercy. Instead, he bore the penalty in His own body, taking our judgment upon Himself and paying the wages of sin. His blood redeems us.

This is where most teaching stops. But this is only the first part of Christ's completed work. Not only did He pay for our sins with His blood to redeem us, but He crucified us on the cross with Him. We can boil it down into a mental sized bite by reviewing the summary of **Romans 6:6**

> Knowing this, that our old man was crucified with *Him,*
> that the body of sin might be done away with, that we
> should no longer be slaves of sin.

Paying for the sin is one thing. Getting rid of the cause of sin is quite another matter. Let's get a word picture. Suppose a food producer has a salmonella outbreak. People are getting sick and dying from eating the food produced from this company. How do we stop the outbreak?

We could contact all the stores and do a recall on the contaminated food, but that wouldn't solve the problem. It would

---

[197] John 3:16, 1 John 2:2
[198] Romans 3:26

Dying to Live

eliminate the immediate threat, but as long as the plant is in operation, everything it produces will still be contaminated. Cleaning up the symptoms doesn't solve the problem. The source has to be eliminated.

Stopping at redemption is the same dilemma. Jesus took all the offenses against us out of the way, nailing them to the cross, but that doesn't fix the sinner. As long as I'm still living for sin, my life will remain infected. I can confess my sins and keep seeking forgiveness, but this is not the promise we have been given. Yet this is how most people view Christianity. We call ourselves, "Sinners saved by grace," but this falls short of the truth.

The sinner must be put to death. I realize I'm rehashing a little bit here, but it is critical that we understand this truth. Jesus did not just die for your sins. He put your old man to death on the cross, and the body of sin has been done away with.

We are no longer enslaved by our old ways, which were contrary to God, but instead we are now free to live as God intended.

The sin factory has been crucified with Christ and the righteousness of Christ is now in its place. The sin-maker has been done away with, and the Righteousness Giver now empowers us. Understanding this truth is important, for it reveals that we have indeed been freed from sin.

People who don't understand grace often ask, "If grace is taught the way some teach it, and the promise is that where sin abounds, grace even more abounds, doesn't that equal a license to sin? Is telling people that Jesus forgives sins, past, present, and future and encouragement to keep on sinning?"

Grace can sound this way unless we realize that we are not only forgiven for sins, but also freed from sin. Our sin maker has been crucified with Christ.

Even this is an incomplete picture. Life cannot be lived in a vacuum. We not only turn from sin, but toward Christ. Dying in Christ is the first step, but we also live in Him. We are buried with Christ, *and* raised as a new creation. Now all things are of God because all things have been made new.[199]

The concept of having a license to sin can only exist if we are still focusing on the flesh. That's an incomplete gospel. We aren't

---

[199] 2 Corinthians 5:17-18

Dying to Live   241 only saying that we have been forgiven and all sin has been paid. We are also not only saying that the sinful nature is dead and gone. The rest of the message is that a new life was resurrected with Christ and we have a new spiritual nature. A nature rooted in the Spirit that is fully experienced through faith in Christ in the Spirit.

If Christ is now the focus, where does that leave sin? Can someone who focuses on grace sin? Jesus is the embodiment of grace. To sin, we must turn from Christ and pursue fleshly desires. But when we focus on the person of Christ – the living truth of grace – how can we do anything but escape from sin?

Remember the woman caught in adultery? Why was she brought to Jesus and not just judged by the Jewish legal system? The Bible says, "We beheld the only begotten of the Father, full of grace and truth."[200] Everyone who beheld Christ beheld grace. Even Jesus' enemies recognized his grace (or favor) toward sinners.

Remember our earlier discussion? Legalism hates grace because it views grace as a threat. The legalists of Jesus' day hated grace because it set people free from the law. Their greatest desire was to catch Jesus in His words and find a way to accuse Him. When they caught the woman in the act, they remembered Jesus and said, "Aha! We've got Him now." They knew Jesus would show her grace, and if they could pit grace against the law, they believed that the law would condemn grace.

"Jesus, we caught this woman in adultery – in the very act. The law says that she should be stoned. But what do *you* say?" The legalists smirked, believing they had set the perfect trap. Let's see Jesus get out of that one.

What irony! Jesus was God in the flesh – the one who gave the law. And now man, who was given the law, was now trying to use the law against the God who gave it.

What was Jesus' reaction? According to scripture, Jesus fulfilled the law completely, and then presented Himself as the perfect sacrifice to bear the penalty for us, who fell short of the law. This woman's sin would soon be paid on the cross, but now He was forced to judge her according to the law before the offering of grace was complete.

---

[200] John 1:14-17

Jesus stooped down and began writing in the dirt. The Bible doesn't tell us what He wrote, but I envision Him writing out the law, and then the heart of its condemnation. The law says do not commit adultery. To look upon a woman and lust is adultery in your heart. The law says not to steal. But to be greedy is thievery in the heart. Covetousness is idolatry. Hatred is murder. On and on He wrote until the woman's accusers became impatient.

"Are you going to make a decision? The law says she must die. What do *you* say?"

I can see Jesus underlining a few convicting parallels He had written and then standing up. "Let the one without sin cast the first stone at her." He stooped down again and circled adultery and lust. Greed and thievery. Hatred and murder.

Each person was convicted by their own conscience, and beginning at the elders, they dropped their stones and walked away. The younger ones looked in astonishment as those they viewed as law keepers conceded to their own guilt. When Jesus looked up, He said, "Woman, where are your accusers?"

"There are none," she said.

Jesus was the only person present who was qualified to throw a stone. Yet the voice of grace declared, "Neither do I accuse you. Go and sin no more."

The law condemns. Grace sets the accused free. Does that freedom point back to sin? No! It gives us the freedom to walk away from sin *and* its condemnation.

Unless you live in the resurrection power of Christ, you cannot fulfill the Christian life given to you. You must first believe Jesus died for your sins to receive forgiveness. You then must believe in His crucifixion, which takes away the sin nature so you are no longer under its power. Then you must believe in His resurrection. Every step of the Christian life is by faith. Everything is an offering of grace, apart from human effort.

Do you trust in God's grace? Do you believe that the grace of God has the power to set you free? Or do you believe as the religious leaders who challenged Christ believed; that the law must protect us from grace? The law cannot set you free and the law cannot root sin out of your life.

People attempt to live life in reverse. The law is given in order to reveal sin and make it exceedingly sinful.[201] The law was never given to make men righteous, but to expose the truth that each person is sinful by nature and in need of grace.

Grace has fulfilled the law, and through grace sin is defeated. Legalism and the law empowers sin. Grace defeats it.

So why do people say that grace is a license to sin? Because they trust more in man's ability to become self-righteous than God's power to transform our lives through grace.

People seem to have an easy time believing that Jesus died for their sins, but then struggle with everything else. Faith comes by hearing, and hearing by the word of Christ.[202] So what happens if we exclude the parts of God's word that don't fit church or denominational traditions? We are interfering with the work of God that calls us to believe by faith. We are to receive the whole counsel of God – not merely that which fits into a doctrinal box that we can keep within our control.

It isn't the church's role to control its members. It is the role of the Holy Spirit to convict hearts, reveal truth through the word (preached and read), and transform believers into the image of Christ. Legalistic rules can only interfere with the Holy Spirit. Non-biblical beliefs take the focus off the Spirit and make people into man-dependent followers of religion. Rules and regulations cannot do the work God has set aside for Himself. Only God can change the heart.

The whole counsel of God must be preached – even if it falls outside of our established belief systems. Until someone hears about Christ's forgiveness, they can't believe in His power to redeem them. Or as the Bible puts it, "How then shall they call on Him in whom they have not believed? And how shall they believe in Him of whom they have not heard? And how shall they hear without a preacher?"[203]

This same truth applies to everything else in scripture. We must also hear about our old life being crucified with Christ. We must also hear about our new life being raised with Christ. We must understand what the Bible is teaching on this topic so we can put our faith in

---

[201] Romans 7:13
[202] Romans 10:17
[203] Romans 10:14

Dying to Live

Christ and live according to His power. Only then can we experience the fullness of God in our lives.

I say that understanding these things allows us to experience God's fullness, but a better way of saying it might be that it opens the door of understanding so we can begin to explore God's fullness, for you will never experience all that God is. Our God is infinite, and a finite person will never reach the end of what God has stored up for us to find in Him.

Each step into understanding becomes a foundation by which we can reach the next step of understanding. You serve an infinite God, and you will never cease from discovering new truths of the word – unless you either resist obedience, don't believe, become lifted up with pride, or fall into the error of thinking you have reached the mountain top and therefore quit seeking.

With all this having been said, let's examine the promise of Christ's resurrection power given to every believer.

You have been raised with Christ

This is a topic that speaks for itself. I am going to recite a number of scriptures that I hope will speak to your heart. These are spread throughout the New Testament, but when drawn together, they paint a wonderful picture of our resurrection power through Christ. **1 Peter 1:3**

> Blessed *be* the God and Father of our Lord Jesus Christ, who according to His abundant mercy has begotten us again to a living hope through the resurrection of Jesus Christ from the dead,

Through the cross, you died. By death, you were freed from the requirements of the law and its claim over your life. While that is good news indeed, the greater news is that you are now a new creation. Take to heart the greatness of the promise in **2 Corinthians 5:17**

> Therefore, if anyone *is* in Christ, *he is* a new creation; old things have passed away; behold, all things have become new.

If you are in Christ, you are not the same person. The old passed away because it died in Christ. You have been crucified with Christ. Past tense. We have already seen the Bible's explanation that the one born of God cannot sin. Now let's bring in this passage from **1 Peter 1:22-23**

> [22] Since you have purified your souls in obeying the truth through the Spirit in sincere love of the brethren, love one another fervently with a pure heart,
>
> [23] having been born again, not of corruptible seed but incorruptible, through the word of God which lives and abides forever,

Let these passages sink in for a moment. Something happens at your conversion. Being converted is not just a mental agreement with the ideology of Christianity. Indeed, there are many who claim the Christian faith in principle only, but this is not who we are talking about. Jesus said, "Unless you are born again, you cannot see the Kingdom of Heaven."[204]

Just believing the Bible is true does not make one a Christian. There must be faith – the answer of God's call to surrender to the truth of God where we release ourselves into God's hands. He takes our life and places us in Christ. This means we have been forgiven of sin because we are under the covering of the blood of Christ. Our old nature has been crucified through the cross of Christ, and we are raised as a new creation through the resurrection of Christ.

Once someone is born again – or is raised with Christ, they are a new creation. At this moment two things happen. God places His Holy Spirit within us and gives us a new nature, born out of that Spirit. We are literally a new person. The new man is born of God, finds its life in God, and because it is of the Holy Spirit, that new life is incorruptible. It cannot sin, for it is born of God. The flesh has no power over the new creation God places within us.

That which sins is destined to die. It cannot live, for once sin occurs, the pronouncement of death is upon it. The soul that sins must die.[205] The only way to purge sin, as we have seen, is death. That is

---

[204] John 3:3
[205] Ezekiel 18:20

Dying to Live

why salvation cannot be found in any other name than Jesus Christ.[206] Only Jesus died on our behalf and paid the penalty of sin. Unless a life is in Christ, death remains the penalty of sin. In Christ we died, and only in Christ has that payment already been made. All who are outside of Christ are still under condemnation and remain destined for the wages of sin – judgment and death.

Our new nature cannot sin. It is impossible. If it could, it wouldn't have its life in God. Anything that sins inherits the wages of sin, which is death. But we have eternal life, cannot sin, and our inner man cannot be corrupted.

If this is true, it begs the question, "If I am new, my old nature is dead, and my new nature is immune to sin, why do I still sin?"

This is one of the great mysteries of faith. A mystery that God has revealed in His word, but most misunderstand. Some say the Christian cannot sin. Others say we are merely sinners saved by grace. While others still make the claim that each time we sin, we fall under condemnation again, and are in need of another salvation.

Eternal life can't die. Those who teach that we lose salvation, are saved again, and lose salvation yet again, simply do not understand the scriptures. Can our inner man die and still remain incorruptible? Can we say that our inner man sins and must be cleansed while remaining consistent with scripture? None of these can be. If life is eternal, it cannot die. If our spirit is incorruptible, it cannot sin. Confusion arises when the line between the flesh and the Spirit is blurred in our understanding.

The flesh cannot be redeemed. All sin is through the flesh. All that is affected by sin must be destroyed. God doesn't put lipstick on a corpse and call it clean. The corpse must be buried. And we see this truth throughout scripture.

Did you know the earth will not be redeemed? God will use the earth as the physical avenue in which to communicate His purposes, but once that purpose has been fulfilled, the earth will be put to death and raised anew. Sound strange? These passages may help to grasp this truth. **2 Peter 3:10-13**

[10] But the day of the Lord will come as a thief in the night, in which the heavens will pass away with a great noise, and the elements will melt with fervent heat; both the earth and the

---

[206] Acts 4:12, John 14:6

works that are in it will be burned up.

^{11} Therefore, since all these things will be dissolved, what manner *of persons* ought you to be in holy conduct and godliness,

^{12} looking for and hastening the coming of the day of God, because of which the heavens will be dissolved, being on fire, and the elements will melt with fervent heat?

^{13} Nevertheless we, according to His promise, look for new heavens and a new earth in which righteousness dwells.

A small picture of this is also found in Revelation 21:1.

This truth of scripture helps to gain an accurate understanding of how we should view this life. Is the world in chaos? Yes. Is it our job to change the world? No. We are called to follow Jesus' picture of outreach. Jesus said, "You are not of this world, but I have called you out of the world." Then He promised that the world will hate those who are not of its system of living.

When the church is living like the church, it will affect the world around us in a positive way, but our focus is not on turning the world into the church. Our focus is to go into all the world and make disciples by calling people out of the world and into Christ.

It's God's job to call hearts to the cross. It's God's job to govern the world. It's our job to become a disciple, take the good news into all the world, and then teach those who respond how to become disciples as well. And what is a disciple? Let's look at **Luke 9:23-25**

^{23} Then He said to *them* all, "If anyone desires to come after Me, let him deny himself, and take up his cross daily, and follow Me.

^{24} "For whoever desires to save his life will lose it, but whoever loses his life for My sake will save it.

^{25} "For what profit is it to a man if he gains the whole world, and is himself destroyed or lost?

There is a cost to discipleship. That cost is losing the world and all we have invested into the world. If anyone loves the world, the love of God is not in him. Consider **1 John 2:15-17**

^{15} Do not love the world or the things in the world. If anyone loves the world, the love of the Father is not in him.

Dying to Live

¹⁶ For all that *is* in the world -- the lust of the flesh, the lust of the eyes, and the pride of life -- is not of the Father but is of the world.

¹⁷ And the world is passing away, and the lust of it; but he who does the will of God abides forever.

Everything our eyes see is passing away. Why love what is dying at the expense of that which cannot die? The church is not called to set up God's kingdom on earth. This is a belief that is growing in popularity, but anyone who studies the word can see that Christ returns to rescue the world from the grip of the evil one. He doesn't come after the church establishes its own kingdom, but after the antichrist establishes his kingdom.

The world is not our focus. It is our mission field, but not our focus. We are going behind the enemy's lines to proclaim that God has rescued any who will receive it by faith. It isn't our work, but God's.

A disciple is one who has abandoned the world and all its empty promises and taken hold of Christ. A disciple is someone who sees the reality of the eternal, and this causes them to realize the falsehood of the temporal. Each believer must realize that dying to this life is how we receive the new life. We don't keep both. Consider the words of Jesus in **Luke 14:26-30**

²⁶ "If anyone comes to Me and does not hate his father and mother, wife and children, brothers and sisters, yes, and his own life also, he cannot be My disciple.

²⁷ "And whoever does not bear his cross and come after Me cannot be My disciple.

²⁸ "For which of you, intending to build a tower, does not sit down first and count the cost, whether he has *enough* to finish *it* --

²⁹ "lest, after he has laid the foundation, and is not able to finish, all who see *it* begin to mock him,

³⁰ "saying, 'This man began to build and was not able to finish.'
...

³³ "So likewise, whoever of you does not forsake all that he has cannot be My disciple.

The call of discipleship is a call to forsake all. We are called to forsake dreams, hopes, possessions, relationships, and any pleasure that does not come from God's hand. Does this mean that we abandoned wives and children? No, but it does mean that we cannot choose the will of others over the call of God. In reality, it is those rooted in the world that abandon the relationship. Knowing this to be a possibility is something we must consider before stepping out by faith.

I met a Jewish pastor who chose to follow Christ. His family threatened to disown him if he didn't abandon Christ. He chose Christ and was disowned and disinherited. Some of his family later came to Christ, but others did not. He willingly forsook all, leaving the relationships into God's hands.

Many don't count the cost, begin to build their life on Christ, and when the cost becomes great, they abandon the call and settle for the world.

The truth is that the cost is small in the eternal scheme of things, but great in this life. Or at least it appears great. Those who view life through the eyes of the world will value the things of the world. And then the cost seems too great. But when someone sees the reality of the eternal, they recognize the answer to Jesus' question, "What profit is there if someone gains the whole world but loses their soul?"

There is no profit. To invest our lives into something destined for ashes is a foolish investment. But the world looks at the Christian, and because they cannot see the eternal, it seems utterly foolish to abandon all the world offers to lay hold of what they think is religion.

It's not mere religion. It is to lay hold of Christ with the understanding that the eternal is what is real, and the world is the mirage.

Don't expect the world to understand faith. Don't expect your friends and family to understand your call. Don't even expect the church to understand your call into the Spirit. Any who view life through the eyes of flesh will scoff at the idea of true faith.

People will give lip-service to faith, but when it comes to the cost, the truth of their focus will be shown. "You have to be practical," they will say. Most people trust God up to the point where they recognize they are becoming truly dependent upon Him. Once someone realizes that God is leading them into a life where they

Dying to Live

cannot meet their own needs and cannot protect themselves should God fail them, most will turn back.

When the way of the cross puts us into a position where God is stripping our confidence away, most will turn back. When the things in this life that we value begin to fall away, our affections are either torn from the flesh, or we cling to our earthly affections and let go of Christ. That is when the cost is too great. We would have begun the tower, but not able to finish. Not seeing God's provision ahead of time would have then been too big of a step of faith to obey. Losing things we once thought were valuable would then have been too big of a step of faith to obey.

When friends and family say you are being a fool, that is when Jesus says, "Anyone who loves father, mother, husband, wife, or anyone else is not worthy of Me."

When your own soul cries out to turn back, that's when Jesus says, "He who does not hate his own life also, cannot be My disciple."

It's a hard calling. It's not hard because the work is burdensome, but because God leads us out of all confidence in the flesh and into complete confidence in Him. Some will be called to abandon careers; others will not. Some will be called to sell all and go into missions; some will not. Some will see their families turn on them; others will see families follow them into the call.

This is where it becomes impossible to tell someone how to walk by faith. What God does in the life of a faithful man or woman will be a great testimony of His faithfulness, but it is not the example of how God works in your life. You follow the call of God as He reveals Himself to you. And that does not come by making a decision based on your own will. It comes through knowing Christ so intimately that you recognize His voice and follow where He leads.

It all begins with the call to die. Die to your life, count the cost, and look to Christ without ever looking back. Then you will see each step of God's leading. Count the cost and then die to this world – and your own life. Then you'll see true life.

Let go of what is passing away and experience true life in the Spirit. That is how we experience the abundant life now, and see the joy of God's promises yet to be fulfilled. When we stand in eternity, the things of this world will be a forgotten mirage. How then ought we to live at this present time?

Discussion Questions:

Does grace give you the power to fulfill the law? Explain.

Did God violate His law to save us?

Read Romans 3:23-26. What does it mean that God was just and the justifier of the one who has faith in Jesus?

Why is it necessary to put the body of sin to death and remove the old nature?

What is the difference between a sinner saved by grace and a new creation in Christ?

Does grace empower people to sin?

Read Romans 7:13. Does the law empower sin or does it create righteousness?

What does it mean that you have become a new creation?

Why is our new nature incorruptible?

What does it mean to be in Christ?

What do we receive when we have faith and are placed in Christ?

What does it mean to hate fathers, mothers, husbands, wives, etc, in Jesus' call to follow?

How do we reconcile this to God's call to express His love to others?

What does it mean to take up the cross and follow Christ?

If God calls someone to quit their job, is that how God works in everyone's life?

How do you count the cost of discipleship?

The Cross – Our Victory Over Sin

2 Corinthians 5:21

> For He made Him who knew no sin *to be* sin for us, that we might become the righteousness of God in Him.

An exchanged life. This is the message of atonement. Jesus Christ took your sin upon Himself, paid the penalty of that sin, and placed His righteousness upon you. It is not your righteousness. The righteousness of God is credited to your account once you surrender by faith.

The problem of our sin is that we don't comprehend our lack of righteousness. Man, in his own heart, believes he is good. As long as we think of ourselves as good, we see no need of salvation, for what are we being saved from? I've done prison ministry and discovered that even the vilest criminal believes he's a good person. "I've done bad things, but I still believe I'm a good person," I heard a prisoner say.

Where there is no recognized need, there is no deliverance. This is the entire purpose of the law. The mind rooted in the flesh believes that rules, regulations, and deeds serve to make us good. If I do good things, I am good, right? This is a mind who trusts in the law. People think the law says to do good and you are good; do bad and you are bad. Or the attitude of many is that our good only has to be slightly better than our bad. If we tip the scales in our favor, then we are good.

Cultural standards are not the measurement of righteousness. Look at Germany in the 1940s. We look back at the holocaust and are appalled that an entire populous could be so cruel. We think of the extermination of the Jews, but the people were not only haters of the Jews, but anyone who didn't fit their narrow focus of being worthy of humanity. They hated the Russians and after capturing millions of them at the beginning of their war with Russia, 80% of the prisoners were allowed to starve to death.

When they invaded Poland, their goal was to subjugate an entire group of inferior people to serve them as slaves. The SS worked the slaves with minimal food and supplies. The Nazis used them like tools, and once they were worn out, they were discarded like trash.

We look back on this attitude and think, how could so many people be so blind? But the truth is, Germany is an extreme example of what happens in every culture. Any populous could have fallen into that same mindset under the right cultural conditioning. In fact, many smaller countries have acted out in similar ways, but because the impact wasn't felt by the world, it has gone largely unnoticed. If the consensus of the culture determines what is right and wrong, the people can always justify their own sins. The reason is that where there are no concrete values in place, the cultural norms shift based on what moves people at that moment. Or the culture can be manipulated by persuasive leaders.

If a persuasive leader arises and his values sound beneficial, the culture slowly shifts to accept his values. Even those who would not normally be given to such actions will adopt the cultural norms being established. It may take a short time, or it may take generations, but what was considered sin yesterday will be accepted today and approved tomorrow. That is unless there is something firm to stand upon.

In time, people lose a sense of right and wrong because they have no moral compass to depend upon. What seems like a pleasure is actually corruption – whether we can see it or not.

The adult 'entertainment' industry passes itself off as innocent fun, but behind the scenes are broken lives and shattered people. Many don't realize that most human trafficking is for the purpose of supplying the seedy side of the industry. Sin presents a pretty face, but behind the mask is always corruption and sorrow.

The culture argues that standards should not be concrete, but apply this logic to anything else? What if accounting was up to the public norm? Who are you to say that my checking account is empty? It's just numbers on the screen and money isn't even real. It's just an electronic transaction and not even a real thing of value. Even the dollar bill is just paper. It doesn't represent anything. Right?

What if science was completely subjective? Could anything be known? Would it lead to order and knowledge, or confusion and chaos? It is only when we have a moral standard that people begin to scoff. The reason is that moral standards interfere with our desire to gratify self.

What we often fail to realize is that every action leads somewhere. Denying that a path leads to destruction does not change the end of the path. Giving soothing words to someone does not change their circumstances. The Bible warns that the end of a thing is better than the beginning.[207] What our life produces is more important than the pleasure of the moment.

The culture says, "Enjoy the journey," and "Live for the moment." But the Bible says to number our days so we may apply our hearts to wisdom.[208] There is an end and it is worthy of our life's investment. The apostles said, "If we have hope in this life only, we are people most pitiable."[209] They sacrificed life now for the greatness of what lay ahead. In fact, the Bible says that the sufferings of this life are not even worthy to be compared to what lies beyond this world.[210]

One question emerges quite often when discussing sin. Why is something a sin? Who is to say what is sin and what is not? Or, why did God arbitrarily decide to make certain things sin?

This can easily be understood by looking at the scriptures. The first thing to note is that mankind was created in the image of God. We were created to be a reflection of God's glory. Yet the Bible says that all have sinned and fallen short of the glory of God.[211] In other words, anything that causes us to fall short of God's glory is sin.

God's law and moral standard are direct reflections of His own nature and character. God has set up boundaries that show us what we must do in order to perfectly reflect the glory of God – for that is what we were created to do. God created mankind for a purpose. As our Creator, He has the right to require us to act within the boundaries He established. It also means that the heart of man will never find rest until it stands in the purpose we have been created to fulfill.

We try to fill the void with pleasures, things, and our own egos, but nothing satisfies. This is what drives man deeper into sin. It is a quest to fulfill by himself what can only be fulfilled in God.

---

[207] Ecclesiastes 7:8
[208] Psalm 90:12
[209] 1 Corinthians 15:19
[210] Romans 8:18
[211] Romans 3:23

Our Victory Over Sin

But as we have seen, man fell through Adam and each person inherits that fallen nature. Human nature cannot fulfill the righteousness of God. It is impossible, for the glory of God is absent and a fallen nature has taken its place. God established the law to do two things. The law reveals the unchanging perfect nature of God and the requirement we must fulfill in order to conform to God's nature. Second, the law serves to show man that he is fallen and can never conform to God's nature. Look at **Romans 3:19-20**

> [19] Now we know that whatever the law says, it says to those who are under the law, that every mouth may be stopped, and all the world may become guilty before God.
>
> [20] Therefore by the deeds of the law no flesh will be justified in His sight, for by the law *is* the knowledge of sin.

On the surface, this passage appears to be a strange contradiction of how we view keeping a moral standard. Who is under the law? Anyone who is not born of the Spirit is under the law. The Bible says, "If you are led by the Spirit, you are not under the law."[212]

Notice one important truth in the above passage. By doing the deeds of the law, you cannot be justified in God's sight. God's moral standard is not presented for you to keep rules in order to please God. These serve only to keep sin in check and show you that you are guilty before God. Once you come to the point where you realize you cannot please God through your flawed human nature, you can then have eyes to see the gift of Christ.

The Weakness of the Law

If it were possible for you to keep the whole law, you still cannot change your nature. The promise of God was never given to those who kept the law, but to those who trust Christ. Let's look at an illustration we touched on earlier in this book – the Old Testament example of Moses and Joshua.

Through Moses, God delivered the law to the people. We often think of the Law as the Ten Commandments, but there were many more than 10. The first five books of the Old Testament are referred

---

[212] Galatians 5:18

to as the books of Moses. Within these books is the whole law given to Israel.

Consider the purpose of Moses. His main purpose was to lead God's people from Egypt (the land of bondage) to God's rest, the Promised Land. As we have already discussed, when God's people refused to trust in God's deliverance, God swore in His wrath, "None of you shall enter my rest." Through Moses (the law), God led the people across the desert and to the Jordan River. On the other side was the Promised Land – God's rest.

The Lord allowed the people to see their opposition. Men of great stature were in the land and the people disbelieved the word of the Lord and put their trust in the flesh. Knowing they couldn't defeat their opponents through human effort, they trusted in fear and rebelled against the Lord.

When the Lord refused to give them the promise, many of the people decided to take it by their own efforts. They formed a party and prepared to enter. God warned those who thought they could inherit the promise by human effort that they could not receive the land unless He led them in. Some tried anyway and were defeated.[213]

The promise could only be received by faith and only when God drew them in. If they had no faith in God's provision, their best efforts could not lead them in. This is similar to the statement of Christ. He is called our rest. Yet Jesus said, "No one can come to Me unless the Father draws him."[214]

The law failed to bring the people in. After wandering in the desert for forty years, the law failed again. Remember when we looked at the failure of Moses? When the people murmured against Moses because there was no water, God commanded Moses to touch a rock with his staff. Out of frustration with the constant complaining of the people, he struck the rock in anger instead of touching it. Because Moses failed in one point, God declared, "Because you didn't believe…you will not enter the land. You will see it with your eyes, but shall not enter."[215]

Moses then led the people to the edge of the promise. God took him upon a mountain so he could see the promise. Though he

---

[213] Numbers 14:39-45
[214] John 6:44
[215] Numbers 20:11-12

earnestly desired to go there, he was only permitted to see it with his eyes, but not enter in. His last effort was to climb the mountain and God said, "I have caused you to see it with your eyes, but you shall not cross over there." And there Moses died and Joshua took his place.

The law took the people to the edge of the promise, but could not take the people into the rest of God. We see this played out in the New Testament. Jesus fulfilled the law perfectly. He took the law up the hill to Calvary, nailed it to the cross and died. The law took him to the point of death to fulfill the law, but the law never brought the promise to mankind. On Calvary the law was both fulfilled and the covenant died. A new covenant was born in Christ and taken down from the mountain of Calvary.

In Hebrew, the name Joshua means, Jehovah (God) is Salvation. The Old Testament was written in Hebrew. The New Testament was written in Greek. In Greek, the name Jesus means, God is Salvation. The law could only see the promise of God with its eyes, but only God's salvation could lead men into that promise. It was not men keeping the law that provided the promise – it was God's salvation that gave the promise.

The law failed in one point and was not permitted to enter. Moses did everything God asked, but in a moment of faithlessness, Moses acted in his flesh and failed. Therefore, the law only proved the inability of man to keep the perfect standard of God. The faithless complainers entered in when they trusted Joshua to lead them, but the law giver could not. Consider the words of **James 2:10**

For whoever shall keep the whole law, and yet stumble in one *point,* he is guilty of all.

Do you think you can please God through keeping a moral standard? Do you think the law can produce righteousness on your behalf? The law keeper will always fail to receive God's promise, but even those who fail miserably receive the promise of God through Christ. This is explained more fully in **Romans 8:3-6**

³ For what the law could not do in that it was weak through the flesh, God *did* by sending His own Son in the likeness of sinful flesh, on account of sin: He condemned sin in the flesh,

⁴ that the righteous requirement of the law might be fulfilled in us who do not walk according to the flesh but according to

the Spirit.

⁵ For those who live according to the flesh set their minds on the things of the flesh, but those *who live* according to the Spirit, the things of the Spirit.

⁶ For to be carnally minded *is* death, but to be spiritually minded *is* life and peace.

What is the weakness of the law? The law is perfect. The law is holy. The weakness of the law is not in God or His perfect standard. The weakness of the law is the flesh. It is human nature – a fallen nature that cannot be perfect. The law only serves to show you the need of a savior. Through the law, you can see the promise with your eyes, but you can never enter in. The promise is only received by faith – apart from the deeds of the law.[216]

Some will say that the Old Testament saints were saved through the law, but this is far from the case. Many wicked men kept the law outwardly, but God said He hated their assemblies, and would not accept their songs of praise or their sacrifices. The truth is that God has always accepted those who looked to Him by faith. The Old Testament saints sacrificed as a foreshadow of what would one day be fulfilled through Christ. We look back to the cross of Christ. Both we and they are redeemed through Christ. Consider **Hebrews 9:22-24, 10:1-6**

²² And according to the law almost all things are purified with blood, and without shedding of blood there is no remission.

²³ Therefore *it was* necessary that the copies of the things in the heavens should be purified with these, but the heavenly things themselves with better sacrifices than these.

²⁴ For Christ has not entered the holy places made with hands, *which are* copies of the true, but into heaven itself, now to appear in the presence of God for us;

Hebrews 10:1-6

¹ For the law, having a shadow of the good things to come, *and* not the very image of the things, can never with these same sacrifices, which they offer continually year by year, make those who approach perfect.

---

[216] Romans 3:28

Our Victory Over Sin

...

⁴ For *it is* not possible that the blood of bulls and goats could take away sins.
⁵ Therefore, when He came into the world, He said: "Sacrifice and offering You did not desire, But a body You have prepared for Me.
⁶ In burnt offerings and *sacrifices* for sin You had no pleasure.

It's a long passage and I encourage you to read it in its entirety. There were a few main points I want to draw your attention to. First, the sacrifices practiced in the Old Testament were copies of what was accomplished in heaven. In other words, they are symbolic and not the actual work of God. In heaven, Jesus paid for sin with the body prepared by God for the purpose of full redemption of man.

Second, notice that it is **not** possible for the blood of animal sacrifices to take away sin. The scripture says that it served as a yearly reminder of sin, but also that it was an act of faith. Those honored by God were not trusting in their own works. They did not trust that killing an animal would save them. They trusted in God and exercised their trust through keeping the commands God gave. As previously mentioned, those who were using works of the law to merit justification had this condemnation – God hates their sacrifices. He hates their assemblies. He even declared that He hated their feast days. All of these things God had commanded them to keep.

In Hebrews chapter 9, the Bible explains the practice of the law, then in chapter 10, the fulfillment of the law in Christ, then in 11, the fact that all these things – both the Old Testament based on the Law and New Testament based on Christ have the same foundation. They are both received through faith. Not done through faith in our practices, but by faith in God's provision of redemption. This is summed up in **Hebrews 11:6**

But without faith *it is* impossible to please *Him,* for he who comes to God must believe that He is, and *that* He is a rewarder of those who diligently seek Him.

While some believe God treated the Jews differently than the Gentiles, the Bible says the opposite. In case you aren't familiar with the word, Gentile, it is anyone who is not a Jew. The Bible often refers to Gentiles as uncircumcised. Circumcision was a sign of the Old Testament covenant. It was the symbolic removal of the flesh of the foreskin which represented the internal circumcision of the New Testament. They had the outer flesh cut away as a foreshadow of what we now experience. We have the inner flesh – our sinful nature – cut away. Both the Old and New Testament saints were saved by faith. This is explained in **Romans 3:29-31**

> ^{29} Or *is He* the God of the Jews only? *Is He* not also the God of the Gentiles? Yes, of the Gentiles also,
>
> ^{30} since *there is* one God who will justify the circumcised by faith and the uncircumcised through faith.
>
> ^{31} Do we then make void the law through faith? Certainly not! On the contrary, we establish the law.

Notice that those who were under the law were not justified by the law; they were justified by faith. Those raised under the law are justified by faith. First faith in God's coming provision, and then of what it represented – Jesus Christ. We who are not Jewish and raised under the law have the same God and the same faith. They kept the law by faith and then turn to Christ by faith. We are justified through faith – apart from the law completely.

Now that Christ has been revealed, we do not need to look to the law for justification at all. All things point to Christ. Where the Old Testament people had the law to convict them of sin, we have the Holy Spirit to convict us of sin. Jesus said that when the Holy Spirit comes, (which was fully realized on the day of Pentecost) He will convict the world of sin.[217]

That's why faith now comes by hearing the word of God.[218] The word is taught and the Holy Spirit convicts the heart of its sin. The realization of sin causes a person to reject God's conviction or it draws them to Christ. Conviction brings us to the realization of sin, and the cross reveals the provision of God's justification.

Then and only then can a person surrender to Christ. Until Christ is revealed by the Holy Spirit, the human mind is the only tool available. And the Bible warns that the natural mind cannot receive the things of God for they are foolishness to the flesh. Yet people still

---

[217] John 16:8
[218] Romans 10:17

Our Victory Over Sin

claim the name of Christ even though they have had no revelation by the Spirit.

When the natural man takes on Christ, human nature molds Christ into an image acceptable to the flesh. This is why someone can say, "Jesus is my best friend," and live completely contrary to Christ. However, Jesus said, "You are my friends *if* you do what I have commanded."[219] And the Bible says that anyone who knows Him will walk as He walked.[220]

The natural man looks to Christ as a supplement to their life in the flesh. Human nature wants a savior, but not a lord. The flesh desires to remain on the throne of our lives while making Jesus subject to our desires. But the call of the Spirit is, "If anyone desires to come after Me, let him deny himself, and take up his cross daily, and follow Me. For whoever desires to save his life will lose it, but whoever loses his life for My sake will save it. For what profit is it to a man if he gains the whole world, and is himself destroyed or lost?"[221]

The natural mind cannot comprehend the concept of dying to self and therefore cannot receive the things of the Spirit.

Escaping the Cruel Husband – The Law

The flesh is born into sin and cannot change its nature. It must die. Let me illustrate this with one other example. Take time to read this explanation in Romans chapter 7. It begins with saying that the law has dominion over us as long as we live. And what does the law say? The soul that sins shall certainly die. The Gospel of John states that Jesus did not come into the world to condemn the world, but to rescue the world from sin. Then scripture goes on to say, "He who believes in Him is not condemned; but he who does not believe is condemned already."

People are not condemned because they don't believe on Christ. People are already condemned, but Jesus came to deliver man from condemnation. The law has power over any who live. That is every person who has been born. For all have been born under the

---

[219] John 15:14
[220] 1 John 2:4-6
[221] Luke 9:23-25

corruption of Adam's fallen nature and all have sinned. We sin because we are sinners by nature. We aren't sinners because we sinned.

Here is the illustration that explains this so beautifully in Romans 7. The Bible uses the covenant of marriage as an example. A woman is bound by the law to stay with her husband as long as both are alive. The law is the husband and we are the wife. The law is a cruel husband. He has all the rights, we have none. We are bound by law to this husband and because we are also corrupted by sin, this husband is compelled to punish us. It is his nature to punish all who sin. We cannot break free unless the husband dies.

But there is a problem. The law cannot die. Heaven and earth will pass away, but the word of God – which is where the law came from – will never pass away.[222]

The heart of the problem is that the law is spiritual, but we are of the flesh. The flesh and the Spirit are at war with each other and can never agree.[223] We have irreconcilable differences, but the law does not permit us to leave our lawful husband and marry another. Yet Christ stands as the merciful husband that loves us and gave Himself for us. He is willing to lay down His life for his bride, but the law will not. The law demands that we lay down our lives as a penalty of sin. For the wages of sin is death.[224]

God will never violate His word, and a woman who divorces her husband and marries another would be an adulteress. Christ will not marry into adultery, yet He loves us and we love Him. But unless our husband dies, we can never be free. And because our husband is the law and is eternal, he cannot die.

Since the husband cannot die, the Bible reverses the solution and declares that the wife can die. Once she dies, the law has been nullified, for the one who dies has been freed from both the law and sin.[225] Since the law cannot die, we must die. Either that or remain married to our condemnation. Death is the call of Christianity. We die in Christ, but we are also raised with Him. In Christ we die and in

---

[222] Matthew 5:18, Matthew 24:35
[223] Galatians 5:17
[224] Romans 6:23
[225] Romans 6:7

Our Victory Over Sin

Christ we are raised into a new life – freed from the law and united with Christ. Look now at **Romans 6:3-7**

> [3] Or do you not know that as many of us as were baptized into Christ Jesus were baptized into His death?
>
> [4] Therefore we were buried with Him through baptism into death, that just as Christ was raised from the dead by the glory of the Father, even so we also should walk in newness of life.
>
> [5] For if we have been united together in the likeness of His death, certainly we also shall be *in the likeness* of *His* resurrection,
>
> [6] knowing this, that our old man was crucified with *Him,* that the body of sin might be done away with, that we should no longer be slaves of sin.
>
> [7] For he who has died has been freed from sin.

This is where Christianity begins. It is also why there is no other way to God. All efforts of man do nothing more than try to make us look better to the law, but the law demands perfection and we can never become perfect. Even if we could suddenly become perfect, we cannot undo the past, and the law doesn't allow for new beginnings.

But to die frees us from what once bound us. Not only are we freed from sin, but we are freed from the sinful nature that produced sin, and we are freed from the husband of the law. The law requires – the wages of sin is death. But in Christ, we have satisfied that requirement, for we have died in Christ.

We are in Christ

We being in Christ is a principle you'll see throughout the scripture. We don't die in the future sense. We died in the past tense. You were buried with Christ. You were crucified with Christ. Never do you see the Bible say that you will be crucified.

This concept is a little hard to understand, so let's bring in another biblical illustration from the Old Testament. Abraham is the father of Israel. He produced Isaac by promise, Isaac bore Jacob, and Jacob's name was changed to Israel. He had twelve sons who became the twelve tribes of the nation of Israel.

When God brought Israel to their homeland, He set the tribe of Levi apart for the priesthood. They were not given an earthly inheritance because God was their reward. Because they were in the priesthood, certain aspects of the law were satisfied without their effort. They were the only tribe permitted to break the Sabbath so they could perform the service of the temple and the act of circumcision for newborn boys.

There was another exemption they were given. Abraham gave tithes to God when he gave ten percent to Melchizedek. When the law was established four hundred years later, the tithe was part of that requirement. Yet Levi was exempted. Why? Because while he was still in Abraham, he gave his tithes through Abraham.[226]

So then, Levi fulfilled the law in Abraham two generations before he was even born. How? When Levi entered the priesthood, God credited him with the works of Abraham by promise. Abraham, who was before the law, fulfilled the law by faith.

The scriptures teach that the believer becomes a king and priest of God,[227] and that we were found in Christ before the world began. Now consider **2 Timothy 1:9**

> ...who has saved us and called *us* with a holy calling, not
> according to our works, but according to His own purpose
> and grace which was given to us in Christ Jesus before time
> began,

You were in Christ before the world began. You were in Christ at His death. You were in Christ when He rose from the dead. How can you be buried with Christ in death? How can you be raised with Christ at the resurrection? It's because your new life is spiritual. It is in Christ now, and it was in Christ before the world began. You have now received it by faith.

How could you die in Christ? How can Jesus bear the sins of the whole world? Jesus doesn't need to be crucified again for each generation. Jesus took upon Himself the sins of the whole world. Not just the world alive two-thousand years ago, but the whole world – the full existence of God's creation. Christ did not merely put your sins to death as in the plural. Jesus condemned sin in His flesh –

---

[226] Hebrews 7:9
[227] Revelation 1:6

Our Victory Over Sin

singular. Sin as a whole was judged, condemned, and executed on the cross. Look at **Romans 8:3-4**

> ³ For what the law could not do in that it was weak through the flesh, God *did* by sending His own Son in the likeness of sinful flesh, on account of sin: He condemned sin in the flesh,
> ⁴ that the righteous requirement of the law might be fulfilled in us who do not walk according to the flesh but according to the Spirit.

The Law, singular, required sin to be judged, singular. Any who are found in sin, will be judged by the law. But any who are in Christ have already been judged. You were judged in Christ, put to death in Christ, and raised in the likeness of Christ. If you are in Christ, all that Christ accomplished is now in you. Not will be. Not you hope to attain this one day. It is an accomplished fact. It has been accomplished without your work.

When you were of the flesh, you were in sin. Now you are in Christ. Jesus completed the work and now invites you to come. We account ourselves dead in Christ. We account our sin nailed to His cross. We now also must account ourselves alive from the dead.

It is faith in Christ alone. He condemned sin in the flesh, crucified us together with Him, and now His life is in us. Look at **Colossians 2:11-15**

> ¹¹ In Him you were also circumcised with the circumcision made without hands, by putting off the body of the sins of the flesh, by the circumcision of Christ,
> ¹² buried with Him in baptism, in which you also were raised with *Him* through faith in the working of God, who raised Him from the dead.
> ¹³ And you, being dead in your trespasses and the uncircumcision of your flesh, He has made alive together with Him, having forgiven you all trespasses,
> ¹⁴ having wiped out the handwriting of requirements that was against us, which was contrary to us. And He has taken it out of the way, having nailed it to the cross.
> ¹⁵ Having disarmed principalities and powers, He made a public spectacle of them, triumphing over them in it.

What is the true circumcision? It is the cutting away of the sinful nature of the flesh. God has put off the body of the sins of the flesh. The sin-maker has been cut out of the life of each believer.

You were buried with Him. You were raised with Him. Your dead works were nailed to the cross. You have been made alive in Him.

Notice that everything was accomplished in the past and everything is in Christ. To have life, you are in Christ. To become righteous, you are in Christ. To have the sins taken from your account, you must be in Christ. To be alive, you must be in Christ. What is contrary to us? What stands against us to condemn our actions? If you are in Christ, nothing. It has been taken out of the way. It has been nailed to the cross. Not only did Jesus take away your sin, but He put to death your old nature. Now all things are of God.[228]

This is the secret to overcoming sin and the weakness of the flesh each day. It begins with receiving this basic truth. Your sins are not just forgiven, the debt has been paid. To receive this you only must believe in the provision of God – faith in Christ.

In the Old Testament, when God's people sinned, the curse of serpents came upon them. When bitten, they were doomed to die. Yet God provided deliverance by placing a serpent on a pole. It was lifted up for the people with the promise, if anyone looked to the serpent on the pole, he or she would live.[229]

Jesus pointed back to this and said in **John 3:14-15**

[14] "And as Moses lifted up the serpent in the wilderness, even so must the Son of Man be lifted up,

[15] "that whoever believes in Him should not perish but have eternal life.

Being lifted up was referring to the crucifixion, where Jesus was lifted off the earth and hung on the cross. Just as any who looked to the serpent in the wilderness would be saved from the poison of serpents, any who look to the cross will be saved from the poison of sin. It is certain death, but looking to the cross by putting our trust in Christ gives us life.

---

[228] 2 Corinthians 5:18
[229] Numbers 21:8

Our Victory Over Sin

Just as the pole had no power to heal in the Old Testament, but instead God honored their faith and miraculously delivered them, we are miraculously delivered through Christ. It isn't the act of looking that saves you. It is God's work on your behalf when you believe upon Him. Look to Christ and believe in His deliverance.

The cross is your victory over sin – all sin.

Discussion Questions:

What is the weakness of the Law of God?

Why did God establish the law?

Did Moses do more good in his life than bad?

Did the law take all his good works into account when he was judged worthy or unworthy to enter the Promise?

Read Hebrews 10:1-4. Could the Old Testament saints be saved through the law (which depended upon animal sacrifices)?

How were they saved?

The Bible uses the illustration of a woman married to the law in Romans 7. Why did the woman and her husband (the law) not have a good relationship?

Why does the Bible switch from hoping the husband dies in verse 3 to us dying in verse 4?

How did Levi pay tithes to fulfill that requirement of the law?

How did we die to satisfy the penalty of the law?

How are we forgiven of sins?

How do we receive life?

If we are in Christ, can we fall outside of God's love?

Explain what faith is.

Our Victory Over Sin

Predestined – a Deeper Look

Since this topic has been touched on a few times, it is necessary to take a direct approach and explain the Bible's teachings on predestination. Unless we understand God's foreordination and the concept of predestination, it is not possible to fully understand what it means to walk by faith. Throughout this book, this topic has arisen a few times through scriptures that mention our roles along with the concept of God's purpose that was fashioned into the world at creation.

Where some teach predestination as a fatalistic concept, the truth is that the Bible presents this in order to make us aware that God is in complete control. Knowing that we are walking on the path of God's purpose should give us great confidence. Not only does this principle show us how we can trust Him, but it also points out the truth that we don't have to figure out how to fulfill God's will. The works have already been prepared, and we are called into God's purpose so we can share in a full inheritance.

Predestination does not mean you don't have a will. It doesn't mean that you have no choice. It means God has already made the way and nothing stands between us and victory. Every threat facing us is a test of our faith, not a hindrance to God's will. You and I can step outside of God's foreordained plan, but we cannot stop God's purposes. And one of the greatest purposes is to provide each Christian with the power to mature in Christ.

God has predestined us to conform to the image of Jesus Christ. In Christ was the perfect marriage of body, soul, and Spirit – for all were completely yielded to the will of the Father. In the same way, our goal as sons of God is to yield ourselves completely to His will.

You have been predestined to conform to that perfect image. To fully grasp this concept of complete transformation, let's look at this in context with **Romans 8:29-34**

²⁹ For whom He foreknew, He also predestined *to be* conformed to the image of His Son, that He might be the firstborn among many brethren.

³⁰ Moreover whom He predestined, these He also called; whom He called, these He also justified; and whom He justified, these He also glorified.

³¹ What then shall we say to these things? If God *is* for us, who *can be* against us?

³² He who did not spare His own Son, but delivered Him up for us all, how shall He not with Him also freely give us all things?

³³ Who shall bring a charge against God's elect? *It is* God who justifies.

³⁴ Who *is* he who condemns? *It is* Christ who died, and furthermore is also risen, who is even at the right hand of God, who also makes intercession for us.

You lack nothing. Let this truth sink into your hearts for a moment. God has given you all things that pertain to life and godliness through Christ.[230] In this passage we see that first and foremost, God has foreordained your life and all the events of your life so that you can receive all His promises and a full inheritance in His Kingdom. Can being dealt a bad hand in life prevent you from conforming to the perfect image of spiritual maturity? No, for it is God who called you, justified you, and glorified you. It is God who raises up those who are weak and rescues those who are distressed.

The circumstances of life may prevent you from becoming what you wanted to be and doing what you wanted to do, but circumstances cannot prevent you from fulfilling all that God has foreordained. If you are trying to force life into the mold of your desires, you will either be frustrated, or you will succeed in pursuing the things that will one day come to nothing.

Can the condemnation of people prevent you from becoming who and what God has predestined for your life? No. For it is God who justifies and who can lay any charge against the person God has elected for His purpose?

Can the sins of the flesh and the life you lived in the past disqualify you from God's calling? No, for it is Christ who died for those sins, and rose to give you a new life in Him.

The question is not, "Can we fulfill God's will?" The true question is, "Can we die to our own will and surrender to God's perfect will?" You were preordained to do these things; therefore, it is not for you to come up with the plan or find a way to do something

---

[230] 2 Peter 1:3

great for God. It is for you to conform to the image of Christ so you will be equipped to do God's will, have eyes to see the path God has laid before you, and have the ears to hear His still small voice speaking in your spirit.

The most common question asked by Christians is, "How do I find God's will for my life?" Well, here is your answer. God's will for your life is to conform to the image of Christ. Nothing else matters. If you learn what it means to walk in perfect communion with God – which is what happens as we conform to His image, you will naturally walk in His will. You cannot miss doing His will. You will do by nature the things that are of God's nature, and this is so because you are walking according to the new nature born of the Spirit. In doing so, you will perceive the prompting of the Spirit to do the works He has ordained you to do.

Don't forget this important truth – you were predestined. If God is for you, who can be against you, for you have been predestined. This means that the path is already prepared for you to walk in (See Ephesians 2:10). If the path is already prepared, God has already ordained you to fit perfectly within His plan, and nothing can prevent God's purposes. What keeps you from fulfilling these things?

Stop for a moment and observe the church. In both the past and the present, the same problems have plagued God's people. Few are the examples of those who we can truly say have become Christ-like. There have always been varying degrees of spiritual maturity, yet all have been predestined to conform perfectly to Christ. How can this be so? God will only work His will in the lives of the spiritually minded.

Let me qualify this for a moment. God does indeed use wicked men to accomplish His will. We see this example with Christ. Jesus said, "I will be delivered into the hands of sinners." The selfish and flesh-driven men thought they were ridding themselves of Christ, but they were actually doing what God foretold more than a thousand years beforehand.

In the Old Testament, God used the wickedness of Joseph's brothers to drive him toward the blessed life. When Joseph's brothers hated him and sold him into slavery, they were actually doing God's will. When the purpose of God came to fruition, Joseph looked at the bigger picture and said, "You meant it for evil, but God meant it for good. This was necessary in order to save the lives of many." He became the hand of deliverance for his people. It was all part of God's plan and Joseph was blessed to be part of what God was doing.

So when I say that God will only work with the spiritually minded, I am referring to the work of fellowship. We are partners in the work. We are not those who blindly act without knowledge. God can use the wicked, but God works through the righteous. The wicked are used, but God's perfect will is for you to inherit the kingdom, not be used as a mere tool in the hand of God.

Does Predestination Create Robots?

This topic naturally arises when discussing God's foreordained will. It is an integral part of scripture and should be an integral part of the Christian's understanding. Don't mistake predestination with Calvinism. They are not the same. Some people have adopted a fatalistic way of viewing this biblical topic, which turns man into automatons. In order to believe the Bible, we must not force the view point that God sovereignty equates to man's automatic response, lacking a will or the capacity to choose. If man had no choice, then God would not have commanded men to choose throughout the Old and New Testaments.

It's beyond the scope of this book to cover the intricacies of sovereignty, predestination, Calvinism, and Arminianism. However, a general understanding is necessary in order to have a grasp on God's will and how we must respond to His call. To put man's will at the center makes God subject to our whims. To stress God's sovereign will at the exclusion of man's will would turn mankind into a robotic automaton who cannot respond, but instead must react to programmed instructions. The Bible affirms both God's sovereignty and man's free will. These two are not mutually exclusive.

To understand God's will, we must reference the passage we looked at earlier. We have been predestined to conform to the image of God's Son. We have been called to walk in the works God prepared beforehand.[231] The Bible also says, "It's not God's will that any should perish."[232]

---

[231] Ephesians 2:10
[232] 2 Peter 3:9

This begs a few questions. One we mentioned already. If we have been predestined to conform to the image of Christ, why do so few people rise to this level? Or maybe we should ask, why has no one fully met this call? If it isn't God's will that any should perish, why do people perish? The Bible gives a great paradox. On one hand, the Bible says that it isn't God's will that any should perish, on the other hand, Jesus said many will take the path that leads to destruction, but very few would find the path that leads to life.[233]

Is God's will thwarted? No. Many erroneous doctrines arise because man is trying to protect God's reputation. Reformed theology states that if we take literally the statement, "It is not God's will that any should perish," but people clearly do perish without Christ, that would mean that God has failed. Therefore, 'any' must only apply to God's elect.

Not so. It is also God's will that we conform to the image of Christ. We are called to walk in the works God prepared beforehand, but Jesus said, "Those who knew the Lord's will and did not prepare himself to do according to His will shall be beaten with many stripes."[234] Jesus is clearly teaching that man can act counter to God's will.

If we are going to take the position that God's will must be fulfilled and man has no choice, then we have to follow that belief to its final conclusion. Every believer *must* conform completely to the likeness of Christ. Every Christian *must* complete the works God prepared beforehand. Everyone considered to be the elect *must* automatically prepare himself and accomplish God's will. This then nullifies the words of Christ where He said the opposite is true.

The Lord has built His will into creation and it runs through human history from beginning to end, but God shows His power in that He calls man to go against his natural human nature and to live contrary to that nature. God calls mankind to do what is humanly impossible so that we understand our utter helplessness and become completely dependent upon Him. Man has no power to do God's will; therefore, we become completely dependent upon the power of God's grace.

---

[233] Matthew 7:13-14
[234] Luke 12:47

It isn't those who hear the word that find the path of life, but those who respond to the call, recognize that God is their life, and look to Him every step of the way. The flesh draws us toward the flesh and the Spirit teaches all things of God as He leads us into the path of life. A path foreordained from the beginning when you were predestined to walk on that path. The path has been prepared and the call has gone out. Now there must be an answer to that call.

If you listen to a great message, are overwhelmed with joy, and determine in your heart to live out God's truth in your life, you will fail. That is unless you take God's truth as a call to the Spirit. In the Spirit, you cannot fail. Fulfillment is a guarantee by God. Jesus said, "He who abides in Me bears much fruit." It's a guarantee. 2 Peter 2 promises, "If you do these things [of the Spirit], you cannot be barren or unfruitful," and "You will never stumble." These also are guarantees.

If God has promised that we cannot fail, then why do we fall into sin? Why does our temper rise up and cause us to say words that wound others or cause division? Why does lust arise in our heart and draw us after the flesh? Why does the critical spirit of the flesh darken our words, attitudes, and actions? Why do we lust for more, covet what we don't have, and become greedy of gaining more? Why don't we have the attitude of Paul, "Whether hungry or full, imprisoned or free, whatever state I am in, I have learned to be content."

Are you content? Do you have perfect peace? A consistent gentle spirit? What about Jesus' words, "You must be perfect, even as your heavenly Father is perfect." Are you perfect?

Clarifying Predestination

The teachings of scripture always serve a purpose. Things God reveals are not merely trivial knowledge, but are intended to provide something that we can apply to our lives. The topic of predestination is no different. It is not merely presented so we can toss it around in debates, but it serves to accomplish a purpose in our faith.

Knowledge alone puffs up, or creates pride in the heart of those who gain it – unless it is knowledge that drives us to love.[235] Learning

---

[235] 1 Corinthians 8:1

about the Bible has little profit, but the knowledge revealed by the Spirit accomplishes at least one of the following purposes:

- Knowledge reveals God's caution against something that will harm us.
- Knowledge equips us with confidence and reveals faith.
- Knowledge calls us to act within God's purpose.

If our view of predestination or any other form of spiritual knowledge does not accomplish one or more of these goals, it appeals to the flesh and does not profit us in the Spirit. The doctrine of predestination can fall short if not understood from the perspective of God's grace and love. For some, it puffs up and creates division, but if understood in light of God's revelation, it accomplishes all three of these things.

Understanding God's foreknowledge and foreordained plan leads us away from harmful beliefs, equips us with confidence, stirs us into faith, and calls us to act according to God's purposes. Understanding this truth is greatly profitable to the Christian's walk. I would go as far as to say that a proper understanding of predestination is necessary in order to walk by faith.

This book has touched on this topic a few times, but it's necessary to be intentional about addressing this controversial subject. Unless you stay within an isolated group, you will encounter this subject many times in your church life. People can be very passionate about this topic because it affects how they view God and their own responsibility to His word.

I once considered myself to be a part of reformed theology. This is because the Bible clearly teaches about predestination and God's foreordained plan. Yet as I listened to the teachings of those who consider themselves reformed, I realized that I can't see eye-to-eye with Calvinism or similar types of reformed thinking.

Approaching scripture with an open mind is critical. It's the Holy Spirit that reveals truth, but we are often blinded to God's revelation because we are filtering it through a belief system instead of allowing the word to speak. When we approach the Bible, only looking at things that fit within our framework of held beliefs, we'll find ourselves explaining away the scriptures that challenge our beliefs and exploiting those which can be manipulated into our pre-supposed position.

Calvinism focuses on God's sovereignty. Arminianism focuses on man's free will. Just so that I can be an equal opportunity offender, let me say that both sides are missing part of the truth. Calvinism draws its inspiration from John Calvin, and Arminianism draws its inspiration from Jacobus Arminius.

It's not the focus of this book to hash out the varying points of both sides, but the teachings of Arminius is not the focus of the Christian life. Equally true, Calvinism is not the gospel as many claim. Some great theologians have said, "Calvinism is the gospel," and I've heard it echoed many times as if it were a fact. It is not.

Calvinism, taken to its furthest conclusion, says that God dictates every event in world history. The thought of man is dictated by the Lord. Salvation is determined by the Lord. Some are lost because God did not choose them and there is no way for them to respond to the gospel. I've heard Calvinists teach that every act we do is within God's foreordained plan. One man who struggled with pornography told me that he believed in Calvinism. "I have no choice," he said. "If God wants to make me stop, He will take away this desire and give me the right desires. Until then, there is nothing I can do."

I'm sure many Calvinists would disagree with this man's words, but when examining the teachings of this doctrine, I believe this statement falls well within the logical conclusion of Calvinism. Man cannot choose good. It has to be imparted into him. Man cannot resist evil, God must change him. If these statements are true, then resisting sin is outside of our control. If we are talking about the unredeemed man, parts of this is true. God has to draw and reveal Himself. But is grace irresistible? Is man without a will? No.

Even Stephen acknowledged this when he said, "You always resist the Holy Spirit."[236] He presented the truth of the gospel, but the people rejected the Holy Spirit. Their hearts were pricked, but instead of choosing repentance, they chose to kill the messenger.

When discussing this predicament with a Calvinist, he explained it this way, "God puts us into the position where we will sin. He doesn't make us sin, He just takes away the option not to sin. It is still man's sin because that is what was already in man's heart."

---

[236] Acts 7:51

I know, there are varying beliefs and varying degrees of Calvinistic thinking, but the main focus of Calvinism is the sovereignty of God. Anything that does not point to God's complete control is considered heresy. However, within the proper framework of faith, that position is correct. I'll explain this shortly.

Most people who hold to Arminianism don't even know who Arminius was. It's less of a theological study and more like a Christian philosophy. Arminianism puts the emphasis on man's will. Salvation is man choosing God, and the focus of evangelism is to persuade people to say a sinner's prayer so they can be saved.

Most evangelistic services are modeled after Charles Finney, who subscribed to this belief system. He used stirring music, emotional messages, and persuasive pleadings to draw listeners to the point of making a decision for Christ. In fact, making a decision was the focus. If the sinner can be persuaded by the fear of hell to receive a ticket to heaven, he will pray a confession and be declared saved.

One of the more dangerous sects of Arminianist teachings is the claim that God is learning as He goes. Some believe that God responded to man's fall by creating the Old Testament Law. The Law didn't work and God learned a better way and sent Christ. This idea is less common, except in the more liberal circles, but when taken to the far end of the Arminianist doctrine, some end up with this assumption.

Do you see a problem with either of these belief systems? Both are focused on something other than Christ. Both would probably also deny that they are not Christ-focused, but since their ideologies draw from quoting teachers, they are by default focused on something other than Christ.

While participating in a study on reformed theology, something was being taught that I believe contradicted the scriptures. I pointed this out by reading a passage that said the opposite. Then I was asked, "Well, do you believe this verse? Or that verse?"

My answer was, "Both. Why should I be forced to choose to only accept part of God's word? Both should be viewed together. If there is a contradiction, it isn't the scriptures that are in opposition; it is our doctrine that is interpreting something incorrectly."

Over the years I have noticed that those who believe in Calvinism ignore or explain away contradicting scriptures. Those who believe in man's free will, explain away any passage that reveals

God's sovereignty or simply pretend they don't exist. On both sides, people tend to say, "Well, some things we just can't understand," when faced with a scripture that opposes their beliefs. Either that or they reword the scripture.

The fact is that the Bible clearly teaches predestination and God's foreordained plan. The fact is that the Bible clearly teaches man's free will to act in obedience to God's word or to rebel against Him.

Free will does NOT negate God's sovereignty. God's sovereignty does NOT negate man's will. You don't have to choose one side or the other, and indeed you should not. When your beliefs are challenged by scripture, you should be asking God to show you the truth – not clinging to a favored belief over the truth of God.

In the remainder of this chapter I am not going to debate for or against the points of Calvinism or Arminianism. I am going to briefly look at the scriptures that I believe paint a clear picture of man's right to obey or disobey, and how that fits into God's sovereign plan.

Understanding these things is both freeing and builds our faith. For once we understand God's plan, the burden of our faith rests on Christ alone, and our lives rest in His plan and His ability to fulfill His work. Yet we also have the joy of knowing that we can freely love God out of choice and that we are not automatons that act like programmed instruments with no real purpose – other than doing God's bidding without a willing heart.

Rejoicing in God's Plan

Let's begin by casting a wide net into the scriptures and discover the bigger picture so we can get a clearer understanding.

The passages we'll be examining will likely challenge many of your assumptions, regardless of which side you stand on. Usually people turn off any challenge to their pet beliefs, but if you stick with this, I believe you will see the clear message of the scripture. Rather than becoming a message of two camps divided (Calvinists vs non-Calvinists), you'll discover that there is a great message in the Bible's teaching.

The goal of this chapter is not to make you believe or disbelieve in predestination, but that you let go of the man-made sides of these doctrines and see the wonderful message of becoming confident in God's purposes and your place in His plan. If you don't close this book, in the next few pages you will see how God reveals His sovereignty as He invites us to join His work. And because His work cannot fail, you will have confidence in the ministry He has called you to do.

It's not a matter of reformed verses non-reformed. It's a matter of looking expectantly to God as you walk confidently in His plan. It's a call to enter the plan, or resist God's call. And yes, people on both sides can miss that call. Jesus said, "Many are called, but few are chosen."[237] To cast a wide net, I want to draw in four passages at once and then discuss them.

John 3:16

> For God so loved the world that He gave His only begotten Son, that whoever believes in Him should not perish but have everlasting life.

1 Timothy 4:10

> For to this *end* we both labor and suffer reproach, because we trust in the living God, who is *the* Savior of all men, especially of those who believe.

2 Peter 3:9

> The Lord is not slack concerning *His* promise, as some count slackness, but is longsuffering toward us, not willing that any should perish but that all should come to repentance.

John 12:32-33

> [32] "And I, if I am lifted up from the earth, will draw all *peoples* to Myself."
> [33] This He said, signifying by what death He would die.

I've seen many arguments as to why these passages only apply to the elect, but the truth is that when you have to add to or take away from scriptures, you have deviated from the truth. Twice the Bible warns against this practice.[238]

It has been argued that the word 'world' actually is referring to the elect, but it is not possible to draw this conclusion if you read the

---

[237] Matthew 20:16, Matthew 22:14
[238] Proverbs 30:6, Revelation 22:18

entire context. Open the Bible and read John 3:16-21. The world is condemned – except for those who believe on Christ. The world was already under condemnation, but those who believed are delivered. God so loved the world (the same world declared as being under condemnation) that He gave His son.

Why does the Bible make a distinction between Jesus being the Savior of all men – especially those who believe? It's because Jesus did not only die for the elect. He died for all men, but only those who believe experience the promise of salvation. If God says all, how can we say, "No, no. That doesn't fit our theology. God you can only love the select few?" God has declared that He loves the whole world, including those who refuse to receive that love. Many are called, but few chosen.

I once had a discussion in a reformed theology group. The teacher boldly declared, "God only loves the elect. He does not love anyone who wasn't preordained to salvation."

I opened the scriptures and read the story of the rich young ruler. (See Mark 10:16-23) When Jesus was calling the young man to follow, He knew one thing stood in the man's way – his love for the world. Jesus said, "Go and sell all you have…come and follow Me." But it's what led up to that statement I focused on. The Bible says, Jesus loved him, and then invited him to follow. The young man walked away sorrowful because he couldn't give up the love of his wealth.

Jesus pointed to the rich young man as an example of why people are prevented from entering the Kingdom of Heaven.

Jesus loved someone who clearly did not receive life. The word used for loved is the Greek word 'agapao', the exact same form of the word used in John 3:16.

God does not only love the elect. He so loved the world that He gave. While some claim that to believe this nullifies the work of Christ, this is not so. It is said, "If anyone dies without Christ that Jesus died for, that would make Jesus' work a failure."

In the words often used by Calvinists, "Who are you to reply against God?" If God has declared His love, just because we don't understand how and why God allows man to respond to that love does not nullify the scriptures claim that God so loved the world, and that men loved darkness rather than light. And that men, who are already under condemnation, remain there because they refuse to

Predestined – a Deeper Look

believe on the Son who died for them. If God said this to be so, and we can't understand it, it isn't the work of Christ that falls short, but our understanding.

To reword the scriptures in order to fit our beliefs is a grave mistake. God does not have pleasure in those who die without Christ. God Himself declared that He has no pleasure when wicked men die in their sins.[239]

There is another important truth that all must realize. You cannot choose God. At least not until He visits you with the call of salvation. Consider the words of Jesus in **John 6:43-44**

> [43] Jesus therefore answered and said to them, "Do not murmur among yourselves.
> [44] "No one can come to Me unless the Father who sent Me draws him; and I will raise him up at the last day.

Until the Spirit of the Father draws us to Christ and opens our eyes, any confession of faith is a work of the flesh. We can't argue someone into the kingdom. You can't preach emotional messages as you persuade people to make confessions. The church is filled with people who made false confessions. In fact, the majority of Christians I've met who were raised in church made at least one false confession before hearing that call.

In a class where people wrote out their testimonies, about eighty percent of the testimonies included the words, "I thought I was saved." These people said a sinner's prayer, thought they were saved, but one day they heard the message and the Holy Spirit revealed the true need to their heart, and they responded and were changed.

The Apostle Peter alludes to this when he says that our enemies may speak evil against us and try to do all manner of evil, but they will rejoice in God's glory on the day of visitation.[240] Until God reveals Himself to an individual, they cannot know Christ, and their words are an act of the flesh. Whether someone responds to the message of the gospel by speaking evil against us, or is persuaded through fear and guilt to say a sinner's prayer, both are acts of the flesh and cannot benefit the confessor.

---

[239] Ezekiel 33:11
[240] 2 Peter 2:12

No one is condemned for speaking against us. The world is already under condemnation and will remain there until God calls and they respond to His drawing.

One of the more common arguments I hear is that salvation has to be automatic because if man has any part in salvation, that is work and salvation cannot come by works.

This argument falls short. Receiving is not work. When the Bible says that salvation is by grace and not by works, it is referring to earning or meriting salvation. Think about when someone gives you a gift. It's your birthday and someone hands you a present. They say, "This is a gift for you." Have you earned that gift because you opened the present? When they handed it to you, did you merit that gift because you let them put it into your hand? Do they have to unwrap the present, open your fingers, and put the gift in your hand in order to insure it is considered a gift and not something earned?

No. If they made you do a favor before you could have your gift, then it really isn't a gift. It isn't an act of works to receive what someone is giving you. So to say that being willing to receive God's gift of salvation is an act of works is a false statement.

> "As many as received Him, to them He gave the right to become children of God, to those who believe on His name."[241]

God reveals His gift of salvation, you believe, and then receive. The only time work comes into play is when someone is resisting the Spirit.

Discussion Questions:

Why does God tell us that He has predestined you to conform to Christ?

Does this predestined call force people to become like Christ?

Read Ephesians 2:10. Why does God say say the works were prepared beforehand?

---

[241] John 1:12

Predestined – a Deeper Look

Does God's foreordained plan mean you have no choice but to fulfill it?

Read Hebrews 4:2-3. God finished the works before calling for faith. If the works were already finished, why didn't the people inherit what God prepared for them?

Does God love only the Christian?

Does God only call the elect?

The Bible says that all things were created for God's pleasure. Read Ezekiel 33:11. Does God have pleasure when someone dies without salvation?

If someone doesn't come to Christ that He died for, has God failed?

Read Romans 8:29. If a Christian doesn't mature in their faith, has God failed?

Receiving God's Purpose

In this chapter, let's look at where the rubber meets the road. How does God's purpose connect with man's will? One of the points of confusion is when we mistake God's purposes as being limited to man's response. If we thing God's purpose can only be fulfilled when the individual is obedient, we fall into error. This applies to both sides of the argument. In reformed theology, man must act in accordance to God's will in order for God's purposes to be carried out. Therefore, if man has a will, then God would be bound, so it is concluded that man must not be able to resist.

In non-reform theology, man needs to help God by becoming a willing vessel, and his cooperation allows God's will to be fulfilled. Some go as far as to make God dependent upon man's effort. Both viewpoints are wrong.

To explain how will and sovereignty work together, let's look at the examples we discussed in previous chapters. We'll start with the Old Testament. When God led His people to the Promised Land, what was His purpose? It was to show His glory to the world by freeing a nation from slavery. He took a helpless people to the land that had been given to Abraham by promise, and said that He would use a nearly defenseless group of people to drive out the idolatrous nations before them.

The people God led out of Egypt arrived to the Promised Land, but could not enter because of unbelief. According to the Bible, the work was already done. Let's revisit **Hebrews 4:3**

For we who have believed do enter that rest, as He has said: "So I swore in My wrath, 'They shall not enter My rest,' " although the works were finished from the foundation of the world.

This passage is comparing us, who received the promise of Christ's rest, with the Old Testament nation of Israel, who disbelieved God.

When was the work complete? Was it done when the people had the faith to enter in? Or when the wicked nations were driven out? No, before Adam was created, God's works had already been completed. This may sound odd, but that's because we are bound by time.

We view time as a moment by moment movement toward the future. God views the entirety of time as a completed work. When God created the world, He had already foreordained His purposes and wove His completed work into the new creation. What you see today, God resolved from the beginning. The purpose of everything is to show His power to us, His glory to us, and His love toward us.

This is why God can say that we were in Christ before the world began. And say those who failed to enter His purpose (the rest from the desert) failed to do so even though the works were already finished.

When the people refused to obey, was God's plan thwarted? No. The purposes of God never changed, but the people who would benefit from that purpose did. God raised up a new generation to enter His rest – one who would follow by faith. They were just as flawed as their predecessors, but they entered by faith. The unbelieving nation died without the promise, but the next generation received it. And we also received it through Christ.

We see the same principle with King David and King Saul. When Saul rebelled against the word of the Lord, God raised up a man after His own heart. What should have been Saul's fell to David. Consider the words of **2 Chronicles 16:9a**

> For the eyes of the LORD run to and fro throughout the whole earth, to show Himself strong on behalf of *those* whose heart *is* completely His.

According to scripture, the word of the Lord goes out as a call to the ends of the earth.[242] This is stated in the New Testament, but it is equally true in the Old. The word of God has gone out and cannot fail to accomplish the purpose God has declared.[243] Then God raises up those whose hearts are completely His.

Let's consider another example. Pause from this book and read Zephaniah 3:9-20. God declared His purpose for Israel. Many of God's declared purposes have not yet been fulfilled. In this passage God promises to visit His people, redeem them from sin, leave a

---

[242] Romans 10:17-18
[243] Isaiah 55:11

godly people who will know the Lord, and ends with the promise that they will have perfect peace, and no one shall make them afraid again. The Lord will dwell in their midst.

That was the purpose God declared for Israel. It's a purpose that shall be fulfilled. It is not dependent upon man's cooperation. In fact, the nation of Israel has never followed the Lord, yet they can still expect to see God's word fulfilled. This is not because of who they are, but who God is. Don't be too hard on Israel. The church hasn't had a very good track record either.

When God declares a purpose, it will be fulfilled. In the book of Daniel we see this often when God declares repeatedly, "The end shall come at the appointed time."[244] God is not waiting for man to prepare the way. The time has already been appointed, and God's completed work will be fulfilled with or without man's cooperation.

There is also the warning that God will not always strive with man.[245] At the end of prophecy, when the wrath begins to fall, cooperation with man decreases and God's purposes are fulfilled in spite of man's resistance. During the judgment of Revelation, God does not invite men to join Him in executing judgment. Wrath against the world is for God alone. But when the eternal work of God is in motion, man is always invited into that purpose. When man fails to respond, God raises up another.

The reason is clear. God's desire is for us to inherit His Kingdom. Though the works were completed at creation, the act of working is fulfilled through those who yield to God and will be inheritors of the Kingdom.

Let's go back to Zephaniah. This passage is what is referred to in Romans 11, where we are told that God has blinded the people of Israel according to the flesh until the time of the Gentiles are fulfilled. After this time has been fulfilled, God will again revisit His people and fulfill the promises of the Old Testament prophecies.

Any who are in Christ are the Israel of God, spiritually speaking.[246] Romans 11 gives a great explanation of the differences between the Jewish nation and the church. It also indicates that once they turn to the Lord by faith in Christ, they also will be grafted in

---

[244] Daniel 8:19, 10:1, 11:27, 11:29, 11:35
[245] Genesis 6:3
[246] Galatians 6:15-16, Romans 11:17-24

Receiving God's Purpose

again and reclaim their place as the Israel of God. Right now, they are Israel by physical means, but we are the Israel of God by becoming the people of God through Christ.

When the foreordained purpose of God is fulfilled, the nation of Israel will discover what the church has already received, and they will join us in the fold of Christ. This is explained by Jesus in **John 10:16**

> And other sheep I have which are not of this fold; them also I must bring, and they will hear My voice; and there will be one flock *and* one shepherd.

While the early Jewish Christians thought the Jews were the fold, the truth is that any who are in Christ are of His fold. And one day the other flock will be joined to the fold. Then we will be one people under Christ.

Because of unbelief, they are not enjoying God's purpose yet. Let's look again at the words of Christ as He spoke over the nation of Israel. Look at **Luke 19:41-44**

> [41] Now as He drew near, He saw the city and wept over it,
> [42] saying, "If you had known, even you, especially in this your day, the things *that make* for your peace! But now they are hidden from your eyes.
> [43] "For days will come upon you when your enemies will build an embankment around you, surround you and close you in on every side,
> [44] "and level you, and your children within you, to the ground; and they will not leave in you one stone upon another, because you did not know the time of your visitation."

What did God intend to give Israel? His purpose was for them to have peace. His coming was meant for their benefit and peace. But what did the nation receive? They rejected God's purpose and He blinded their eyes and raised up another people (the Gentiles) who would walk in His purpose. Instead of peace, they found destruction.

When God's people were led through the desert out of the bondage of slavery in Egypt, it was a twelve-day journey to the Promised Land. God led them straight to the promise. It was meant for their good, rest, and peace. But they could not believe and instead found the destruction of the desert.

In both cases, did man's unbelief thwart the purpose of God? No, the purpose was fulfilled and will be fulfilled. But those who could have obtained the promise did not. Knowing beforehand how His people would react, God foretold of their rejection, but also declared His unchangeable purpose. It wasn't God who decided beforehand to tease the people with a promise and then snatch it from them. He meant it for their benefit, but they chose not to believe. Man's will hindered man from becoming a part of God's purpose, but did not hinder God's purpose.

In the same way, you are called into a royal priest hood. Look at the promises of God offered to every believer. Is God dependent upon your response? Or is it an invitation for you to become an inheritor of what God intends to give? Consider this passage from **Romans 8:28-32** again:

> [28] And we know that all things work together for good to those who love God, to those who are the called according to *His* purpose.
>
> [29] For whom He foreknew, He also predestined *to be* conformed to the image of His Son, that He might be the firstborn among many brethren.
>
> [30] Moreover whom He predestined, these He also called; whom He called, these He also justified; and whom He justified, these He also glorified.
>
> [31] What then shall we say to these things? If God *is* for us, who *can be* against us?
>
> [32] He who did not spare His own Son, but delivered Him up for us all, how shall He not with Him also freely give us all things?

What is God's purpose for every believer? To freely give you all things. You were called into God's purpose. God knew you before the foundation of the world, and He wove His purposes into your life. There is nothing that can stand between you and the fulfillment of God's purposes – except unbelief. Just as God's people were called into His purposes and He led them to the promise, the works were already accomplished, the path was already preordained, and God's purposes were established and could not be thwarted. Yet look at **Hebrews 3:19**

So we see that they could not enter in because of unbelief.

And we are given the same warning in **Romans 11:20**
Well *said.* Because of unbelief they were broken off, and you stand by faith. Do not be haughty, but fear.

Now let's revisit Romans 8. You were predestined to conform to the image of Christ. How many Calvinists have been perfectly conformed to Christ's image? How many non-Calvinists have conformed to that image? Not one person in history has perfectly conformed to Jesus' likeness. Even the Apostle Paul, the one God used to pen two-thirds of the New Testament, lamented over his inability to be the godly man he desired to be. And what was the reason?

Sin dwelled in his flesh, warred against his mind, and sought to overcome him and conform him back into a fleshly way of thinking. Sometimes it got the best of him. Other times he rejoiced in the fact he learned to rest in Christ. In the rest of Christ, the flesh had no power, but sometimes he lost focus and fell to sin's manipulation.

Did God condemn Paul when He fell? No. He returned his focus to Christ and rejoiced that his mind now served the Lord. Just because we have been predestined to conform to Christ does not mean that we can't fall short of God's purpose. Also consider this passage from **Hebrews 12:14-17**

[14] Pursue peace with all *people,* and holiness, without which no one will see the Lord:

[15] looking carefully lest anyone fall short of the grace of God; lest any root of bitterness springing up cause trouble, and by this many become defiled;

[16] lest there *be* any fornicator or profane person like Esau, who for one morsel of food sold his birthright.

[17] For you know that afterward, when he wanted to inherit the blessing, he was rejected, for he found no place for repentance, though he sought it diligently with tears.

Beware lest you fall short of the grace of God. It's not God's purposes that fall short. It is we who fall short of that purpose and miss what God intends for our peace. How do we fall short? In this example, bitterness can take our eyes off of Christ and put us into a worldly mindset. The world seeks to rob us of God's promises. It isn't God's promises that fall short, but our focus on God's grace that falls short.

We are called to pursue what God has set before us. In the example above, the focus is peace and holiness. Note that we are called to pursue – not produce. We lay hold of what Christ has provided. Either Christ is the focus, and all He provides is ours, or the world is the focus, and we inherit all its passing sins and dying provisions.

This is why you can be predestined by the Lord and not fulfill that which you have been foreordained to accomplish. The foreordained plan of God has woven everything we need to fulfill a life of perfect godliness. It is already in our path of obedience. God leads us down the paths of life, but the flesh calls us back to the world. God's purposes will be fulfilled and God invites us into that plan. But while God is leading, the world is calling.

We fall short, but God's purpose continues. Man's free will allows him to be a part of God's purpose so we can receive a full inheritance. Man's free will also allows him to step off God's foreordained path and pursue that which is destined for destruction.

Why did Esau lament? It wasn't because something bad happened to him, but because he invested his life into what was passing and missed the promise. In the same way, God is beckoning you to follow Him so you won't miss the promise. The Bible points to Esau's example as a warning for us. Why? Because God's foreordained plan doesn't force you into righteousness. God calls you to lay down your life in this world and willingly choose the eternal path of life He is revealing.

You have the God-given right to pursue what is passing. Sin will present the world, polished and shiny, but God calls for faith in what is not yet seen, but will never pass. It's the call to walk by faith and not by sight. It's the call to walk in the Spirit and not in the flesh. It's the call to follow the will of God and say, "Not my will, but yours."

You will blow it. No one is predestined to blow it. No one is predestined to not blow it. Any one of us can step outside of God's purpose for our lives, and if necessary, God will raise up someone to

Receiving God's Purpose

be a part of His purpose without us. God's will is going to be fulfilled. Period. However, don't mistake what is being said. When you blow it, you will fall short, but that doesn't mean that God has cast you off. Step back into God's purposes, set your eyes on Christ, and pursue the promise of His goodness. God doesn't bless flawless people, but people who walk by faith. Our perfection is in Christ and our goal should be to abide in Christ so we can follow His call.

God's message is good news indeed. All we must do when we blow it is to focus back on Christ and follow Him back into His will. God's will is that you know Him. God's will is that you inherit the kingdom. God's will is that you become a partaker of Christ and enjoy being a partaker of His glory – both now through intimacy with God, and in eternity when you will see Him face-to-face.

Blowing it does not take you out of God's purposes. Choosing to follow the flesh and rejecting the call of the Spirit does exclude us. God's not calling for people who are perfect in themselves. He doesn't demand mistake-free godliness. He calls for those who will trust Him, receive from Him, and follow Him.

God has not only built into your life the things that make for your peace, but also the things that will lead you back into His way of righteousness. God did not only foreordain you to fulfill your calling, but God also foreknew you and is not surprised when you blow it. God's grace unweaves our minds from the flesh, and one step at a time, He weaves our lives into His purpose. Growing in Christ is learning how to trust Him – even when you fall.

Let's wrap up this topic with the parable of the laborers in Matthew 20. Jesus compared the Kingdom of Heaven as a field owner who hired laborers. He went out in the morning, found men needing work, and promised them one day's wage. A few hours later, he found other workers and promised them the same. At the end of the day, the master came across men who had been idle all day because they couldn't find work. He said, "Go and work the last hour, and I'll give you what is right."

He called each laborer and paid them a day's wage. Those who came in at the last minute got the same as those who labored all day. Those who had worked all day complained, but the master's answer said it all, "Are you angry because I am good? I can do what I will with my own money. I have decided to be good to those who came in last the same as I did for you."

When I see this truth, it gives me hope. God is not measuring me based on when I gain the understanding of truth, but because He is good and desires to show goodness to any who will follow Him.

The message of this parable is not that we earn any reward. The message is that God calls and any who answer will be treated based on His goodness and not our merits. The life founded on grace does indeed work, but not to earn favor, rewards, or approval. We labor because we are yoked to Christ and we are going where He leads. We will work. We will do good works. We will have righteous acts. But these are born out of a relationship with Christ. They do not create that relationship. Nor can works earn God's kingdom. Christ paid your debt on your behalf. A debt you can never repay. How then can works put God in debt to us and earn us anything?

You might read this book and realize that you've spent your life pursuing meaningless religion, or selfish desires, or that you have blown it so many times you fear God's patience is running thin. The truth is, look to Christ and be transformed into His likeness. God doesn't measure you based on when you 'get it'. Just that you get it. And that you respond to His call.

God's purposes may have passed you by because you have been distracted by the cares of this life. Leave what is behind in the past. Follow Christ now, and experience His purpose. It is the Father's good pleasure to give you His kingdom. He is not rewarding you based on how much labor you have accomplished. The measuring standard is faith. Did you believe Him and follow Christ. This is the work of God, that you believe on Christ.[247]

You have been predestined to conform to the image of Christ. Follow Christ and be changed into His likeness.[248] God has prepared your works beforehand that you should walk in them.[249] You are His workmanship. The ministry is not your workmanship. Walk where He leads. If you have wandered off course, walk where He leads. If you have blown it – badly, walk where He leads. In the flesh, we have all blown it. In the Spirit, we have perfect peace and intimacy with God.

---

[247] John 6:29
[248] 2 Corinthians 3:18
[249] Ephesians 2:10

Receiving God's Purpose

God isn't measuring your righteousness based on what you have done or not done, but on the work of Christ and whether you are found in Him.

This also should give you great confidence in ministry. Success is not the measure of works. Obstacles are not the determining factor of our direction. If God is for us, who can be against us? His purposes will be accomplished. They cannot fail, because the works were finished from the foundation of the world.

Our only concern is are we Christ focused and are we walking on the path where He leads. Everything else has been foreordained. The only variable in the Christian life is, will you come and follow Christ. Everything else rests on God's shoulders.

Discussion Questions:

Consider the people God led across the desert. Was it God's will for them to die in the desert over the coming 40 years?

What effort did God require in order for them to inherit the promise?

According to Hebrews 4:3, when were the works completed?

Read Luke 19:41-44 and Luke 13:34. What was God's purpose for the people?

Did God want the people to miss the day He visited them?

Read Romans 8:32 and Luke 12:31-32. What is God's purpose for each Christian?

Review Romans 8:28-19 and Hebrews 12:14-17. How do these two verses work together to unveil God's plan for our lives and what is our responsibility?

Read Matthew 20:1-16. What does this parable tell us about the promise of God?

Is the reward earned by the amount we labor or our faithfulness to His call?

If we have wasted the days of our life, does this mean we have missed our opportunity?

What is the difference between God's purposes for each individual and God's purpose for all of creation and time?

Does God need us in order to fulfill His purposes?

Why does God call people into His purpose?

Expelling Wrath

Few people actually live with the knowledge they are under grace. Many make this claim, but rarely does a Christian abide in the grace of God. We have this misconception that God is watching our every move with a critical eye. When we do something good enough, He tosses down a blessing. If we fall short, He strikes us with the rod of anger.

Many times I have heard well-meaning people say, "God took me behind the woodshed," as though we misbehaved and a strict Heavenly Father grabbed us by the ear, dragged us behind the house, and beat us until we could take no more. This is not the message of faith God has revealed.

Equally dangerous are those who look at the good things in their life and say, "I must be doing something right."

We do not live under a merit system. Let me reiterate this again for emphasis. God does not bless based on a merit system. If you have this worlds goods and are experiencing happiness, this is not the evidence of God's blessing. If it were, how do we explain the godless pleasures of the wealthy? Look at Hollywood. How many multi-millionaires live godless and immoral lives, yet they have everything their heart desires. Look at professional athletes. There are plenty of examples of rich athletes that live contrary to God. Many atheists have wealth.

The opposite is also true. Hardship does not equate to God's judgment. Many who do things we recognize as illegal and immoral escape judgment. How many crime lords murder and oppress, yet die after a long life without any evidence of God's wrath on them?

Certainly God will bless and God will execute wrath on those who do not know God. But God's higher goal is to lead those unworthy of mercy to the cross where they also are offered grace. God extends His unmerited favor to the criminal and the gentleman. He extends grace to the prostitute and the virtuous woman. Grace is offered to the thief as well as to the honest, hardworking man or woman.

Grace is not merited, nor does any depth of sin exclude a person from God's invitation of grace. It is offered to all, but all will not see the value in it.

Limited grace is a manmade idea. Meriting blessings is also a manmade idea. Both ideas blind God's children to the work He is doing in their lives. The Bible has promised, that once we are in Christ, there is no more wrath. God's anger was poured out on the cross. Any who enter the covenant of the cross by faith have escaped wrath. Period.

If you belong to Christ, wrath will never be part of your life. We mistakenly equate chastisement with anger, wrath, and judgment. Let's take a deeper look at the passage many misunderstand as punishment. Look at **Hebrews 12:5-6**

> [5] And you have forgotten the exhortation which speaks to you as to sons: "My son, do not despise the chastening of the LORD, Nor be discouraged when you are rebuked by Him;
> [6] For whom the LORD loves He chastens, And scourges every son whom He receives."

There is one key phrase you must not overlook, "Whom the Lord loves, He chastens." The word 'chasten' comes from the Greek word, 'Paideia', which means, the complete training and education of children. This training is founded upon love. God's goal is for you to inherit His kingdom and receive every promise. The promises of God were given to us because God wants us to have them. They are not a vague hope, but a real offering from the hand of God.

The Bible says, "God is love."[250] This means that everything God does is out of His love toward us. God's love is called 'agape', or unconditional outward focused love. It is a love that is expressed through action without considering whether someone is worthy or not. God does not love us because we are worthy. God loves us because He is love and love (agape) requires itself to be expressed to the benefit of others.

When the Bible speaks of chastening, don't view this through the lens of a flawed fleshly way of thinking. Our parents get angry and often punish out of wrath and frustration. God cannot get frustrated, for He sees the end from the beginning.[251] He knew your misbehavior before you decided to go the wrong way. He also knows what you will do if not corrected. God sees the end of your ways.

---

[250] 1 John 4:8 and 1 John 4:16
[251] Isaiah 46:10

Expelling Wrath

When that way is harmful, God corrects your way. It isn't for His benefit that God chastises us, but for our benefit. The Lord discourages us from pursuing the path of destruction while leading us into the promises and path of life.

Some children will rebel, even against the most nurturing environment. God does not drag us toward the paths of life against our will. He uses external circumstances to chastise us, while at the same time His Holy Spirit leads us by communing with our spirit in order to draw us to seek Him and receive His eternal favor. The goal is not wrath, but blessing.

Blessing is eternal, not temporal. I think getting a house is a blessing. To a small degree it may be. However, houses are temporal, but God's eye is on the eternal. What I think is good is based on human understanding, but God judges what is good based on its eternal benefit. I've had people look at an object and say, "God has blessed you," but I've never had someone look at my trial and say, "God is blessing you." Yet a house has never changed my life or shaped my character. Hardship has.

God is constantly expressing His love toward us. His love is our blessing. Hardship is a blessing because God uses difficult circumstances to shake loose what is bad and reveal what is good. Sometimes blessings come in the form of our comfort and pleasure, but not always. God is always blessing. He is either expressing love in the mountaintop experience, or guiding us back to His presence where the greater blessings can be realized. Even when we are near Him, God will wean us off the flesh through difficulties so we learn that the flesh isn't the true blessing. The Spirit is.

In the Christian life, hardship is not judgment; it is a blessing. Pain is not wrath, but a blessing. Tribulation and trials are not God taking us behind the woodshed, but the blessing of a loving God. We are instructed not to despise God's chastening, because He is training us to become eternal children. He is leading us into the path where we are more than conquerors. The Lord is teaching us how to wean ourselves off of a life in the flesh and live in the Spirit where we begin enjoying the true blessing now.

If you are a child of God, nothing in your life comes out of wrath. You have escaped wrath and now everything is the nurturing hand of God. When you live in the mindset of God being angry, it is impossible to live in faith and experience the joy of fellowship. Expel that thought each time it arises. You are not appointed to wrath, but are saved from it. Now you are a child, and God has no greater joy than to delight in your way as He leads you to His best. Take these passages to heart.

1 Thessalonians 5:9
For God did not appoint us to wrath, but to obtain salvation through our Lord Jesus Christ,

Romans 5:17
For if by the one man's offense death reigned through the one, much more those who receive abundance of grace and of the gift of righteousness will reign in life through the One, Jesus Christ.

Do you see the greatness of this passage? If our inherited sin nature reigned to bring about death and sorrow, how much greater is the blessing of God's grace that overcomes that sorrow? The sin that entered the world corrupted our lives and caused great pain. Yet much more does God's gift give us life. He didn't say that Christ matched the consequences of sin. Scripture does not say that God merely tipped the scales on our behalf. The message of grace is that God's abundant favor much more abounds above what sin had destroyed.

Grace abounds *much* more.

If you are walking in God's gift of grace, sin may have robbed your life, but grace much more blesses your life. God not only overcame sin, but sent a tsunami of grace to completely wash it away. The consequences of sin cannot stand in the presence of grace.

Are you still wrestling with this idea? Let's dig a little deeper in

Romans 5:8-11
⁸ But God demonstrates His own love toward us, in that while we were still sinners, Christ died for us.
⁹ Much more then, having now been justified by His blood, we shall be saved from wrath through Him.
¹⁰ For if when we were enemies we were reconciled to God through the death of His Son, much more, having been reconciled, we shall be saved by His life.
¹¹ And not only *that,* but we also rejoice in God through our

300   Expelling Wrath

Lord Jesus Christ, through whom we have now received the reconciliation.

Stop for a moment and meditate on this passage. God demonstrated His love toward us while we were sinners. We were enemies of God, and rather than pouring out judgment, the Lord entered our world and provided the way of the cross as an escape from the judgment of sin.

If God did this while we were alienated from Him, how much more will He express His great love toward those who have now been justified in Christ? Why then do those who received reconciliation from their past sins now resist the grace offered more abundantly to them as a child of God?

As if this weren't already enough, we now have a life that rejoices in the reconciliation we have received. In other words, our lives should be centered upon the truth that we are reconciled with God. Not merely forgiven, but everything that created a breach has been removed and we are completely reconciled to God.

Reconciliation means fellowship. If a husband and wife are separated and then reconciled, the differences that separated them have been resolved and the relationship restored. Unlike human relationships, God performed both sides of the reconciliation and does not carry hard feelings and baggage into the new relationship. While we were sinners – those whose sins were irreconcilable to God and His holiness – Christ died for us. The wages of sin is death, so Jesus took our sins to His own account, paid the penalty, and then rescued us from the condemnation that bound us to judgment.

If that is true, and it is, how much more will God show His great love toward those who are now in Christ? If God loves the sinner this much, how much more does He express His love toward those whose sins have been taken out of the way? We were saved from our sins by His death, now much more are we daily saved through Jesus' life?[252] A life that we also now possess.

Stop living under the fear of wrath and start living as one who is reconciled fully to God. You have the right to be in God's presence. Your rights were given to you by God, by grace, through the cross.

---

[252] Romans 5:10

It's the new covenant. A covenant is an agreement made by two people, and it cannot be broken.

The Bible says that because God could swear by no one greater, He swore by Himself to confirm the covenant.[253] God cannot lie and cannot break His word or His covenant. The oath of the New Covenant was sealed by the blood of Christ. The Bible says that God purchased us, His church, with His own blood.

You have no power to make or break that covenant. It was sworn and confirmed between the Father and the Son, Jesus Christ. The covenant was sealed by His blood, and confirmed through the resurrection. All you can do is walk in that covenant, or walk outside of the covenant. By faith, we believe God's promise and answer His call. When we disbelief God's promise, we walk as those who have no assurance.

Your sins cannot break the covenant, for you are not the guarantee of the covenant. Walking in the flesh does not break the covenant, it merely causes us to reject the benefits of God through His covenant. You can't sin your way out of the covenant. You can only trade the benefits of God's grace for the temporal pleasures of the world and the flesh. You can't trade away salvation, but you can invest your life in worthless works that will be devoured by the fire of Christ judgment. Nothing that is not of God can pass over. Anything God works through us shall pass over and will be rewarded.[254]

If you sin, don't run from God or grovel in your misery, turn from the flesh and walk in the light of Christ according to your new nature. The forgiveness has already been given, for the debt has already been paid. You have not added new charges to Christ's account. Believe God's promise and look to the cross. He has already paid.

Once again the question will arise in the minds of many, "Isn't this a license to sin? If my sins are paid before I committed them and I'm already forgiven, does this mean I can walk in sin without fear of consequences?"

The answer is both yes and no. If you choose to snub God's love and walk away from communion, you are free to do so. Will

---

[253] Hebrews 6:13
[254] 1 Corinthians 3:14-15

Expelling Wrath

God boil with anger and avenge you with His wrath? No. If you are born again, you have a new spirit and are no longer under wrath.

However, there are consequences. Living contrary to God does have consequences, but wrath is not one of them. First, you have the Holy Spirit within you. There can be no peace or confidence in your life outside of God's will. Your inner man will be troubled. It is possible to sear your conscience to the point where you no longer grieve over sin, but you also will no longer experience the peace that surpasses all understanding.

Sin will judge you, not God. Sin is a curse. Sin is part of a fallen world and while it gives a temporary pretense of satisfaction, it requires more from us than it gives. The more we sin, the more we are giving control of our minds to the flesh and the greater bondage we'll experience. Sin is a deception. It causes us to believe we are in control, but it is the flesh seeking control over us. Consider **Romans 6:14-18**

[14] For sin shall not have dominion over you, for you are not under law but under grace.

[15] What then? Shall we sin because we are not under law but under grace? Certainly not!

[16] Do you not know that to whom you present yourselves slaves to obey, you are that one's slaves whom you obey, whether of sin *leading* to death, or of obedience *leading* to righteousness?

[17] But God be thanked that *though* you were slaves of sin, yet you obeyed from the heart that form of doctrine to which you were delivered.

[18] And having been set free from sin, you became slaves of righteousness.

If we willfully sin, we are submitting ourselves under sin's bondage. We become its slave. So how do we become free again? Look at the passage above. You are free. Sin only rules us when we submit ourselves to it. Hit has no power over our lives, but sin tries to convince you that the old man lives and rules over you.

In the 1800s, the Emancipation Proclamation freed the slaves. Like the power of sin, the slave owners refused to set their captives free. The south was defeated and slavery was officially outlawed. Many liberated men rejoiced in their new freedom, but do you know what most of the freed slaves did? They willingly stayed in bondage because they didn't feel free. Land owners bluffed them into service and they lived like their freedom had never been given.

This is sin in your life. Christ defeated your master, destroyed the old nature, and set you free. Yet sin rises up and denies your right to freedom. Though it has no power to enforce its will, most Christians are stuck under the mindset of the old man and when the flesh says, "Serve me," they serve it. They don't know they are free.

When you realize you are serving sin or the flesh, submit to God. The way to break the stronghold of sin is to stop submitting to it. And we do this by submitting to righteousness. You don't have to perform rituals, bargain with God, or perform some type of penance.

There are those who deny Christ and claim we have to break generational curses by searching out and confessing the sins of our fathers and forefathers. But Jesus said, "Whom the Son makes free is free indeed." If you are under bondage of an assumed curse, you are denying the work of Christ and submitting yourself to sin. You are already free. Free from your sins. Free from the sins of your fathers. Free from the sins you will commit tomorrow. Live like someone who has liberty!

Each of us will serve something. We either become enslaved to sin through fleshly passions and desires, or a slave to righteousness. We either serve in the Spirit, or are ruled by the flesh. Both require submission, but righteousness calls for willing obedience while sin applies the shackles and refuses to relinquish control willingly.

In the Old Testament, Samson had God-given strength so that no man could bind him. In one incident, he willingly allowed his people to shackle him and deliver him to the enemy. However, the shackles had no power over him. The Spirit of God came upon him and he broke the shackles as if it were a thread touching a flame.[255] The same Spirit breaks you free from bondage. The shackles sin has placed on you are threads in the flame of the Holy Spirit. Break them off, for the enemy has already been defeated.

Slavery to sin invests our lives in a world that is passing away. There is no inheritance in this world. Righteousness is an investment in God's kingdom. In that kingdom, our willing submission to

---

[255] Judges 15:14

Expelling Wrath

obedience will be transformed into an inheritance given to all children of the King.

The investment into the world is without fellowship. There are no eternal relationships or true intimacy in the corruption of sin. However, the Kingdom of God is all about our relationship with our Father. Fellowship begins now, grows deeper as we mature into God's image, and then becomes sight. The joy of reconciliation will never pass away. Things aren't the focus. Pleasure isn't the focus. Knowing God on an intimate level is the focus. We enjoy this life with Him now, and we'll enjoy the Kingdom of Heaven through that fellowship then.

The rich in this world often complain of loneliness, but there will be no isolation in grace. It's all about knowing God and enjoying fellowship with Him, both now and forever. When our focus is on our fellowship with God, things and pleasures will have the correct place in our life and we'll have the right perspective by which to enjoy life without sin.

Discussion Questions:

Is a trial, hardship, or problem the evidence that God is angry?

Why does God love us?

Is God's love based on what we have done, or who He is? Explain.

Do you ever feel as if God is angry at you? Why or why not?

What does it mean, "You are not appointed to wrath?"

Does this mean that God doesn't care if we sin?

What turns our heart toward God when we stray, His anger or His grace?

When we sin, can we break the covenant of grace? Why or why not?

The Bible says that those who sin are slaves of sin. When we sin, how are we made free?

Does grace lead us to sin?

Growing in Intimacy

2 Peter 3:17-18

[17] You therefore, beloved, since you know *this* beforehand, beware lest you also fall from your own steadfastness, being led away with the error of the wicked;

[18] but grow in the grace and knowledge of our Lord and Savior Jesus Christ. To Him *be* the glory both now and forever. Amen.

Ask the average Christian how to avoid being led into wickedness and they will likely point to something you do. Read your Bible. Pray. Go to church.

What did the Apostle Peter tell the church just before he was led to his execution? The warning was to beware, or be on guard against the false leading that draws is toward wickedness. The solution was to grow in grace and the knowledge of Christ. It isn't doing that draws us closer to the Lord. It isn't doing or resisting that overcomes the call of sin. It is growing in God's grace.

Grow in grace. The only limit to our intimacy is our desire to seek and know Him. By this point, the word grace should stir in your mind the realization of what God has given you. And what He has done for you. You are not growing to find grace, but growing in the grace – or favor of God – you have already received. The Bible does not say to find grace, but to grow in His grace.

Everything Jesus possesses has been given to you. Any who are in Christ are in grace and have the mind of Christ. Intimacy with God grows as your knowledge of Him grows. Grace and knowledge are interwoven.

Knowledge alone puffs up and creates pride.[256] When knowledge is something we acquire in order to feel as if we have achieved something, it becomes a fleshly mindset. But knowledge of grace has the opposite effect. Knowledge ceases to be something I know, but begins to be an understanding of who God is, how much He loves and favors me, and a full realization of what He has done. It also gives me the understanding of how dependent I am upon Christ.

---

[256] 1 Corinthians 8:1

I don't support Christ; He supports me.[257] It isn't merely knowledge, but knowledge of His grace.

I once met a man in church who memorized scripture for the purpose of gaining an advantage. It was nearly impossible to have a reasonable conversation with him because he would pound you over the head with scriptures. He didn't want friends. He wanted subjects. Any time someone shared something, he would barrage them with criticism and Bible quotes. He knew the words of the Bible, but did not understand the scriptures.

According to the Bible, knowledge puffs up, but love edifies. Yet we are also told that to know God is to love Him. Many times we are commanded to know the word, study to show ourselves approved, and promised that the word corrects, instructs, provides doctrine, and reproves what is wrong – so we can be complete, thoroughly equipped for every good work.[258]

The word, mixed with faith, built on an understanding of grace (God's favor toward you) has power. It is the word of God and it will accomplish what God purposes. Yet for some people, the word passes through them and they look to only use it for their purposes. Others, who are founded upon grace, see the word of God empowering their lives and renewing their minds.

The fleshly mind uses the word to assist the flesh. Knowledge for that person puffs up. The spiritually minded seeks God through His word. For that person, the word reveals the love of God and His purposes. Once we see the truth of God's love in the word, we believe God and release our will to Him, and His Spirit takes the word and accomplishes God's purposes in us. He then uses us to accomplish His purposes in ministry to those around us.

God's word will accomplish His purposes. The question is, are we going to be in that purpose, or are we going to focus on our own purposes. These things are meant for your peace, but many miss that peace because of other things crowding their lives and choking out the word.[259]

Those who understand grace have the foundation to understand. They understand that God is out for their good and He is the source of

---

[257] Romans 11:18
[258] 2 Timothy 3:16-17
[259] Mark 4:19

Growing in Intimacy

all good. They also understand that anything outside of God's goodness is a distraction. The favor of the world may sound good, but the favor of God *is* good. The favor of the world is a moment. The favor of God is eternal.

To grow in grace is to mature in the faith. It is to fully understand that God is out for your good, and that the commands of scripture are His staff of guidance so we find all He has for us. Take time to read Psalm 23. Most of us have heard this many times, but in this psalm, we see how God's desire is to lead us to everything we need.

I love the passage where David says, "I will fear no evil, for Your rod and staff, they comfort me."

Compare that to the view of most Christians. We think of God's rod as something for our backs when we do wrong. I don't know about you, but when I was a child, if my father reached for the rod, I wouldn't feel comforted. It was David's comfort because he understood that these were for his protection, not punishment.

The rod was for David's enemies. The picture is a lamb following a shepherd. If something came after the lamb, the enemy found out the purpose of the rod. The shepherd would strike the enemy with fierce blows while the lamb stood safely behind his master.

The staff was a hooked stick. It was intended for the sheep, but not to strike it. When the sheep wandered off course, the shepherd would reach out and retrieve the sheep and guide it back on course. It was not punishment, but guidance. No good shepherd would beat a sheep back into the fold. Sheep are helpless animals that are short-sighted. They often wander off course, but because the shepherd cares for the sheep, he leads them to safe ground, protects them in the dark valleys, and guides them back each time they stray.

If you are honest, you can look at your life and see a constant straying. Yet you are still with the Lord. Why doesn't God just abandon us and say, "I'm sick of these wandering sheep?" Because He is the good shepherd who laid down His life for the sheep.

God knows you will wander. When we wander, He guides us back – not in anger, but in patience and love. He favors us and is guiding us to the fullness of His grace. This will not fully be realized until we see Him face-to-face, but many expressions of grace are for you in this life.

The truth of the Christian life is that you cannot miss what God has for your life if you are growing in grace. Certainly you will wander and at times you will make bad decisions. Many times what we think is a good decision leads to negative circumstances we cannot foresee. We can't see our future, but God can.

Sometimes difficulties force us into a direction that we did not want to go, but later discover it was good. Or circumstances force us away from what we were certain was good. Sometimes we are stubborn and press hard against the staff. Sometimes God intervenes in order to stop our harm. Sometimes He allows us to suffer some consequences so we see the worthlessness of the world and the trustworthiness of His guidance.

If you are seeking Christ and walking in His will, God will not allow you to miss His blessings. Your flawed decision-making is not a barrier to His grace. God is not surprised when we wander off course. He is not surprised by the curveballs of life. While we lament over our bad choice, God is already leading us to the right way. What seems like a loss to us is part of God's plan to lead us to a greater gain. We view the temporary, but God sees the eternal.

I say all of this to point out one important truth. God's grace / favor is the foundation of intimacy. Regardless of what you have done or the mistakes you will make, you must not stay focused on anything but God's favor. Deal with the issues that draw your focus away from intimacy, but don't live in your mistakes. Grow in grace – that is the first foundation of intimacy. Grow in the knowledge that God favors you, and everything in your life is designed to lead you into His goodness and the fullness of His joy.

Forget what is past. Turn from what is presently in our life that is contrary, and receive God's favor. If God favored you enough to go to the cross, why would He abandon His grace now that the work has been done? The only thing standing between you and intimacy with God is this: faith in His favor.

God favors you. Period. If your sins disqualified you, then the cross was a wasted work. Certainly there are consequences to sin, but the nullification of Jesus' work on the cross IS NOT one of those consequences.

Grow in grace and the knowledge of Christ. The more you know Christ, the more you will see and experience His favor. Knowledge is important, for if you do not understand what God is

Growing in Intimacy

doing, you can't receive it. If you don't see His favor, how can you rejoice in it?

It is no accident that the Apostle Peter ended his last words with the reminder to focus on grace. You must grow into the knowledge of what Christ has done for you. And what He is doing for you. The work is already accomplished, but your understanding is an ongoing growing process.

The more you understand grace, the closer you will grow to the Lord and the more the fruit of the Spirit will emerge in your life. Knowing rules and regulations cannot produce maturity, cannot root sin out of your life, and cannot produce the fruit of the Spirit.

Certainly we want to obey, but obedience is not our act of meriting God's favor. Obedience is our acknowledgement of God's favor and the act of trusting in God to bring about the change in our lives that His word has called us to live out. Obedience outside of faith is legalism. Faith founded upon grace produces obedience.

Studying is important in the Christian's life, but there is a legalistic way of studying and a grace way. If I'm studying in order to feel accepted, that is legalism and profits little. I say little because it's possible that I could study for the wrong reason and God still speak to me. But He would then be leading me out of an erroneous way of thinking.

Legalism says that I have to read a certain number of chapters a day. Or I must spend so many hours in study. Or spend x number of hours in prayer.

When I was younger, our church read about a man who dedicated his life to prayer. He made the statement, "If you are not spending two hours each morning in prayer, you aren't prepared and won't have victory."

What was the result? We were taught that the only way to have victory was to spend at least two hours in prayer each day. According to the book, that was the minimum. The result was a legalistic way of thinking. And guilt when I fell short. What was worse is that my prayer life didn't improve – even when I met the two-hour requirement. Why?

I wasn't seeking God in prayer. I was fulfilling a mandate He did not place on me. And this is one of the great flaws in the Christian church. God dealt with this man and called him to prayer. Each of us are different and God deals with us in different ways. We are called to pray without ceasing, but that is a heart of constant communion with God. We indeed set time aside for prayer in order to be more focused, but the length of time is not set in stone. My prayer life is not for you to imitate. Nor is your prayer life the standard by which I measure my own life.

Later I met a man who thought pool tables were evil. He was appalled when he discovered a couple had a pool table in their home. He called them worldly and sinful. But were they? No. He came out of a lifestyle where playing pool, drinking, and fighting was the norm. He associated the pool table with his old life, but in reality, the pool table was merely an inanimate object. It was neither good nor bad; it was his behavior that was sinful, not the object he used.

When I first began to preach, the pastor of my church pressured me to quit my job and go to seminary fulltime. I had two young kids and I was the sole income earner. There were four of us in ministry with him, and he persuaded two of them to quit work. His rationale was, "When God called me to preach, He called me to quit my career and start preaching. The doors opened up and I never had a time when I wasn't preaching somewhere."

I sought the Lord much and finally got an answer. The Lord unmistakably affirmed that I was where I should be and I decided not to exit the workforce. Two other guys did. One went into bankruptcy and the other fell into financial hardship and returned to work. He is no longer in the ministry.

The point we should note is that God called this pastor to take this drastic action, but not those he was discipling. Unless God calls others to do this, it is a work of the flesh and cannot be successful. God called one man to devote his life to prayer, and while prayer is important in every life, one man's calling does not equate to the way God works with everyone. Putting a burden of a specific number of hours takes our focus off seeking God and on fulfilling a man-made requirement.

Bible study is the same way. Do not set a limit on your Bible study. Do not say, "I must read for one hour," or "I must read 5 or 10 chapters." Set time aside to seek the Lord and then seek God through His word. A scripture may come alive and you might spend all your time on one passage. Other times you might feel led to read in quantity to gain a wider perspective. Knowledge is important and

Growing in Intimacy

both quantity reading and deeper study is important. However, once it becomes a regulation, we are no longer seeking God, but seeking to make ourselves feel self-righteous.

As I began to preach more frequently, I realized that I was getting mixed messages and was preaching what others were telling me and not what God was revealing in my own life. The Lord led me to dedicate an entire year to reading nothing but the Bible. I determined not to read theological books, listen to sermons, or do prepared lessons. My goal was to get a fuller understanding of the word.

What I intended for a year stretched out into more than three years, almost four. In those years, I read the Bible cover to cover more than a dozen times and some books of the Bible, I read more than thirty times. At some point, I felt God release me from this desire and though I still read the Bible as my primary spiritual input, I've read some great books that added to my understanding. Some books have put into words what God was already doing in my heart, and it became an 'aha' moment. "Aha, this is what God is doing. This writer has put into words what I have already been experiencing, and now I understand it better."

This was how God worked in my life. It would be an error for me to say, "You must read only the Bible." Just as it was a mistake for one man to tell another that he must quit work and go to seminary. Or to tell others that they must pray a minimum of two hours a day. Or another book that put me into bondage where a man decided to give God 90% of his income and was greatly blessed. Others tried to follow that formula and couldn't pay their bills.

Follow the Lord. What God does in the life of another is for His purposes and for the benefit of the one God is teaching. We can glean from what others learn, but we cannot imitate God's calling in their life. Nor should we expect others to have our passions that God has given us.

You see this often in churches. Those whom God has touched to reach the homeless become critical of others who don't have that passion. Those who have a passion for the unborn often criticize those who don't share that passion. Some have a deep love for doctrine and become critical of those who don't spend hours studying Greek, digging out lessons, and teaching the word.

The truth is that God has appointed each member in the body as He wills. As you grow in intimacy with God, your passions will emerge. But don't assume that the passion God gives you is the passion God expects of everyone. God has gifted you and appointed you as He sees fit for the purpose of edifying the body. Your calling (and my calling) is not to heap guilt upon those who do not experience what we are experiencing, but to edify the body in love as God gives us the opportunity.

The Apostle Paul was sent by God to preach Christ to the gentile world. Many were opposed to this idea because they thought God only dealt with the Jewish church. They thought the gentiles must convert to the Jewish law, and then trust in Christ. God gave Paul the passion for the gentiles, and God gave Peter a passion for the Jewish people. Both learned to focus on Christ alone.

Paul could have criticized Peter for ignoring the world. Peter could have criticized Paul for ignoring the Jews. But the truth is that God gave each man a passion to fulfill God's calling. Neither man chose his passion.

I recently read an article calling each Christian to missions. The article indicated that every person must be a missionary in order to fulfill Jesus' call to go into all the world. He argued that every Christian should serve on the mission field – if even for a short time. Not so. God has laid this call on his heart, but if I decide to become a missionary out of obligation or guilt, God will not bless the effort. Then it would be a work of the flesh and not a calling of God.

Not to mention that once you step out of the prayer closet you are in the world. The mission field is all around you. Some God calls to go to far away lands. Others are called to reach the inner cities. Some to reach their neighborhood. Some to reach the world through the internet. Follow God – not the mandate of others.

God has given me a passion for the word and a passion to write. When I write, the word comes alive and jumps off the pages of scripture. This is how God deals with me. Because my frame of reference is in the writing world, I could easily assume that in order for you to know the word deeply, you must write. I could say, "If you write, the word will come alive. Anyone who doesn't write isn't seeking God."

That would be false. You might try to imitate my methods, and if you hate to write, you would be forcing yourself to fulfill a task of drudgery and never experience what I experience. Another person might spend hours in prayer and say that the scripture comes alive as they pray them back to God. Then they might claim, "If you aren't praying the scriptures back to God, you aren't seeking the Lord. This is how you grow closer to God."

The truth is that God deals with us as individuals and different passions arise in different ways. I believe this is by design, for if there was one way, Christianity would be reduced to methodology instead of intimacy. God wants you to know and experience Him on a personal level. He does not want you to follow processes and procedures, but instead He calls you to seek Him and know Him. And God reveals Himself as He draws and you respond. You might see His word come alive through poetry, song, writing, prayer, or any number of other ways. Answer the Spirit's calling, not a demand others claim is the way to know God.

Also take care not to impose your calling onto others.

If you seek God, He will reveal Himself to you. If you seek to imitate a process, your growth will be limited to the framework of someone else's process.

Seek God in prayer that you may know Him. Let prayer be a communion with God. If God gives you a passion for prayer, follow that passion. If you feel as though your prayer time has fulfilled the burden of your heart, don't force yourself to continue in a formal prayer just for the sake of measuring up to an arbitrary standard. Let your prayer life be a constant communion with the Lord – whether it is dedicated prayer time or the communion of God throughout daily life.

The same is true for studying, reading, writing, singing, witnessing, or any other outlet for our spiritual walk. The goal is to have fellowship with God. Your life can be in constant communion with the Lord. That doesn't require a specific regulation or dedicated prayer time. Some people indeed benefit from dedicated time. The point is not to do away with these things, but to allow them to encourage us in our growth into intimacy, and not to displace intimacy with God by focusing on Christian rules and regulations.

Know God. There is no formula for this. God's promise is that if you seek, you will find. Seek as God draws. Don't limit God's work within the boundaries of what others have experienced.

Grow in grace – or God's favor – and the knowledge of Christ. No man can tell you how to know God. A teacher can share biblical principles that can be applied to your Christian walk, but God reveals Himself to you and draws you into a deeper fellowship. Seek Him through the word. Seek Him through prayer. Commune with God as a lifestyle. Trust in His favor, enjoy His expressions of love, and learn to walk with Him. You will not fall short when Christ is your focus.

Intimacy is to know God. Let Him reveal, and let your heart respond. God is always calling and always drawing. Look to Him and let everything else cease from being a distraction. Seek because you are growing in grace – not because you feel an obligation. Enjoy the fellowship of God.

Discussion Questions:

Review 2 Peter 3:17-18. What does Peter teach as a contrast to being led away by error?

Psalm 23 illustrates God's leading with a rod and staff. Do you think God uses the rod on His sheep?

Read Proverbs 14:27 and Psalm 19:8-11. What does it mean to fear the Lord?

How does grace cause us to grow in intimacy with God?

Why does knowledge puff us up with pride?

How do we grow in knowledge without being lifted up in pride?

How much Bible study should you do each day?

Can prayer, Bible Study, and Christian disciplines become a distraction from intimacy with God? If so, explain.

If someone condemns you for not sharing their passion, should you feel guilty?

Does God lead a person into apathy?

How do we discover the passion of God's calling?

Should we pray each day?

How do we pray without ceasing and still not make it a legalistic practice?

Can legalism lead to intimacy with God?

Repentance – the setting of the mind

This chapter will examine repentance from the perspective of a life focused on the Spirit. There is a godly repentance, and there is a worldly repentance. One grovels in sorrow, the other shifts our focus to what brings joy. Look at **2 Corinthians 7:10**

> For godly sorrow produces repentance *leading* to salvation, not to be regretted; but the sorrow of the world produces death.

The topic of this chapter will not be on salvation, but the principle equally applies to those who have received salvation. If we draw our concept of repentance from the world, it always creates regret. As Christians we should sorrow over our fleshly behavior, but not grovel in it. The joy of grace should turn us to the right way and draw us out of the flesh. It is sin that creates sorrow, not repentance.

Repentance does not create sorrow. It actually produces joy.

Keep in mind that when you are born into the Spirit, a new nature is created and becomes the foundation of your life. Before we were born again, sin did not create sorrow within our old nature. We might have sorrowed over the consequences, but it isn't until something is threatening, shaming, or harming us that we even thought about sin. We sorrowed over the consequences, not the sin.

Now that we have a new nature, our inner man desires to live according to a godly standard. When we live according to the flesh, our spirit will be troubled and we won't be comfortable in sin. Nor will we be at peace when we draw our attitudes and actions from the flesh. God's Spirit communes with our spirit and reveals the will of God. Our minds exercise what has been revealed and it comes out in our lives. The only time this doesn't work is when our minds are focused on the flesh. And that is what repentance is all about.

Sorrowing over ungodly behavior may lead us to repentance, but repentance does not mean to sorrow. Sorrow is the realization that something is wrong. In the scripture above, immorality was in the church, it was confronted, and the person living in sin sorrowed over his behavior and found restoration. But sorrow is only one road that leads us to repentance. According to the Bible, the goodness of the Lord also leads us to repentance.[260]

So we should understand that repentance does not mean to sorrow. Sorrow is not necessary for repentance. Both joy and sorrow can lead us to repentance because to repent means to turn the mind.

The word 'repentance' comes from the Greek word 'metanoia', which literally means: to change one's mind. It is to take our mind off of one thing and to place it on another. We are thinking one way, then we see the correct perspective and recognize it is different than what we have been thinking, and we change our focus onto what is correct. In this chapter we'll examine three main passages that deal with this. Start with **Romans 8:5**

> For those who live according to the flesh set their minds on the things of the flesh, but those *who live* according to the Spirit, the things of the Spirit.

So what is repentance in this case? It is to realize that we are in the flesh by examining our patterns of thinking. If our minds are in the flesh, we'll see fleshly patterns. Do little things bother you? Are you stressed? Stress is a part of life, but the flesh handles stress by building pressure and reacting against perceived threats. The flesh crumbles under the weight when stress gets too heavy.

Faith says to not be anxious, but to turn our minds from the cares of this life and focus on something greater. Faith doesn't deny problems; faith looks for God's working through our problems, and releases our cares into God's hand. The flesh says, "I must double my effort." Faith says, "All things work together for those who love God and are called into His purposes. It is God who works in you to accomplish His purposes."

The flesh is stuck on the immediate. The one walking in the Spirit by faith looks beyond the immediate and endures all things with God's joy set before them.[261] **Philippians 4:6-9** is a great passage on repentance:

> [6] Be anxious for nothing, but in everything by prayer and supplication, with thanksgiving, let your requests be made known to God;

---

[260] Romans 2:4
[261] Hebrews 12:2

^{7} and the peace of God, which surpasses all understanding, will guard your hearts and minds through Christ Jesus.

^{8} Finally, brethren, whatever things are true, whatever things *are* noble, whatever things *are* just, whatever things *are* pure, whatever things *are* lovely, whatever things *are* of good report, if *there is* any virtue and if *there is* anything praiseworthy -- meditate on these things.

^{9} The things which you learned and received and heard and saw in me, these do, and the God of peace will be with you.

Do you see the call of repentance in this passage? Do you see that it is the goodness of God that calls you to repent, or change your mind from a negative way of thinking in the flesh to a positive way of thinking in the Spirit?

When someone has anxiety, does it work to say, "Don't worry?" No. Resisting the flesh isn't the answer. The call of repentance isn't to resist the temptations of the flesh. Keep in mind that temptation is not only enticing you to do something blatantly sinful. Temptation is the luring of the flesh. It's the call to turn from the Spirit and put confidence in the flesh.

We worry because we are confident that our problems have the power to cause us harm. We lust because we are confident that a pleasure will bring us satisfaction. We think vengeance will bring us justice. Name the object of our flesh's attention and at the heart of it is trusting in something other than God. When we are anxious, we fear something because we believe it has the power to overcome us. So is the answer to convince ourselves not to worry? Is it to deny the existence of problems? Or to turn a problem into an object and think of it as small?

None of the methods people employ work. When a problem is small, we might have limited success, but when the problems are numerous or something threatening is looming over us, denial does not work. Using human effort is merely trying to overcome the flesh through the flesh.

The Bible's answer is to set our minds on these things listed above. The instruction not to be anxious begins with prayer and supplication with thanksgiving. This means that even our petitions to God for help are founded upon a heart thanking God. How can you be thankful during your problems?

This is why this book stresses the importance of understanding predestination. It isn't possible to fully understand faith without a basic understanding of God's foreknowledge and plan. Problems surprise us, but they don't surprise God. In fact, the solution has already been worked out before you were born. Those who don't understand this basic truth will look at problems as something that God is not in control of.

When God allowed Satan to test Job, the Lord said, "You can touch this part of his life, but not that." God set boundaries and though Satan could make Job think he had power, the truth is that he has no power outside of God's command. Before Peter fell, Jesus said, "Satan has desired to sift you as wheat. But I have prayed for you, that your faith should not fail. When you have returned to Me, strengthen your brethren."[262]

Peter was going to be tested. Satan was going to push Peter beyond his human ability. Peter was going to fall. In Peter's eyes, he failed. He thought his faith failed. What could be worse than denying he even knew Jesus? He had invested his entire life in Christ, and suddenly it was gone. His reputation was destroyed. His strength was overthrown by a servant girl who accused Peter of being with Jesus. To protect himself from potential legal consequences, he denied he had ever met that man. His faith failed him. Or did it?

No. Peter's flesh failed him, but when Jesus rose from the grave, He restored Peter by putting his focus on God's calling by faith. Satan sifted Peter's flesh, but could not overthrow his faith. From the temporary perspective, it was a total defeat, but what Peter did not realize is that when he fell, he found the true source of strength.

Once his own abilities failed him and all confidence in the flesh was removed, then Peter was confident in the Spirit and boldly preached Christ before the very crowd who had shouted, "Crucify Him." Then he was threatened but never wavered. Peter was no longer his own strength. Peter's faith was no longer in his abilities. Suddenly Peter was strengthening the brethren by pointing to Christ as the true strength, and faith in Jesus name was the only source of life.

---

[262] Luke 22:31

That is repentance in action. Satan desires to sift each one of God's people. The Lord will allow this to happen – in the flesh. And the goal is to sift away the chaff of the flesh so your confidence is solely in His power.

That is when you become anxious for nothing. When life looms over you, your flesh will cower in fear. If your strength is in the flesh, you cower with it. But those who have learned to set their minds on the things above look at the problem and say, "Lord, You have already worked out the resolution. Whether you carry me through the valley, or knock down the fortress with a mighty hand, I will trust you."

God leads you down the path of life. Temptation calls you out of that path to pursue the flesh. Temptation tries to scare you off the path with threats. If our eyes are on the problems, they will be too great for us. But if our eyes are on the Lord, the problems don't matter.

When you sin, God is not demanding you to grovel in the shame of your sin. God calls you to repent. Sorrowing over our sin is the natural reaction of our spirit because we are violating the new nature and not acting according to who we are. And you know what? God knew you were going to fall. He isn't shocked. While you are saying, "Why do I keep doing this," God is already working in your life to teach you how to walk in the Spirit so you are not ruled by the flesh. But you have to stop sorrowing in the flesh and start trusting in the Spirit.

Jesus has already paid for your sins. Two-thousand years before you were born, Jesus paid for your sins on the cross. Before man was even created, you were in Christ.[263] Your sin isn't a shock to God. Your sin is not unanticipated. Just as God foreknew Peter would deny Him, but already made a way for his return, God foreknew you and has already provided for your peace.

When your problems arise, whether that be internal temptations or external stresses, rest in Christ. He not only foreknew what you are going through, but He has already cleared the path to see you through it. Not only to make it through, but to emerge with an eternal perspective that He will use to strengthen the brethren. But if you put

---

[263] Ephesian 1:4

Repentance

your trust in the things of the flesh, you are robbing yourself of God's best.

When you blow it, God has already forgiven you. Don't be faithless, but believe. Just as the prodigal son rehearsed a meaningless speech, we pray meaningless prayers. "Father I have sinned," was an acknowledgement that the son had turned his back on the father. Then while the son was crying, "I'm not worthy to be called your son," the father wasn't listening, but instead was calling out, "Bring the best robe and a fine ring to put on my son."

All the groveling the prodigal was putting himself through was needless and ignored by the father. Your groveling is also meaningless and is ignored by your Heavenly Father. God is looking for repentance, or a change of the mind from the flesh back to the Spirit, not a speech about our worthlessness. God knows the lack of value of our lives in the flesh. But He has also created an incorruptible life in the Spirit that carries the worth of Jesus' sacrifice on the cross. Do not call what God has cleansed worthless or unclean.[264]

In the prodigal's life, repentance was to turn away from what was destroying him and back to the father who loved him. The same is true for you. There is nothing wrong with saying, "I have sinned and I'm sorry." Sorrow is a natural response when we act contrary to who we are in Christ. But praying, "Please forgive me," is a prayer of unbelief. According to the Bible, you are already forgiven. If you are in Christ, your debt is paid. Instead of begging God for forgiveness, we should be praying, "I've blown it because I took my eyes off of You and pursued the worthless pleasures of life. I am sorry I turned from You. But I thank you for your mercies and the promise that I have been forgiven through Christ. I thank you for your grace. You have given me favor I don't deserve. I am favored, not because of what I've done, but because of who You are."

Repentance is not begging for forgiveness. It's to set our minds on what is of God. It is to trust in what God has already declared to be true. I'm not trying to win God's approval. I am rejoicing in God's approval through Christ. You are favored, not because you have earned it, but because you believed in Christ and received what God

---

[264] Acts 10:15

promised. You believed God and your faith was accounted as righteousness. Don't turn from that faith now.

Stop praying for God to make you godly. Start believing in the finished work of Christ. Stop praying for God to make you holy. Believe His word, which says you are holy in Christ. Stop praying for God to sanctify you. Start believing that God has placed a spirit within you that is already sanctified and set apart for Himself. Stop praying that God would keep you from sinning. Start believing God's word – the one born of God cannot sin because they are born of God. Live like who you are in Christ and not who you were in the flesh.

True repentance is to take our minds off the flesh, and set our minds on the Spirit – by faith believing what God has said and allowing Christ to transform your outward behavior into who you are in the inner man. Consider these truths:

You were sanctified – Jude 1:1, Hebrews 10:10

You are forgiven – 1 John 2:12

You are holy – Ephesians 4:24

You are righteous – Ephesians 4:24

You are already clean because of God's word – John 15:3

Your old sinful nature has already been put to death – Romans 6:6

We are these things because of Christ, not personal achievement. According to scripture, because the religious seekers sought for their own righteousness, they did not find the righteousness of God.[265] We are commanded to seek God's kingdom and God's righteousness, and all we need will be added to us.[266] None of these spiritual attributes originate from you or your behavior. All of this comes from God. We seek His righteousness, not our own. You are partakers of God's nature,[267] not the producer of godliness, righteousness, sanctification, or any other eternal benefit.

Act like who you are by faith and stop living like you are that old man who was put to death in Christ. Either you believe the word of God, or you believe the flesh. You either set your mind on the truth of Christ, or the achievement mentality of the flesh. Striving to

---

[265] Romans 10:3
[266] Matthew 6:33
[267] 2 Peter 1:4

produce godliness is a submission to the law. Set your mind on God's truth of who you are in Christ. Look at **Colossians 3:1-4**

[1] If then you were raised with Christ, seek those things which are above, where Christ is, sitting at the right hand of God.

[2] Set your mind on things above, not on things on the earth.

[3] For you died, and your life is hidden with Christ in God.

[4] When Christ *who is* our life appears, then you also will appear with Him in glory.

This is repentance at its core. And it is God's goodness that leads us to it. Your life is hidden with Christ in God. Set your mind on what is above. Your performance is of the earth. Your sins are of the earth. Your failures are of the earth. Adopt the attitude of the Apostle Paul. Forget the things you are leaving behind and reach ahead to what is eternal.[268]

You sinned. Leave it behind. You failed God. Leave it behind. You fell short and blew it badly. Leave it behind. It is of the flesh and will not follow you into the Spirit. Leave it behind and reach for what is above. That is how you become like Christ.

Believe God's word that you are what He has declared you to be in Christ. You can't change the flesh; you can only leave it behind. When it deceives you into sin, repent by acknowledging it as a worthless work of the flesh, agree with God, believe His promises, and set your mind on what is above and leave what is behind in the past.

We needlessly carry the burden of guilt and failure. None of these will pass over when we pass through the judgment seat of Christ. Why then should we hold on to them now? They are of the flesh, but we are in the Spirit.

Repent by setting your mind on Christ and put off the deeds of the old man. The old nature is dead. His deeds are dead. Leave it with the dead flesh. It is not who you are and has no place in your life. Your life is hidden in Christ. You are a new creation born of the Spirit.

---

[268] Philippians 3:13

Live like the new creation and the flesh loses its power. Or as the scriptures put it, "Walk in the Spirit and you will not fulfill the lust of the flesh." It has no power over you. Believe God and walk in this truth.

Discussion Questions:

Read 2 Corinthians 7:10 and Romans 2:4. What leads us to repentance?

What is repentance?

Does repentance only mean to turn away from willful sinning? Explain your answer.

How is thanksgiving a form of repentance?

How did Peter's denial of Christ bring him to true repentance?

Where was Peter's confidence before he fell?

Where was it after he fell?

Did Peter have a change of mind?

How did that affect the rest of his life?

When we sin, what is God's reaction?

What does God expect of us after we sin?

Review Colossians 3:1-4. Where do you see repentance in this passage?

How does believing who we are in Christ lead us to repentance?

The Greatest of These is Love

1 Corinthians 13:13

> And now abide faith, hope, love, these three; but the greatest of these *is* love.

Not long ago I wrestled with this passage. I had no problem believing that faith, hope, and love were the most important things in the Christian life, but I didn't understand how love could be the greatest of these. Shouldn't it be faith, for without faith it is impossible to please God. We are saved by grace through faith. Without faith, how can we experience the love of God? That should mean that the greatest is faith, or so I reasoned.

It's true that by faith we experience love and establish ourselves in hope, but the foundation of everything is love – agape. The reason love is the greatest is because love is God's expression toward us. Everything is founded upon God's love. Everything. It isn't just love, but the expression of God's love. What we call love is based on a human standard, but this is agape love and it's found in the person of Jesus Christ.

God so loved the world that He sent Jesus Christ, and he is full of grace and truth.[269] Grace is the expression of God's love in the person of Jesus. He came to reveal both grace and the truth about God that was once hidden from man's eyes. His love is eternal, but until Jesus covered sin, the veil of the Law's condemnation covered the love of God. The veil stood between fallen man, and God's expression of love.

In the Old Testament, God appears cruel and harsh. But the God we see in the Old Testament is the same God of the New. Why such a drastic difference between God's demands in the Old Testament and God's expression of favor toward us in the New Testament? Sin has been done away with. Sin, by its nature is an affront to God's character and nature. It is selfishness personified. Selfishness and love are in direct opposition to each other.

Add to this, the Law of God condemns men in the flesh. The Law is the perfect standard of God, based on who God is and what

---

[269] John 1:14

His nature requires. Can that which attacks the nature of God stand in God's presence? Can anything that opposes God or attempts to bring corruption into His nature stand in communion with God? No. Sin collapses in God's presence. Sin can make an assault upon God, but sin cannot affect God, for nothing can change God's nature.

Consider how God interacted with Moses. The people who stood afar viewed God as a terrible threat, but Moses viewed God as a friend. Even in the midst of the revelation of the Law that condemned man, we see the love of God shining through. When the people sinned, Moses stood up to intercede for the people and asked for God's mercies. Mercy is when people don't get what they do deserve, but grace is showing favor we don't deserve.

God agreed to Moses' petition of mercy, and then Moses saw an opportunity. He wasn't satisfied with getting something from God. He wanted to see God. Let's pick up the conversation in **Exodus 33:17 - 34:1**

> ^{17} So the LORD said to Moses, "I will also do this thing that you have spoken; for you have found grace in My sight, and I know you by name."
> ^{18} And he said, "Please, show me Your glory."
> ^{19} Then He said, "I will make all My goodness pass before you, and I will proclaim the name of the LORD before you. I will be gracious to whom I will be gracious, and I will have compassion on whom I will have compassion."
> ^{20} But He said, "You cannot see My face; for no man shall see Me, and live."
> ^{21} And the LORD said, "Here is a place by Me, and you shall stand on the rock.
> ^{22} "So it shall be, while My glory passes by, that I will put you in the cleft of the rock, and will cover you with My hand while I pass by.
> ^{23} "Then I will take away My hand, and you shall see My back; but My face shall not be seen."

In this passage God declared His favor toward Moses, but then made it clear that Divine favor did not change the fact that Moses in sinful flesh could not survive in God's presence. No flesh can stand in God's presence and live. Yet God took Moses as close as possible to seeing the full glory of God.

What was the result of this encounter? When Moses saw God's glory from a distance, he was so affected by God that his face reflected that glory for many days to come. It was so bright that Moses had to put a veil over his face so people could look upon him.

This was only a small glimpse of God's passing glory. If Moses, in his sinful state, had stood in God's presence, he would have died. This is what happens to sin in God's presence. Sin does not affect God, but God has a drastic effect on sin. Do you also see why beholding the glory of Christ – God's full measure of grace – doesn't promote sin? Rather than becoming a tool for sinning and getting away with it, grace transforms us into the glory of God.

A man or woman abiding in God's presence will shine with the glimpse of the glory they behold. Instead of rushing to sin because we can get away with it, we shine with His glory and sin is dispelled.

The glory that once threatened man because of sin is now revealed in man because of the love God showed the world. In Christ, the sin has been taken away and we behold God's glory. We see it in part, but one day we are promised to abide with God in His full glory. In fact, we will share in His glory.

So what would once destroy man because of sinful flesh will now be the treasure of man through Christ. And this treasure is now hidden in our earthen vessels[270] through the love expressed through Christ.

What greater love could God possibly show than to bear the penalty of sin for us? The God whose presence destroys sin loved us enough to come in the form of man and destroy sin, so we could be free to enter confidently into His presence. What was once the fear of man has been taken out of the way. Now we can abide in perfect fellowship with God without fear. We fellowship freely now, and we have no fear of judgment when we stand before Him. All our sins have already been judged on the cross.

There is nothing greater than agape love. Love is the foundation of the Christian life. Without love, faith could not exist and hope would never be seen. Truly the greater of these is love.

Love is God's care for us, and is greater than man's faith – or faithlessness. The love of God is greater than man's hopelessness. When we recognize the love of God, faith is born, along with hope.

---

[270] 2 Corinthians 4:7

God's love is not dependent upon man's faith. Consider **2 Timothy 2:11-15**

> [11] *This is* a faithful saying: For if we died with *Him,* We shall also live with *Him.*
>
> [12] If we endure, We shall also reign with *Him.* If we deny *Him,* He also will deny us.
>
> [13] If we are faithless, He remains faithful; He cannot deny Himself.
>
> [14] Remind *them* of these things, charging *them* before the Lord not to strive about words to no profit, to the ruin of the hearers.
>
> [15] Be diligent to present yourself approved to God, a worker who does not need to be ashamed, rightly dividing the word of truth.

In this passage, to deny Christ doesn't mean we do as Peter did. At his moment of weakness, he feared the people and denied he knew Christ. But did Jesus deny Peter? No. Jesus restored him and showed him what it meant to have strength in Christ alone. In the passage above, deny is to reject God. The word deny comes from the Greek word arneomai, which means: to deny, to prove false to himself, to act entirely unlike himself, not to accept, to reject, to refuse something offered. In the context above, I believe 'to refuse something offered' is the correct interpretation.

In this passage, the context is God's faithfulness, whether we are walking by faith or not. In context, I believe to deny Christ is a sidebar comment to those who deny Him as Lord. They will be denied the right to be children of God. This is not saying that if a Christian is fearful during persecution and falls into the flesh as Peter did, they will lose salvation. No. The meaning is not directed to those who are weak in the flesh, but to those who deny Christ.

Also, to make sure the translation I'm using is not a distraction, I want to address another word in this passage. Some translations say, "Study to show yourself approved," but the word study is not in the text. The Greek word is 'spoudazo', which means to exert one's self, endeavor, or be diligent.

Notice that the diligence is so we can receive our full inheritance, not so we can merit God's love. Even if we are faithless, God remains faithful. He remains with us, even if we do not remain focused on Him. God cannot deny Himself. Since God's Spirit is within us, we are always in Him and He in us. We may not abide in Christ by living in agreement with His will, but our spirit always remains in Christ. In other words, we may not walk with Christ in perfect fellowship, but God remains with us because He has placed us into divine fellowship.[271]

That's one of the important truths we must always remember. Our spirit is always in Christ, but our lifestyle and self-will can step outside of God's will and become worldly and carnally minded. Our will may not abide in Christ, but our life is always hidden in Christ. Or as **Colossians 3:1-4** puts it:

[1] If then you were raised with Christ, seek those things which are above, where Christ is, sitting at the right hand of God.

[2] Set your mind on things above, not on things on the earth.

[3] For you died, and your life is hidden with Christ in God.

[4] When Christ *who is* our life appears, then you also will appear with Him in glory.

This passage goes on to warn us against sin and the works of the flesh. Many instructions are given to the believer as we are commanded to live according to our new nature, but notice the foundation of this truth. We don't set our minds on eternal things so we can find God's favor. We do these things because our life is hidden in God through Christ. This is true even if you sin.

There are consequences to sin, just as there are rewards to those who abide in God's will. Our goal is to experience the full reward.[272] God's goal is for you to share in His glory and receive of His kingdom – in other words, that you receive the full inheritance He intends for you.

Even if you depart from God's will, you do not depart from God's love. If you are faithless, God remains faithful. His love is not dependent upon your ability to perform. You are accepted in Christ because of what He has done, not because of what you have done or are doing. Don't forget that God so loved the world that He gave us deliverance through the cross. This is while we were still sinners. Take to heart **Romans 5:8**

---

[271] 1 Corinthians 1:9
[272] 2 John 1:8

But God demonstrates His own love toward us, in that while we were still sinners, Christ died for us.

If while we were sinners God loved us and expressed His favor towards us, how can this be any less true now that we have been adopted as His children? For some reason we can believe God loves us as sinners and receive Christ, but we think the nature of God's love changes into judgment after we become Christians. If God did not require us to merit His love while we were children of disobedience, why would God now require love to be earned? God never changes – even if our behavior does. Grace, or the expression of God's favor toward us, never changes. Grace is unmerited, so it cannot be performance based.

The God of the Old Testament is the God of the New, but what could not be received through sinful flesh can be received through Christ. In Christ, we have everything the Old Testament saints could not receive and what the prophets foresaw, but could not experience.[273] What they saw far off through the lens of the law, we experience through Christ.

Love – the perfection of the Saints

People have many ways of viewing God, and in the scriptures we see many descriptions of God's action. The Bible says that God is a consuming fire, is our refuge, is our strength, is our healer, is good, is just, is holy, is merciful, is pure, is righteous, is Spirit, is faithful, is wise, and is light. Nothing captures the essence of who God is like the short statement, "God is love." This is why love is greater than all things. Love is the essence of God, and in order to understand all doctrine, and our own lives in Christ, we must view it through the lens of God's love.

Most have heard of the chapter of love, 1 Corinthians 13. This chapter views the love of God in comparison to man's works. All the good works done outside of love (agape) are meaningless. Even to offer our own bodies as a burnt offering to God has no value, for human effort cannot produce or replace love. There is another chapter of love I want to explore before we conclude this topic. It shows that

---

[273] Luke 10:23-24

the Christian life must be founded upon the love of God and how that love flows into everything of value. Carefully read **1 John 4:7-21**

[7] Beloved, let us love one another, for love is of God; and everyone who loves is born of God and knows God.

[8] He who does not love does not know God, for God is love.

[9] In this the love of God was manifested toward us, that God has sent His only begotten Son into the world, that we might live through Him.

[10] In this is love, not that we loved God, but that He loved us and sent His Son *to be* the propitiation for our sins.

[11] Beloved, if God so loved us, we also ought to love one another.

[12] No one has seen God at any time. If we love one another, God abides in us, and His love has been perfected in us.

[13] By this we know that we abide in Him, and He in us, because He has given us of His Spirit.

[14] And we have seen and testify that the Father has sent the Son *as* Savior of the world.

[15] Whoever confesses that Jesus is the Son of God, God abides in him, and he in God.

[16] And we have known and believed the love that God has for us. God is love, and he who abides in love abides in God, and God in him.

[17] Love has been perfected among us in this: that we may have boldness in the day of judgment; because as He is, so are we in this world.

[18] There is no fear in love; but perfect love casts out fear, because fear involves torment. But he who fears has not been made perfect in love.

[19] We love Him because He first loved us.

[20] If someone says, "I love God," and hates his brother, he is a liar; for he who does not love his brother whom he has seen, how can he love God whom he has not seen?

[21] And this commandment we have from Him: that he who loves God *must* love his brother also.

I didn't feel at liberty to exclude anything in this passage because all of it applies directly to grace and walking in the Spirit. Do you believe in the love of God (verse 6)? That is the essence of faith.

Don't reverse the order of these instructions. We don't love the brethren in order to prove our love to God. Nor do we love God in order to accomplish anything. Love is not what we are doing, but rather it is the evidence of what God is doing in us. Or another way of saying this is that our expressions of God's love is the evidence that we believe in His love and are allowing His love to rule in our hearts.

When we love our fellow believers, it is the evidence that we have received the love of God. When we love God, it is the evidence that we have already received that love from God. We are receiving what God is providing into our lives, and allowing it to be expressed back toward God and out toward others.

It is because God so loved us that we love one another. We have known the love of God and believed (or put our faith in that love), and therefore we abide in His love. You don't love others by human effort, but because you have received the love of God. Loving God is not an act of human effort, but it's the act of loving God with the love He has first given us. It is an act of faith – believing in God's gift of love.

The command is that he who loves God must love his brother. Why? Because if God has given us His love, it is not merely for our self-indulgence, but so we can express it outward. Agape, by its very nature, is self-giving and outward focused. The only way to not love is to resist the love being given and turn our focus to the flesh.

I was taught, and believed, that love was an act of our will to love God and love others. Yet the love of God does not come by the will of man (See John 1:13). We are born of God because of God's will, and His love is poured into our hearts by the Holy Spirit, not by the will of man. In the same way, our will does not produce love back to God or out to others. Any self-willed love is an act of human effort and is of the flesh. The love of God is already present within us. We either believe in His love as the passage above states, or we believe in the flesh. We either express God's love outward through the Spirit, or we express ourselves through the flesh.

We abide in Him and He in us because He has given us of His Spirit. According to Romans 5:5, His Spirit pours God's love in our hearts when we are born of God. Then drop down a few verses in 1 John above, and we are told that any who confess Christ, the Son of God, God abides in him and he in God. In the next verse abiding is again mentioned. Those who believe in God's love abide in God and He in us.

The message is clear. You cannot receive Christ without receiving the love of God. Christ is the Word made flesh, God in human form. Since God is love, any who have the Son have the love of God. Any who have the Spirit have the love of God. Any who are born of God have the love of God.

Love is not what you do, but what you have received from God. We then take what we have received of God, and express it in what we do. The love of God will always produce acts of God's love outward. Outward toward God, outward toward the brethren (fellow believers), and finally outward toward those in the culture around us – or as Jesus said, our neighbors.[274]

Notice that the message is the same as we discussed throughout this book concerning Christ. How are we changed into Christ's likeness? We are changed as we behold Him. It's an act of expectant faith. How do we receive God's love? How do we apply love to our lives? By trying harder?

Our efforts should never be the focus. We behold the love of God, put our trust in that love, and as we behold God's glory, we are transformed into that likeness. God is love, and as we focus on God's agape, love naturally flows outward from our spirit, into our lives, and out to others.

God's love produces action, but our actions can never produce God's love. The foundation of agape must first be built by the Spirit, and then God flows through us. Then we know that we are in the love of God because of His Spirit within us and the outflow of that Spirit back to God and outward to others.

This is also why Jesus said, "Love your enemies and bless those who persecute you…that you may be children of your Father in Heaven."[275] A child of God has the love of God within them, and that love must be expressed. Otherwise, we are living for the flesh and are not living as a son or daughter of God. Whoever has been born of God loves, for God is love.

---

[274] Luke 10:27-37,
[275] Matthew 5:44-45

Most Christians are not living based on who they are in Christ. They are walking in the flesh, so the love of God cannot be perfected in them. Consider the words of **James 4:1**

> Where do wars and fights *come* from among you? Do *they* not *come* from your *desires for* pleasure that war in your members?

Within the life of the Christian is the love of God. Those who set their minds on the love of God begin to manifest the love of God in their relationship with God, then toward each other, and finally toward the neighbors in the culture around us. Yet when the focus is on ourselves and satisfying the flesh, what happens? Wars arise and fights emerge in the church. Instead of becoming outward focused children of God, we act like inward focused carnal people of the flesh. We become what our focus is upon. Let's allow James to continue. **James 4:3-4**

> ³ You ask and do not receive, because you ask amiss, that you may spend *it* on your pleasures.
> ⁴ Adulterers and adulteresses! Do you not know that friendship with the world is enmity with God? Whoever therefore wants to be a friend of the world makes himself an enemy of God.

When we set our minds on things above, we will value what God values. When we set our minds on things that please the flesh, we'll value the world and then act like the world. Anyone who has been in church for any length of time has seen this truth. What do people fight about in church? Do they fight for the opportunity to give of themselves and become more outwardly focused? No, they fight about not getting recognized. They fight about someone offending them with a slip of the tongue. They fight about self-benefiting programs, positions in the church, music, food, decorations, and countless other meaningless issues. If we are not Christ focused, by default we'll become fleshly minded and self-focused.

Wars come out in other ways. Fighting spawns Denominationalism and even break off churches within denominations. Human nature and the flesh will always create divisions. Look around. Denominations fight against other denominations, church against church, sects within the church fight with other sects. Is this God's way? How does this affect the impact of the church?

According to Jesus, "By this shall all men know you are My disciples, by your love for one another." Sadly, all the world can see is Christian against Christian and organization against organization. They don't see Christ. They see masses of people who claim the name of Christ but can't get along or agree on anything. Of course there will be differences in how we view certain teachings of scripture. At times, people will be completely wrong in their beliefs.

The problem is that we turn non-essential beliefs and preferences into dogmas. People have drawn circles around themselves and now declare that anyone outside of that circle is the enemy, and to get inside you must follow man-made tenants.

Disagreements are part of life, yet everything should be founded upon what God has declared to be the greatest command. These three remain: faith, hope, and love. The greatest of these is love. This is the greatest commandment, to love God with all your heart and to love your neighbor as yourself. Yet once the church was born, a new commandment was given. **John 13:34-35**

> [34] "A new commandment I give to you, that you love one another; as I have loved you, that you also love one another.
> [35] "By this all will know that you are My disciples, if you have love for one another."

Whereas we once had to love our neighbor as ourselves, now we are commanded to love our fellow Christians with the love God has given us. That is greater than the love we have for ourselves. God is love. God has taken of Himself, placed it into the heart of the believer, and then gave us a new commandment. Love the brethren with the love I have given you.

This command didn't exist before because man never received God's own love before Jesus paid our penalty and opened our hearts to receive the Holy Spirit. Now we have been given what no one else has ever received. Along with this great love comes the greatest command – take what God has given, abide in it, and allow it to flow unhindered into the church. And then the world will see something that has no other explanation than it has to be of God.

This is a command that can only be fulfilled by those walking in the Spirit. As the Christian and the church slip farther into a carnal way of thinking, the expression of God's love is lost from their behaviors and the witness to the culture falls short. Instead of revealing the love of God through our lifestyles, we become dependent upon man's programs and efforts. But nothing can testify to the truth of Christ more than a church expressing the love outward that comes from the fountain of love flowing from the Spirit.

The church has failed in this calling. We've failed because we are looking to ourselves and trying to live out our faith by human effort. Humanly speaking, love is conditional. I love because I receive. I love based on my feelings, abilities, personality, and preferences. But God has given us the power to step out of the human way of thinking and into the Spirit. In Him is perfect love. In us, the love of God is perfected when we abide in it and allow God's power to transform our way of thinking into His way of thinking.

We are so caught up in sectarianism and self-focused ideals that we are drawn into the flesh instead of into the Spirit. If you are walking in the Spirit, you cannot help but to love the brethren. Instead of having a critical spirit, you will love and care for those in the household of faith, regardless of denomination, race, or region.

I have been guilty of this. Very guilty. In the past I thought it necessary to criticize those who did not hold to the exact same doctrine. Sometimes the people I criticized were wrong. Is calling them out and making a public spectacle the right solution to this? It took a long time to realize this truth, but rebuking the church is not the call of the Christian. In a moment we'll explore the Bible's answer, but I am now confident that creating division is the last alternative. And unless Christ is being rejected, becoming divisive is not an option at all.

Certainly false teaching must be addressed and confronted with the love of the truth. But what we see is truth without love, knowledge without revelation, mockery of others, name-calling, and criticism. The goal has shifted from edification of the body to destroying perceived enemies.

Do we need to hunt down every heretic and create a public spectacle in order to make the world know there is error out there? When someone falls into error, do we restore them by calling them evil, mocking them, or using bitter sarcasm in our debates? How does

The Greatest of These is Love

truth overcome error? How does light overtake the darkness? Darkness is dispelled by the presence of light. You don't have to convince the person in the shadows that they are in the darkness. When the light is shining, darkness is evident. Anything not in the light is darkness.

In the same way, correcting errors in the church isn't accomplished by attacking churches that are teaching poorly. False teaching isn't eradicated by name-calling and mockery. At this moment, the world sees the false church and those mocking the false church. It sees the true church mocking other true churches for petty differences. It sees fighting and wars among the members.

Jesus did not say, "The world will know you are my disciples because you ridicule those who claim My name but teach error." No, the world will know the true church because of the supernatural love that has no other explanation than, "God must be with them."

Let the darkness fight against the darkness. Our mission is to know the love of God and abide in that love. When we follow this command, the Bible says that we will then be to the world as Jesus was to the world. Then men will either be drawn to Christ or they will hate us as they hated Him.

Even if someone has errors in their beliefs, it does not nullify the command, "He who loves God must love his brother also." To find a loophole, people often claim someone isn't a believer and is therefore an enemy of God. Then it's okay to hate God's enemies, right? Not so. We are also commanded to love our enemies. We can't escape God's call to love.

The love of God is perfected in us when we take what God has given, abide in it, and then allow God's love to do its work in our lives and out to those around us. Love is directed first to God, then to the members of Christ, and then to the world around us.

Destroying others is not the work of the Christian – on any level. God's ways are higher than our thoughts and what we think is right is often the opposite of how God works. We think we must defeat the world from a position of power, but God says that the weak things overcome the mighty. We lift ourselves up in order to overcome, but God says to humble ourselves under His hand and then God will lift us up in His time. We think we get rid of error by stamping it out, but God says not to return evil actions or words, but to overcome evil with good.

The Greatest of These is Love

The truth is that the world is already under condemnation, so there is no need of condemning. The error is already under destruction, so we don't need to destroy it. The world is under the power of the devil, and it isn't our job to remove the enemy. Our job is to let our light shine, for we are not converting the world, but calling men out of the darkness of the world.[276] Let's look at the message of **1 Peter 2:9-12**

> [9] But you *are* a chosen generation, a royal priesthood, a holy nation, His own special people, that you may proclaim the praises of Him who called you out of darkness into His marvelous light;
>
> [10] who once *were* not a people but *are* now the people of God, who had not obtained mercy but now have obtained mercy.
>
> [11] Beloved, I beg *you* as sojourners and pilgrims, abstain from fleshly lusts which war against the soul,
>
> [12] having your conduct honorable among the Gentiles, that when they speak against you as evildoers, they may, by *your* good works which they observe, glorify God in the day of visitation.

What do we proclaim? Do we proclaim that this teacher is false because of an error in doctrine? Or do we declare a denomination as liberal? Or rigid? Do we condemn traditionalism? Condemn liberalism? No. we proclaim Christ and hold up His praises. It is He who calls us out of darkness. Have you ever watched a debate end by one person saying, "I was so wrong. You have convinced me?" Has anyone ever abandoned their organization because you called their leader an antichrist?

I've yet to hear such a testimony. But I have seen people come out of cults and false religions when they understood the message of Christ. As they grew in understanding, the error became evident. It wasn't revealed by studying the error, but instead the error couldn't stand in the presence of the understanding of truth.

Notice a few key points in the passage above. You were called out of darkness and into His light. You are sojourners and pilgrims. You are those who are traveling through a land that is not your own.

---

[276] John 17:16, John 15:19

Abstain from the lusts of this land. Have an honorable conduct around the lost. They may label you as evil, but when God visits them, they will glorify God by your good works. How you live and conduct yourself is the greatest witness you can have.

That conduct is based on the love God has poured into your heart. God has poured His Spirit into your heart, and now you have everything that pertains to life and godliness. Obedience is not what you do for God. Obedience is taking what God has given you and living in it. God has given you His love – the very essence of God – and now He asks you to abide in what He has given you.

Allow that to become your essence and express His love toward others. That is when the world will look at the church and say, "What makes you so different." It isn't you. It is Christ within you. And the only way they can experience that kind of love is through coming to the Lord they see in your life. The love of God is perfected in those who first believe in His love, and then abide in the love He has given.

Problems arise when we think God's love isn't sufficient. We then will use human effort and fleshly methods to try to do the work of God. We don't think that revealing the love of God expressed in the scriptures will transform a life. So we beat them over the head with the Bible, insults, and bitter words. We don't believe God's promise that love perfects us, removes fear, and leads others to truth. So we use hatred to convince others that what we disagree with is bad, and present ourselves as messengers of wrath instead of people who are perfected in God's love.

How can we as people be perfected? It isn't what you do. It is what God has done. You will make mistakes. In fact, as you grow in truth, you'll find that many of the things you thought were true fell short of the gospel. Yet you will also look back and see that God used you and showed grace to you in spite of your errors in thinking. But God doesn't change your way of thinking through anger and rejection. He guides you with a loving hand as he opens the word to you, enlightens your understanding by the Spirit, and brings people into your life to present truth you have not yet grasped.

God is asking you to show the same grace toward others that He is revealing to you. When we blunder, we don't want God to strike us with the rod of anger. Why then would we want to show that attitude toward others? We are called to judge, not by pointing out failures in others, but by directing others to the truth of Christ.

Five times in the letters to the churches the apostles confronted error by saying, "I am pleading with you," or similar statements. We are pleading with a hopeful heart for others to see the truth. We are pleading with an upward hand, not with a downward pointing finger. Once someone grasps the truth, the error has no place to hide. Even your own errors will continue to fall away as you learn of Christ.

This is the call of the Spirit. To set your mind on Christ, be transformed into His likeness, and then you will fulfill the Christian life because you are abiding in your new nature and not drawing from a mind that is focused on the flesh. Let's conclude this book by looking at the words of scripture again:

> And we have known and believed the love that God has for us. God is love, and he who abides in love abides in God, and God in him.
> Love has been perfected among us in this: that we may have boldness in the day of judgment; because as He is, so are we in this world.

How do we abide in God? By believing in His love. How are we perfected? By abiding in His love. How do we correct error? By pointing to the true love of God. How do we reach the culture around us? By expressing His love toward each other as we abide in what God has revealed to us.

By this shall all men know you are My disciples, your love for one another.

By this we abide in God, believe the love God has for us.

By this we walk in the Spirit. Abide in His love. Look to Christ, allow the word to reveal His likeness, and be transformed into that image.

Submit, don't labor.

Transformation is the natural process of conforming to His image when we look to Him and live according to the new nature He has given us. We have been given everything that pertains to life and godliness. Past tense. Believe, look expectantly to Him, and abide in that truth. And never forget, the greatest of these is love.

Discussion Questions:

Why does the Bible say, "The greatest of these is love?"

Why was God's love unrealized in the Old Testament?

Was the veil that prevented man from touching God for God's benefit or mans?

Why was that veil removed?

If we are faithless, does God stop working in our lives? Check your answer against 2 Timothy 2:13.

Have you seen God work in your life when you weren't trusting Him?

Read John 14:23 and Colossians 3:1. How can Christ be above and still abide within us?

Read 1 John 4:19. Do we love God in order to receive love?

How do we love God and love each other? Where does that love come from?

How are we transformed out of a fleshly way of thinking and into God's expression of love?

Read John 13:34-35. What is the new commandment?

How was this different from the previous commandment to love?

How does the world know we are Jesus' disciples?

Review 1 John 4:12. How is the love of God perfected in us?

Are we perfecting the love? Or are we allowing God's love to complete God's purpose?

Why does perfect love cast out fear?

What causes people to fight within Christian circles?

How can we deal with error and problems without losing our focus on love?

Is it possible to fight for self and remain focused on the perfection of love?

How do we deal with someone who is bitter and harsh in the church?

What is the greatest command in scripture? How do we fulfill it?

Acknowledgements

My first acknowledgment must go to my Lord and Savior, Jesus Christ. It has been a long and wonderful journey to get to this point in my spiritual life. I can't imagine what He has already prepared for me to discover in the coming days and years.

I'd like to give a special acknowledgement to Carlton Rivers, pastor of Grace Café Church and author of The Freeing Power of Grace.

When I met Carlton, God had already revealed most of this book and it was close to completion. I was almost 'there', for I had a good concept of grace and was experiencing what it meant to walk in the Spirit, but something was missing. Through much prayer I wrote this book, and at the right time, we crossed paths.

In the book of Acts, Pricilla and Aquila encountered a man named Apollos. The Bible said that Apollos was mighty in the scriptures, but these two godly people recognized something was missing, took him aside, and explained the way of truth more perfectly.

Though I'm no Apollos, I believe Carlton has been faithful in instruction as Aquila and Pricilla once were. Carlton challenged me with the scriptures, I took the challenge and began digging into the word and trying to see how grace could be better explained in my life and teachings. For the next several weeks, I prayed, read the word, and looked at the scriptures with an eye open for God to show me the meaning of grace. Then it clicked. While preparing one of the chapters of this book, my eyes were opened and it was like a veil lifted. Grace wasn't just one of the teachings of scripture. Grace was what every teaching was founded upon.

Jesus said, "Peter, you are a stone," then referring to Himself, Christ continued, "On this Rock I will build My church." The Bible says that Jesus is full of grace and truth. He is the embodiment of grace, and the Rock everything is built upon. Once I realized this, everything changed from trying to be, to trusting in what He has done.

I am grateful that God crossed our paths at the time when needed it and was prepared to see it. Walking in the Spirit abiding in grace cannot be separated, so this book could not effectively explained the Spirit without founding that upon the understanding of grace.

For this reason, Carlton deserves a special word of thanks. Without being willing to explain this message more perfectly, I would have had an incomplete book.

Contact the Author

You can contact the author at one of these locations:
Personal Website: www.eddiesnipes.com
Ministry site: www.exchangedlife.com
Email: eddie.snipes@gmail.com

Other books by Eddie Snipes:

I Called Him Dancer – Christian Fiction
Simple Faith: How every person can experience intimacy with God
The Promise of a Sound Mind: God's plan for emotional and mental health